Everyone Sent to Multiply Everything

Robin Wallar

Hamilton, Ontario, Canada

Everyone Sent to Multiply Everything
Copyright © 2020 by Robin Wallar
Edition: 1.0

Unless otherwise noted, all Scripture quotations have been taken from the Christian Standard Bible®, Copyright © 2017 by Holman Bible Publishers. Used by permission. Christian Standard Bible® and CSB® are federally registered trademarks of Holman Bible Publishers.

References cited as NIV are from the New International Version. THE HOLY BIBLE, NEW INTERNATIONAL VERSION®, NIV® Copyright © 1973, 1978, 1984, 2011 by Biblica, Inc.™ Used by permission. All rights reserved worldwide.

References cited as ESV are from the English Standard Version. The ESV® Bible (The Holy Bible, English Standard Version®). ESV® Text Edition: 2016. Copyright © 2001 by Crossway, a publishing ministry of Good News Publishers.

References cited as NASB are taken from the New American Standard Bible® (NASB), Copyright © 1960, 1962, 1963, 1968, 1971, 1972, 1973, 1975, 1977, 1995 by The Lockman Foundation. Used by permission. www.Lockman.org

References cited as MSG are taken from The Message. Copyright © 1993, 1994, 1995, 1996, 2000, 2001, 2002. Used by permission of NavPress Publishing Group.

Cover Design By: Mikaela Fergusson
Cover Art By: Emma Lelea

To order more copies visit https://liftchurch.ca/esme

Contact Information:

        info@liftchurch.ca
        P.O. Box 89120
        991 King St. W.
        Hamilton, ON
        L8S 4R5

Table of Contents

Acknowledgements — V
Preface — VI
Introduction — 8

Part 1 Everyone Sent to Multiply Everything

1 Everyone Sent to Multiply Everything — 13
2 Who Is Everyone? — 18
3 What is Multiplication? — 29
4 The Discipleship Pipeline — 36

Part 2 Discipleship Potential

5 What Is Discipleship? — 44
6 Gospel Fluency — 56
7 Secure Identity — 85
8 Missional Living — 105
9 Radical Generosity — 133
10 Crucial Conversations — 147
11 The Work of Discipleship — 170
12 Discipleship Multiplication — 189

Part 3 Multiplication Power

13 How We Multiply: The N+2 Leader — 204
14 Multiplication Imperatives — 226
15 Thriving as a Multiplying Leader — 247

Part 4 Leadership Position

16 Empowering to Multiply — 256

Part 5 Apostolic Life-Cycle

17 Apostolic Life-Cycle	282
Conclusion	290
Appendix: The Story of Scripture	292
Scripture Index	294
Endnotes	300

Acknowledgements

Many people have made this work possible. Thank you to the entire LIFT Church family. Without your friendship and support, these ideas would not be written down; this is your story. I wrote down these ideas on discipleship with all of you, past and present, close to my heart.

In particular, thank-you to Dan Lupo, who tirelessly reviewed the work and refined the ideas. Thank you to Alex Busch and Jeff Webb, who helped to develop the concepts. To the many others who helped to bring it to life: Ellen Bedecki, Nicole Haverkamp, Tarrah Martin, Anny Ko, Emma Lelea, Mikaela Ferguson, Graham White and many others!

To the Gracepoint Church family, thank you for your hospitality and encouragement in providing space and time to develop the content.

Thank you to my wife Laura. Your support in all the late nights, early mornings, long weekends and missed family time has been an unseen burden. I could never have done it without you. I love you. Thank you for making disciples with me.

Preface

In the summer of 2018, we began to formalize the LIFT Church discipleship framework as we seek to see people made fully alive in the hope of Jesus through a network of multiplying churches thriving across our nation. The driving force behind all our work, by the grace of the Holy Spirit, is the power of multiplying discipleship. This book is an effort to articulate what exactly we mean when we are talking about multiplying discipleship.

We have been on an incredible journey over the last 13 years. We have discipled thousands of people, mostly post-secondary students, through a growing network of churches. None of the ideas originated in a vacuum or private study. Instead, all of the ideas were tested in the life-on-life discipleship relationships of our church; the good, the bad and the ugly.

The content of the book is aimed to empower the discipler, in any context, to think clearly and systematically about how they can intentionally invite, model, train and empower people to be multiplying disciples themselves. I have aimed to tackle the theology, content, culture and systems that enable disciples to reproduce.

I wrote this book with three audiences in mind. First, it was written for our church as a tool to help us move with unity and clarity as we multiply disciples and plant churches.

Second, this book was written for church leaders who are wondering if and how they can call those in their churches to radical, sacrificial and powerful New-Testament style discipleship. You can.

Last, this book was written for ordinary disciple-makers. Ultimately, it is you, wherever you are, that Jesus has sent into the world to bring his glorious hope, joy and life through the call to discipleship and church planting.

I have intentionally limited the usage of illustrations or examples. The primary objective of this book was to engage in a discussion on the clarity and consistency of an overarching discipleship system. I would caution readers from trying to copy and paste the LIFT Church Discipleship Pipeline into your context. Rather, I would encourage you to wrestle deeply with the concepts, study scripture yourself and contextualize your learnings to your unique situation. The intention is that forthcoming handbooks will help the discipler apply the framework in their context.

On a personal note, I was reticent to commit to writing a book on discipleship. Time is precious, and I was hesitant to invest the time into something that no one would read. However, my wife wisely counselled me towards simple obedience. If the Lord was putting it on my heart to write, then I had to write. In his grace, there has been much beautiful fruit that has come from the process. He is good, and his call to be a disciple-making disciple is the best invitation anyone could ever receive.

Stay tuned for the accompanying discipleship handbook that will be released in the second quarter of 2020. Additional copies of this book, and the forthcoming handbook, as well as additional resources, are available at http://liftchurch.ca/esme.

Robin Wallar
Hamilton, Ontario
January 2020

Introduction

It begins with ordinary, unremarkable people. People like you and me. People from all walks of life, backgrounds, preferences, histories and stories. People from all over, each with their own story, but who are finding their story is woven together with hundreds, thousands of others. These are ordinary people who do not possess any special giftings or talents. In a world of celebrity, these are those who find themselves in the crowds. Ordinary people who have stories of hope, joy and beauty. They also have the memories of past hurts and shame, of a life lived in a broken world in desperate search of answers. They are ordinary people because they have moments of faith and moments of doubt.

But, these ordinary people are not ordinary at all. They are saints whose names have been written into eternity. They are disciples whose lives are defined by the passionate pursuit of him who has conquered sin and death in history and in them. They are those who have discovered and received the glorious grace of Jesus. This Jesus is no mere person, but the author of creation who has spoken life into everything that lives and breathes — including them! They were dead, alone, isolated, separated — desperate in their sin. But that's not the end of their story; no, now, they are fully alive.

Transformed into weapons of righteousness, these ordinary sinners' lives are testimonies that declare that no failure is so great or so complete that it cannot be redeemed by the grace of Jesus.

These disciples, followers and saints live at home in this place of grace. They know who they are because they know *whose* they are. They have accepted his invitation to receive life, and a desire for his presence fuels them. They have received everything they need from him who gives more than they could ask or imagine. They do not wish to be confident, bold, secure and passionate, they choose to be confident, bold, and passionate because they know whose sons and daughters they are.

These disciples pursue the holy way of Jesus with all they have. They reject the allure of sin and the trappings of temptation. As recipients of the love of Christ, they are truly free. They choose to walk as holy people, allowing the self-sacrificial way of Jesus to be their aim. They forsake the temptations of the world because they know Jesus is better. That is their mantra: Jesus is better. Jesus is better. Jesus is better. In everything they do, they know that nothing will satisfy like Jesus.

Every aspect or component of their lives is a tool in Jesus' hands. Nothing is theirs and everything is his to be used as an instrument of his glory. That is the mission of their lives and the deepest longing of their souls — to see Jesus glorified. There is nothing else that they desire; everything else pales in comparison to the purpose of Jesus glorified.

So they live their lives on a mission, a mission that is the inevitable outcome of people who have encountered the goodness of God. As they are transformed, their outlook on the world is transformed. As they have received, they long to give. Their lives are conduits for glory and grace. They become carriers and ambassadors who are longing, pleading with our world to receive the life that he has to offer.

They give with open hands. A generosity that is driven by the generosity of God who did not even spare his own son. They can give because they are content in Jesus, so they cling to nothing because they know that nothing is theirs. Whether the Lord gives much or little they are content, for their satisfaction is in him. They are abundantly generous with their lives, opening their homes and their hearts — inviting people to see this goodness of Jesus.

They are not alone. This is a movement of disciples working together for that which is greater than any one of them. They commit to deep relationships. Through a common bond in Christ, and a desire to see the nations know him, their relationships transcend personal attraction and chemistry and the family of God is forged. They know that what they can accomplish together is far greater than what they can do alone. They walk with a profound humility towards one another; they submit to another.

As iron sharpens iron, they invest in one another, encouraging each other to chase after Jesus. They forsake their personal preferences to serve the needs of the whole. They know it's not about them but about him and his Church, so they willingly lay down their wants and deny themselves to serve others. They see every person as critical and valuable because they know that what they do together thrives on the faithfulness of all rather than the gifts of a few.

Such commitment to each other and the mission creates the environment for deep trust and deep discipleship. They willingly and eagerly take on the mantle of discipling others to know Jesus by urging and empowering one another to chase after Jesus. They build a bold, audacious faith in each other.

They proclaim Jesus with authenticity, eager to share with whoever will listen to the news about what Jesus has done for them. They do not have to force their faith on others: instead, they live with a bold passion that is contagious, attractive and unavoidable to those who see it. They serve the most vulnerable because they know it is in the darkness that the light of Jesus can shine the brightest.

So it grows. It multiplies. One, then another, then another, then another. Those who were ordinary have become saints and disciples who passionately lead others to Jesus. As the heart for Jesus grows in them, their desire to see the world know him overflows. So they ask, "Where can I go to proclaim his name?"

So they are sent, not separate but as a part of the whole. These people begin to spread out into difficult places. A family of disciples spread across the nation. The campuses of our nation become infused with the word of Jesus, transforming ordinary people who were dead in sin into fully alive ambassadors of grace. Bound together as a family of grace, they send people forth with eagerness because they know the pain of sending is worth the gain of seeing those who are dead raised to life.

This is the picture of a discipleship movement. A picture of a church surrendered to Jesus. Ordinary people, fully alive in Jesus, gathering in unlikely places, working in unity to multiply passionate disciples, influence nations and see Jesus glorified.

Why do we aim for the nations? Why do we go together? Why do we multiply? Very simply because it is the heart of God and the command of Jesus that we do so. By God's grace, we will see a discipleship movement birthed.

How will God accomplish all this? What follows is a picture of how we believe we can implement a vision for multiplying disciples across nations.

Part 1

Everyone Sent to Multiply Everything

1

Everyone Sent to Multiply Everything

Matthew 28:19

Go, therefore, and make disciples of all nations

'The Great Commission' has been the focus of many sermons, podcasts and books. Yet, for all its popularity, true multiplying discipleship can seem out of reach for the average believer. Discipleship seems like something that 'leaders' and 'strong Christians' do, but unattainable for the everyday follower of Jesus. Further, the command that we are to make disciples of All Nations" can seem like hyperbole at best or completely irresponsible at worst. Understanding that readers of this book may likely find a similar narrative in their mind, we need to begin with a confession: we believe fulfilling this mission is possible!

Across the world, discipleship movements are fulfilling this great commission and seeing people come to faith in vast numbers. This is often without fame or recognition for those involved. In fact, there is often no reward beyond the supreme joy of seeing people come to know and walk in relationship with Jesus. Yet despite the lack of rewards and the often huge sacrifices, we are seeing discipleship movements grow like wildfire across the globe.

The question we asked is: how?

How do we lead disciples to become disciple-makers and churches to become church-planting churches? How do we see new believers replicate the transformative work that Jesus has done in them into others? What do we do when we have multiplying discipleship happening at a large scale? What roles do leadership, culture and values play in building a discipleship movement? How do we hold people accountable and to what? How do we protect against the influx of culture and the temptation to compromise? What does a radically missional life look like?

Ultimately, the question we seek to answer is: how do we raise disciples who can consistently raise up healthy disciples so that we see viral movements of multiplication and discipleship happening?

Foundational to the idea of a multiplying discipleship movement is a concept that we call the "Apostolic Imperative." This idea derived from the very passage above can be summarized in a simple statement: *Everyone Sent to Multiply Everything* (ESME). While the statement is simple and memorable, there are in fact three important declarations being made:

Everyone Sent to Multiply Everything

Everyone

... all nations...

Firstly, we believe that every person is invited to not only be a follower of Jesus but someone who can invite others to follow him as well. In fact, these two invitations are inseparable. For this reason, we believe that every person has the potential and the invitation to see the world around them made fully alive in the hope of Jesus.

This means everyone. Especially those who are different from us.

Fully living into this idea of everyone involves questioning our own inherent biases and prejudices. Who do we subconsciously disqualify from discipleship? We need to take a deep look to identify any prejudices we hold on gender, age, socio-economic status, physical/mental ability or even personality type and interests.

In saying that everyone is called, we are also saying that there is no room for a consumer mindset. There is no "us" and "them"; there are no "volunteers" and "staff." The church is a family of disciples on a mission together to make more disciples. Everyone is invited to participate in this mission and to be refined by a commitment to know Jesus.

Saying that everyone has the potential to be sent as a multiplier for the Kingdom of Jesus does not mean that everyone should, needs to or even can do everything. It does, however, mean that everyone can and should live their lives with the focus of declaring the name of Jesus into the world around them. The degree of their influence and the nature of their multiplication is contingent on their Commitment, Character and Competencies. The essence of this aspect of the imperative is that we are committed to identifying and developing in our people what they may not even see in themselves.

We will examine how to live out the value of 'Everyone' in more detail in Chapter 2, but it is important that we don't gloss over this fundamental starting point. 'Everyone' may seem simple, but it is much more difficult to live out.

Sending
Go...

Churches exist to equip and send people; that is what it means to be apostolic.[1] Every person who is a disciple of Jesus is sent into this world to see other people know Jesus. The Church does not exist to merely receive people, it exists to send.

We send because Jesus was first sent. The importance of this cannot be overstated. We are sent into the world in response to the fact that Jesus was sent into our world so that we could be made fully alive. This is important not just as a theological statement but also as a practical reminder that being sent and sending others is costly. It was profoundly costly for the Father to send the Son — yet he chose to do it.

We do likewise. We are sent into this world to see people know Jesus and, in turn, to be sent into their world. This means that instead of clinging to relationships as things to hold onto, we look at our lives and relationships through the lens of the mission to the world.

Being sent is to be continually looking outward to the world around us with compassion, love and grace saying to the Lord, "Here I am, send me." We are people who put our hands up to do the difficult and challenging. We are the people who look at the unknown future and instead of seeking confidence in the outcome; we respond in faith to a God who desires the world to know him.

To be sent and to send means that we do not primarily look to our own interests but to the interests of others. The Church is always looking beyond its own immediate interests to ask the question: how can we see more people made fully alive in Jesus?

Of course, part of sending people is preparing them to be sent. This means leading people to know Jesus and grow in their discipleship and multiplication capacity.

Multiplication

> *... make disciples...*

Multiplication is what happens when we see the intrinsic potential of every person, invite them to join us on the mission and send them to do likewise with others.

In short, we are not merely disciples: we are *disciple-making disciples*. Every disciple, from the moment they come alive by the grace of Jesus, has a responsibility to train additional disciples to make disciples.

Leadership is not rewarded based on charisma, popularity or having the "it" factor. Instead, leadership is a natural product of multiplication. An effective multiplier is a person who will naturally find themselves in a position of influence and leadership attained simply by virtue of their ability to mobilize and send others.

This means that every leader is continually looking around them to see who they can invite to know Jesus and subsequently raise and send to see others also know him. They should constantly be asking, "Where can I multiply?" A multiplying leader is a person who naturally takes initiative to invite the people in their world to participate in the mission of Jesus. It is proactive, intentional and purposeful.

For this reason, multiplication is not restricted to the "spiritual" activities of the church (if there were such a thing). In multiplying "everything," we mean that in everything that we do we are continually asking the question: *"Who can I invite to participate in the mission?"* In everything we do, there exists the opportunity to invite someone to participate in the mission.

Summary

A discipleship movement is based on these three principles working together. When all are called and then sent to be disciple-making disciples, the church transforms from an hour and a half gathering once a week, into a movement of believers bringing hope, life and joy into a broken and hurting world. We will be returning to these concepts throughout this book, as they form the foundation on which everything else stands.

Part 1 of this book will continue to expound on these theological principles and set up the framework on which the rest of the book is built. Part 2 will explore the depths and nuances of discipleship and will explain what exactly we desire to multiply. Part 3 will focus on the culture and values of multiplying disciples. Part 4 will outline the importance of leadership systems in multiplying discipleship movements. Finally, Part 5 will take these principles and apply them on a macro scale, illustrating how a discipleship movement quickly turns into a thriving church-planting movement.

2

Who Is Everyone?

The Apostle Peter makes a massive declaration in 1 Peter 2:9 when he asserts that we, in Christ, are a holy nation, a royal priesthood. The Apostle John reasserts this bold claim in Revelation, calling followers of Christ a "*Kingdom of priests*" (Revelation 1:6). These statements come from Jesus' closest followers and two of the most influential leaders in the early church. They knew that Jesus' trial and subsequent execution centred on claims surrounding authority over the temple, and by extension, the priesthood (Matthew 26:57-68).

The Apostolic Imperative, Everyone Sent to Multiply Everything, is predicated on a compelling, yet straightforward idea: the Priesthood of all Believers. In Christ, we are all priests and ministers of the presence of God! For many Christians, if you were to ask them if they had ever thought of themselves as a priest, they would respond baffled and confused, believing that they are not called or holy enough. However, our mere befuddlement pales in comparison to the response of first-century Jews. It would have been nothing short of an assault on the holiness of God! Paul joins Peter and John in rewriting the rules around sacrifices and temples in his letters to the churches (1 Corinthians 6:19, Romans 3:25).

To see "everyone sent" we must understand what qualifies us to be sent and authorizes our boldness and courage to announce the Kingdom of God to a broken and hurting world. Our invitation to be priests in Christ is a supremely high and holy calling that is a serious blessing and privilege. It is our responsibility to baptize, multiply and disciple, and to do so we must dismantle the notion that a special few are called to ministry while others are not. We must eradicate the concept of "calling to ministry" as it gives permission for believers to build lives where consumption and "being fed" are prioritized over being equipped and sent for missional engagement with a broken and hurting world.[2]

Paul, Peter, John and, most importantly, Jesus' words about his kingdom, priests, nations, temples and sacrifices were spoken with thousands of years of history and the story of the Israelite nation in full view. To live as a priest today, we must first know what it meant to be a priest in Jesus' day.

Korah's Rebellion

Numbers 16 tells the story of a Levite named Korah who had taken exception to the rigid set of qualifications surrounding who could enter into the priesthood, most notably the office of High-Priest. Under the leadership of Moses, and by the hand of God, the nation of Israel had been liberated from the tyranny of slavery in Egypt. As the Israelites were solidifying their identity as God's chosen people through which the nations would be blessed, God communicated the priestly order to Moses for him to implement.

To be a priest was a high and holy calling, and only a very select few were permitted to participate. Of the twelve tribes of Israel, only the tribe of Levi was permitted to serve in the temple or tabernacle. Of the tribe of Levi, only men born to the lineage of Moses' brother Aaron could enter the official priesthood and offer sacrifices on behalf of the rest of the nation of Israel (Numbers 18:1-3). Of the lineage of Aaron, only a single male could be selected as the high-priest to enter the presence of God (Leviticus 16). The privilege of administering God's presence was reserved for the chosen of the chosen ones.

Accompanying the stringent requirements for admittance into the priesthood were strict requirements surrounding the behaviour and livelihood of the Levites in general, and the priests more specifically. God wanted to make it absolutely clear that the responsibility of administering his presence was severe and dangerous work. God needed to make it abundantly understood that he would not tolerate or accept sin near him, so he separated the Levites from the people. Levites were not permitted to own land. In fact, they depended on the rest of the Israelite nation to supply their needs. There was no room for selfish ambition in the life of the priest; it was a life of service and sacrifice — metaphorically and literally (Numbers 18:20)! God was to be their supplier, and they would learn to trust him and lean on him for all of their needs. Of the gifts the community gave them, they were to give the best of what they received to God as an offering; they could not hold onto anything for themselves.

The priests were to be the exemplars of righteousness and holiness to the entire Israelite community. In addition to following the whole law, they were called to an exceptional standard of behaviour and lifestyle. They were to be physically, spiritually and ceremonially perfect. Even the hair on their head was legislated. Leviticus 21-22 contains a long list of requirements of the holiness of priests. If they were going to administer God's presence, they needed to be perfect to do so. It was not enough for the nation of Israel to be counter-cultural by itself. The priests needed to be the leaders of the counter-cultural statement about God's holiness and his character. They were to declare to the world around them that God's presence was serious business. So serious, in fact, that the Most Holy Place, the place where God's presence rested, was separated from the rest of the tabernacle by a thick curtain; a veil, which separated the nation of Israel from the presence of God. Only the High Priest could enter beyond the curtain, and even then, only once a year!

Korah was well-positioned to enter this calling, or so he thought. He was a direct descendant of Levi, the first cousin of Moses and his brother Aaron. However, he was not satisfied to be relegated to mere tabernacle maintenance. In his pride, he wanted access to the presence of God for himself and others, without following the requirements set out by God. He wanted to be the one to offer sacrifices. He protested to Moses, "You have gone too far!

The whole community is holy, every one of them, and the Lord is with them. Why then do you set yourselves above the Lord's assembly?" (Numbers 16:3)

His protest escalated into a full-on rebellion with 250 men and their families joining the protest to open up access to the presence of God to all people. They were not satisfied to merely care for the tabernacle — they wanted direct access to the real thing. Moses calls them out for directly opposing the Lord and offending his holiness. God's presence and the privilege of administering sacrifices were not open to all, despite the protests of Korah and his followers. The issue at stake was the holiness of God.[3]

To settle the issue, Moses challenged them to enter the tabernacle and take the incense that facilitated the presence of God and distribute it among themselves. God was deeply angered by this assault; who were they to barge into his presence? In response, an earthquake opened up and swallowed the rebellious Levites. They were swallowed into the place of the dead: the grave, or as it is commonly known in Hebrew, Sheol. Their pride and sin were met with the wrath of God. They had no right or claim to the presence of God.

We are all like Korah. We want the benefits of God without the authority and sovereignty of God in our lives. We want to be king without surrendering to the King. We have no intrinsic right to the presence of God. We live in our pride and have sought to establish ourselves as equal with God. We do not want to submit to his kingship or his rules. God has absolutely no reason to grant us a relationship with him; we do not deserve it and we have not earned it. In fact, we cannot earn it. We deserve what Korah and his followers earned: death!

God's presence, and by extension the opportunity to be a priest, are dangerous. To enter the presence of God is to totally and completely surrender to the his holiness. He is king, He is Lord, He is God. The whole establishment of the rigorous sacrificial system of the Mosaic law was to show that we do not have a claim to the presence of God without the necessary sacrifice (Hebrews 9:22).

Thankfully, Korah was not the end of the story. His ransacking of the tabernacle was not the final word on the call to be ministers of God. As Korah entered Sheol, another would come who would also enter Sheol, but he would not stay there.

His name was Jesus.

Christ's Redemption

Jesus too made bold claims about the temple, claiming that he could rebuild it in just three days (John 2:17). Jesus boldly forgave a man's sins in Matthew 9, a task reserved for priests! Following these statements, the Jewish people, possibly with people like Korah in mind, were horrified and wanted to kill Jesus.

However, Jesus was not talking about physical temples when he made his bold proclamations. He was describing a new future where access to the spirit of God would not be limited to a few elite men, but would be accessible to all those who would call him Lord (as foreseen in Isaiah 66:1-2).[4] From the beginning, God's desire was always our hearts. It was always about a relationship with us!

All of Jesus' boldness would have amounted to nothing if he had suffered the same fate as Korah. He would have made bold proclamations, subsequently descended to the place of the dead, and that would be the end of the story. As Jesus breathed his last breath, an earthquake violently broke out (Matthew 27:51-53). The temple was shaken, ransacked by the force of the earth tearing itself apart. The veil separating the most sacred place of the temple from the rest was torn in two. As Jesus died, the place reserved for the elite of the elite was exposed to the entire world.

As Jesus entered Sheol, he descended into the grave as Korah did. But he did not enter Sheol as a violator of God's presence, initiating a rebellion based on pride. Jesus entered Sheol with the authority to proclaim freedom (1 Peter 3:18-20). He suffered death, bearing the weight of our sins into his body because the Father had asked him to. Unlike Korah, who claimed the sacrificial system was irrelevant and God's holiness a manufactured idea, Jesus entered the grave to satisfy God's holiness.

Jesus was both priest and sacrifice. He was proclaiming freedom and forgiveness while offering himself as the means that purchased our freedom (Galatians 3:13). Then Jesus rose from the dead, rising from the grave, from Sheol. If death was the price to be paid for rebellion against God, Jesus had demonstrated that death was not the final word. His resurrection emphatically declared that God is for us, that he wants a relationship with us and that he was willing to purchase it with his own life!

Jesus' death and resurrection provided a new way. His righteousness becomes ours. When God sees us, he sees Jesus' righteousness. Although we should not have any reason to believe that we can be ministers for God, Jesus has paid the price that we should have and we can boldly step into the very presence of God (Hebrews 4:16). This is grace. We deserve death, but we get life. We deserve isolation and loneliness, yet we get relationship. We get the very presence of God![5]

We have absolutely nothing to bring to the table, except for our sin, pride, rebellion and selfishness. In ourselves, we can only multiply our sins, but by Jesus' grace, we are invited to become multipliers of God's grace, presence and Kingdom.

The call to be a priest has absolutely nothing to do with our natural talents, knowledge or behaviour. We are a nation of priests because we recognize that there is nothing in us that could possibly qualify us for the job. When Peter and John declare that we are a nation of priests, they are inviting us to a place of total surrender and submission to Jesus. We are not qualified by what is in us. Instead, we are qualified by the shed blood and the resurrected body of Jesus that declares that we are forgiven and empowered.

Yes, there may be designated responsibilities, in accordance with commitment, character and competence. Crucially, this is not a matter of spiritual superiority, but rather one earned through faithful obedience as servants and ministers. All of us are equal before the throne of God because we are all there by the grace of Jesus, not by anything we have done.

Korah was wrong because he thought the priesthood was open to all because the holiness of God did not matter. The priesthood is opened to us because of the grace of Jesus. To receive Jesus as Lord is to receive the call to become a priest. The ordinary person, those who would never have a hope of accessing the presence of God, could and can now carry it in themselves!

In 1520, the German theologian Martin Luther, having recovered this teaching, began to affirm it boldly:

> *A cobbler, a smith, a farmer, each has the work and office of his trade, and yet they are all alike consecrated priests and bishops, and everyone by means of his own work or office must benefit and serve every other.* — Martin Luther[6]

In Christ, we are all equally called to be ministers for the Gospel. The moment we confess Jesus as Lord, we are called to a life of sacrificial service of his Kingdom. At that moment, everything we have, including the very breath in our lungs, is given in service to our great God. We do not say, "I could never do that." Instead we say, "What could God do through me, his called and chosen one?"

The call to become a priest is always dangerous, sacrificial and requires total dependence on the supremacy of God. The priesthood of all believers does not change that. In fact, we have been called to an even higher counter-cultural standard than the original Levitical priests! Unlike the ancient priests, our high calling is not so that we can earn the right to enter God's presence. We have been given access to God's presence, and that comes with responsibilities that we cannot ignore.

Living Temples

Jesus' upending of the priestly system resulted in the priesthood dramatically and forever changing. Formerly, the temple housed the presence of God. Through Christ, we become living temples; we house the Spirit of God in us. As priests, the presence of God is no longer found in temples made with human hands. It is carried in the bodies of those who proclaim Jesus as Lord (1 Corinthians 6:19-20).

Jesus' selection of his first disciples included those who would be the least likely to be priests, much less *living* temples! He selected run-of-the-mill fishermen, rebellious zealots, traitors and tax-cheats. Likewise, many of us would not typically be chosen to be priests. We are not skilled, good, bold, spiritual or wise enough. Yet, as living temples, we become those who are confident, secure, loved and powerful because the Spirit of God resides in us.

As those who house the presence of God, we carry power and authority. We are given the ability to read scripture, hear the voice of God, pray with power and expect God to move in and through us. As carriers of the presence of God, we can proclaim the Gospel, administer communion, baptize believers and see people subsequently filled with the Holy Spirit.

We often respond to the leading of the Holy Spirit with an attitude that says, "I could never." Yet the blood of Jesus in us cries that, on our own, we cannot do anything for the Kingdom of God; but the Spirit of God in us can and will do whatever he pleases! To be a living temple is to live outside of our comfort zones. We must learn to live reliant upon the grace and power of the Holy Spirit within us.

Immediately after calling us to the priesthood, Peter reminds us that the call to be priests and living temples means that we will forever be foreigners and exiles in the culture around us (1 Peter 2:11). Our culture fills our minds, thoughts and bodies with trash. We offend the holiness of God, the blood of Jesus and our own created purpose when we allow the culture around us to seep into and corrupt our thinking. As priests, we are not made to be the same as the culture around us; we must be clearly and distinctly different. The shape of our lives should be immediately evident as distinct from the culture around us. We do so by modelling after our high priest, Jesus. We lead with forgiveness, grace and mercy, even in painful and messy situations. We give with abundant generosity and fear no lack. Part of the calling of a priest is to be a blessing to the nations and to help redeem and restore creation to relationship with God. We cannot do this unless we ourselves are different from culture, while also still living in relationship with it.

We are called to live and lead holy lives. We do not do so to earn the favour of God; that's impossible. We do so because there is no higher or greater joy than to live in harmony with the spirit of God within us! We look at the promises of our culture, be it fame — sex — comfort — or success, and say that we have something infinitely more precious. As priests, we endure suffering with joy because we carry the hope of humanity, the Spirit of God, in ourselves. We are bold, courageous, confident and eager to announce the good news of Jesus.

Living Sacrifices

The primary responsibility of the priest was offering sacrifices on behalf of the people of Israel to restore them to right relationship with God. The actual sacrifices were required to be perfect, without defect or stain. Jesus was our sacrifice once and for all (Hebrews 10:10). We should not be able to give our lives to God; we are not worthy. In Christ, however, we have been made perfect. Jesus has made us holy so we can offer our lives to God simply because he is worthy. As Paul says, we are living sacrifices (Romans 12:1).

The call to live as a sacrifice means that we give up our lives for the benefit of others and the cause of Christ. Our cultural obsession with individual autonomy and pursuits of success have no room in the life of a living sacrifice. How can we give our lives to God and for the purposes of God as an act of worship while selfishly serving ourselves?

The Levites gave up their rights and privileges to serve the nation. To be a sacrifice, we learn to walk in community as a family. It is no mistake that immediately after Paul invites us to the high holy calling to be living sacrifices, he reminds us that we are a body (Romans 12:4). Our call as living sacrifices is worked out and expressed by submitting to one another in the body of Christ. Collectively, we seek to offer our lives so that the world around us can be restored to a relationship with God.

Our culture tells us that life is found in a careful balance of the right work, the right vacations and the right relationships. When we can balance work and play, we are promised peace and prosperity. We spend our lives in pursuit of an elusive harmony in our lives where everything is "just right," and we are to avoid stress. By that measure, living sacrifices are hopelessly unbalanced. We give our lives for the benefit of others because we already have the hope of humanity in us. The metaphor of our lives is not that of a scale carefully being balanced but of a sacrifice that is given. Paul, in prison and full of joy, knows that he will give his life for the name of Jesus, so he describes his own life as a sacrificial offering (Philippians 2:17)![7] If the approach to our lives does not work in a prison cell, remote village, urban city, in poverty or riches, then it is not Biblical theology, but rather an indication of our privilege.

> **Philippians 4:11-13**
>
> *I am not saying this because I am in need, for I have learned to be content whatever the circumstances. I know what it is to be in need, and I know what it is to have plenty. I have learned the secret of being content in any and every situation, whether well fed or hungry, whether living in plenty or in want. I can do all this through him who gives me strength.*

As living sacrifices, we can pour our lives out for others because Jesus has rescued and redeemed us, and in him, we have everything we need. He is the counterbalance to our trials. He is our rest. He is our joy. He is our hope. He is our salvation.

Mission

The story of Korah's rebellion does not end with him falling into the pit. For the nation of Israel, it gets much worse. Following the rebellion of Korah, the nation of Israel was angry with Moses. Rather than repenting their sin and offence before God, they were stubborn in their pride. They deserved the same fate as Korah. A plague broke out amongst the people as they suffered the just reward for their sin. Moses and Aaron respond by falling on their faces and pleading with God to be merciful. Moses subsequently instructs Aaron, the High Priest, to make an offering for the people amongst the people. Aaron stands there with the offering, between the living and the dying. In that place of danger and fear, Aaron halts the plague and brings hope to the dying.

What a powerful picture of the nature of a priest! The priest stands between those who are living and dying to bring hope and salvation. Jesus was the ultimate High Priest who stood between the living and the dying so that we could have life.

We, as priests, are sent on the same mission. We are sent to stand between the living and the dying so that those around us may be made fully alive in Jesus. The world around us is desperately searching for hope, meaning and purpose. Our commission as priests is to enter that place, between the living and dying, and to bring hope and life. Our job is to boldly call those in that place of death, to confess Jesus as Lord and to receive the new life that he offers. To be a priest is to give our lives to that purpose.

> *Therefore I would be glad to find this word priests becoming as common as it is for us to be called Christians... This belongs to the office of a priest, that he be a messenger of God, and receive from God himself the command to preach his word... And this is the way in which your preaching is to be discharged, that one brother proclaim to another the powerful work of God: how ye have been ransomed from sin, death, hell, and all evil, by him, and have been called to eternal life. Thus shall you also instruct others how they may come also to the same light. For your whole duty is discharged in this, that you confess what God has done for you; and then let this be your chief aim, that you may make this known openly, and call every one to the light, whereto ye have been called. Where you see people who are ignorant, you are to direct and teach them as you have learned, namely, how a man may be saved through the virtue and power of God, and pass from darkness to light.* — Martin Luther (ca 1517)[8]

3

What is Multiplication?

In the introduction, we painted a picture at a very high level of what a multiplying discipleship movement looks like. The Apostolic Imperative, "Everyone Sent to Multiply Everything," is one of the bedrock ideas woven throughout scripture. The instruction for multiplication is an affirmation of who God intended us to be as his prized creation and an invitation to continued partnership with him. Genesis 1 so beautifully describes our pre-fall condition:

> **Genesis 1:27-28**
>
> *So God created man in his own image; he created him in the image of God; he created them male and female. God blessed them, and God said to them, "Be fruitful, multiply, fill the earth, and subdue it. Rule the fish of the sea, the birds of the sky, and every creature that crawls on the earth."*

In essence, we were created to multiply. When we multiply, we are living our created purpose to be image bearers. Multiplication is an expression of God's character; God is a multiplying God. Our purpose is to continue the creative work of God in partnership with him. In essence, we are most alive when we partner with what God is doing in this world. Unsurprisingly, life is most beautiful when God's purposes become our purposes.

God's desire to see creation know his Glory is manifest *through* our partnership with him. God, in his sovereignty, has chosen to use us to see his glory amplified. He did not have to include us, but in his grace and desire for relationship, he has![9]

However, in our selfishness we start to live for our own glory, rather than Jesus' glory. Such selfish desire is what initiated our fall into sin. The corruption of our created purpose to partner with God is powerfully expressed in the story of the Tower of Babel in Genesis 11.

> **Genesis 11:4**
>
> *And they said, "Come, let us build ourselves a city and a tower with its top in the sky. Let us make a name for ourselves; otherwise, we will be scattered throughout the earth."*

Their sin was deeper than simply desiring their own glory, though that was bad enough. In the Tower of Babel, we see a violation of creation at a fundamental level. Rather than fulfilling the mandate to multiply, they desired to gather in the safety and security of their own glory. Multiplication requires faith, stepping into the unknown, taking risks and glorifying God. In our fallen condition such a bold, selfless life is unthinkable. The Tower of Babel is a story of our rejection of partnership with God — our rejection to multiply and fill the earth so that he will be glorified. God's response to the rebellion of the people of Babel is to confuse them and forcibly scatter them by eliminating their ability to communicate.

What does this have to do with church multiplication? Everything. So much of our thinking about the church is based on this mindset of "let's gather in safety." The church often has looked eerily similar to the Tower of Babel. This is what theologians have come to call Christendom, and it governed our way of thinking for centuries. In Christendom, the church sought to gather in seclusion from the world and establish our own communities of safety and security.

While we may have operated out of a desire to know Jesus, our method and thinking were not multiplication oriented. They were what we call 'addition' oriented — "How can we gather more people?" In 'addition' thinking, the priorities quickly become programs, providing religious goods and services, and attracting people by the skill or quality of our preaching.

In an 'addition,' or 'Babel,' model of thinking, we expect people to come to us. We grow churches by adding more people to our programs. In exceptional cases, we can build especially successful programs, perhaps reaching thousands or even tens of thousands. In this model, the effectiveness of the whole is limited to the impact of just a few people. Rather than scattering and multiplying for the Kingdom, we end up gathering primarily for our own benefit. The diagram below illustrates the way that addition oriented thinking is all about adding people to the inside of our group, club or building. Once inside, it's not clear what the people are supposed to be doing other than being entertained.

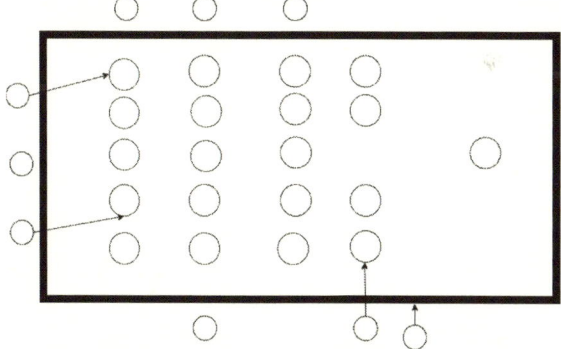

How can we add more people?

The story, thankfully, does not end with the Tower of Babel and the scattering. In Matthew 28, Jesus re-affirms the commandment from Genesis 1, but now he does so in light of his death and resurrection. This is crucial; the Great Commission is an invitation to participate in the mission of God that we were invited into at the dawn of creation!

Matthew 28:19

Go, therefore, and make disciples of all nations, baptizing them in the name of the Father and of the Son and of the Holy Spirit

When we are participating in the Great Commission, we are actually entering into what it truly means to be human; what it means to be fully alive. Jesus gave us a commandment to grow through multiplication! The church is an echo of Genesis 1, not Genesis 11. The commandment to multiply everything is an invitation to partner with the work of God — to be fully human. This can seem like a heavy and difficult call. However, while it definitely requires a high degree of intentionality, it is, as Jesus says, a light burden; when we embrace it, we become more alive in the goodness of Jesus.

With this background in mind, it is incredible that the consequences of Babel are reversed in Acts 2!

Acts 2:4-5

Then they were all filled with the Holy Spirit and began to speak in different tongues, as the Spirit enabled them. Now there were Jews staying in Jerusalem, devout people from every nation under heaven

In light of the resurrection of Jesus and by the power of the Holy Spirit, those who were scattered had been gathered and given a new mandate to multiply. Crucially, the gathering in Acts 2 was the launching point of a broader movement. It would have been so tempting to settle into a comfortable rhythm right where they were, but God's purpose in this was to see all creation know his goodness and have an opportunity to respond to the grace of the Gospel. If we fast forward to Acts 8, they were subsequently scattered to multiply!

Acts 8:1,4

… all except the apostles were scattered throughout the land of Judea and Samaria… So those who were scattered went on their way preaching the word.

The remarkable thing about the church in Acts is that it was everyone *except* the apostles who were scattered. It was the *ordinary* believers who had been mobilized and empowered to be ambassadors for the Kingdom. They went to introduce people to the grace of Jesus who would subsequently be sent to do likewise.

When we plant churches, we are not just planting churches — we are planting churches that plant churches. When we make disciples, we are not only seeing people know Jesus, we are raising disciple-making disciples.

The defining characteristic of multiplication is that those who are sent mobilize others to do likewise. The diagram illustrates the way that in multiplication oriented thinking, everyone is mobilized as a participant, not a consumer. The diagram below helps to illustrate the power of relational networks; what keeps people together is a common mission, facilitated through relationships. In contrast, in addition oriented thinking, the quality of the product or program is what holds people together.

Multiplication Oriented Thinking

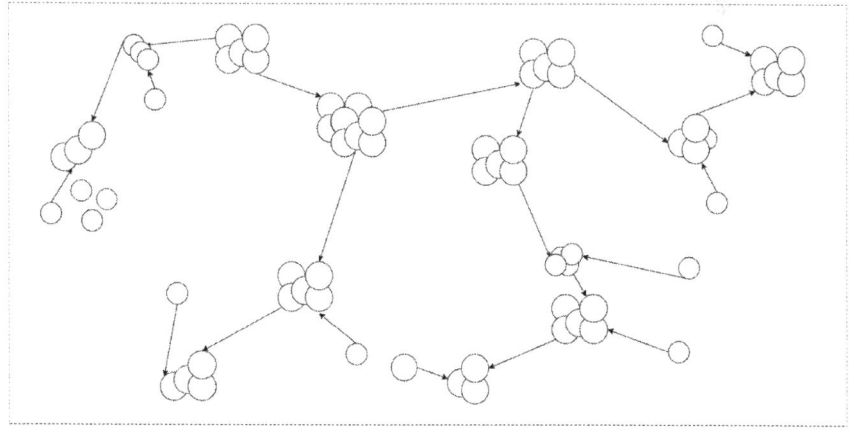

How can we mobilize everyone for mission?

It should be clear, at this point, that multiplication and sending are intertwined. If we multiply, we will send. And if we send, we will multiply. Perhaps this is one of the reasons why multiplication is hard: it is costly. We must be willing to sacrifice what is immediately comfortable for ourselves to fulfill what Jesus has invited us into.

The largest churches in the world may reach a few tens of thousands of people at a time. Rocket-like growth may include adding a few thousand attendants in a year. It is tempting to be impressed by these metrics, but they pale in comparison to the impact of multiplication. Historically, the most influential movements of the church have always been built around mobilizing ordinary saints to multiply the goodness of Jesus to those who have never heard his name.

Multiplication starts slow. It begins with 1 and grows to 2, then 4, then 8. In fact, if we take a multiplication path, it is slower and harder initially because it requires life-on-life discipleship. However, if we stay the course, slowly the movement gains momentum and the impact reaches far beyond what we could imagine. Each person becomes catalytic to the movement. When we speak of a discipleship movement, we are describing the process of ordinary people, transformed and empowered by the Holy Spirit, sent into the world to have an impact; one that far exceeds what we could possibly do through larger events or services. For example, there are multiplication movements in Latin America and India that in a single year will plant 15,000 churches between them, reaching well over 200,000 people with the Gospel for the first time.

Multiplication is about ordinary people, empowered by the Spirit and sent as ambassadors for the Kingdom of Jesus. Through the new covenant made possible by the blood of Jesus, and the "word of their testimony" (Revelation 12:11), the saints overcome the power of the enemy and see the mission of God brought to the world. It is their stories of transformation that will ultimately see disciples multiplied.

The grand narrative of scripture can be described entirely in multiplication language. Multiplication is not advanced discipleship, nor is it simply evangelism. It is, in fact, the very bedrock of the work of God in creation!

The invitation to multiplication is a whole new way of thinking about church. Living sent is an invitation to embrace the full life that Jesus has promised. It points all the way back to Genesis 1 where we are invited to participate in the mission of God in the world. By Jesus' grace, and his grace alone, we get to participate in the mission.

4

The Discipleship Pipeline

With the theological foundation of multiplication and the priesthood of all believers, we can understand that the Apostolic Imperative, Everyone Sent to Multiply Everything, is not simply a statement about organizational growth; rather, it is a statement about relationships. Multiplication, discipleship and sending are, at their core, relational activities.

When we observe Jesus' ministry, it is abundantly clear that discipleship can only happen in the context of relationship. This is critical; the Church is not an institution with a set of tasks to accomplish, but a community calling one another to deeper levels of discipleship and evangelism. Sometimes the church can fall into the temptation of prioritizing the completion of tasks over the formation of meaningful relationships and spiritual maturity. We can see the apostle Paul calling us to a deeper level of relationships in referring again to the analogy of the body:

> **1 Corinthians 12:24-26 [ESV]**
>
> *But God has so composed the body, giving greater honour to the part that lacked it, that there may be no division in the body, but that the members may have the same care for one another. If one member suffers, all suffer together; if one member is honoured, all rejoice together.*

The relationships we form in the church are different from those that we tend to form around common interests, work or family. The church is a body of people who are united together in a common mission: to see people know Jesus! It is this mission that allows people from diverse backgrounds to be united together in heart and mind as we saw in Acts 2.

This causes us to ask the question, how do we create a scalable environment where everyone is sent to multiply everything, while also living in deep relationship with the wider body of the church? As the community grows, it becomes more difficult to ensure that everyone is being sent and multiplying in an effective, strategic and relational way. The more the desire to see sending and multiplication is actually lived relationally, the more this question becomes critical to address. It becomes exponentially more difficult to maintain and develop these relationships at scale, let alone engage in mission. This is not a problem unique to our context; discipleship movements across the world and across time have run into this same barrier. We can see both the problem as well as the solution in the early church.

Shortly after the beautiful passage in Acts 2 where the believers share everything and have everything in common, they start to run into challenges. They may have deep relationships, but it soon becomes challenging to maintain those relationships and engage in mission.

Acts 6:1-7 [NIV]

In those days when the number of disciples was increasing, the Hellenistic Jews among them complained against the Hebraic Jews because their widows were being overlooked in the daily distribution of food. So the Twelve gathered all the disciples together and said, "It would not be right for us to neglect the ministry of the word of God in order to wait on tables. Brothers and sisters, choose seven men from among you who are known to be full of the Spirit and wisdom. We will turn this responsibility over to them and will give our attention to prayer and the ministry of the word." This proposal pleased the whole group. ... So

> *the word of God spread. The number of disciples in Jerusalem increased rapidly...*

How did they tackle the challenges introduced by large numbers, a big mission and deep relationships? The answer is not surprising: structure. The introduction of structure allowed two very important things to happen: healthier relationships and a bigger impact for the Kingdom of Jesus!

The Discipleship Pipeline is a means by which we can create an environment for discipleship that will clearly engage, integrate and mobilize every person in the church. In turn, those disciples can be mobilized and sent to continue multiplying new disciples in places, near and far, where the Gospel is not yet being proclaimed.

The introduction of systems and structures allows for the following:

1) Healthier individuals by helping answer the core questions people are asking.
2) Healthier relationships by providing them direction and purpose.
3) Greater ability to accomplish the mission of the Church: to see people know Jesus.

The Discipleship Pipeline

This leads us to the Discipleship Pipeline. The Discipleship Pipeline is a tool that we can use to establish clarity around the process of multiplying disciples. It serves to provide clarity on how the church is made of many people, each serving uniquely according to their gifting, capacity and experience.

The Discipleship Pipeline creates an environment where people are consistently growing in their discipleship and leadership capacity on three axes simultaneously: Leadership Position (Where do I multiply), Discipleship Potential (What do I multiply?) And Multiplication Power (How do I Multiply?) as seen in the diagram below.

Three Dimensions of Discipleship

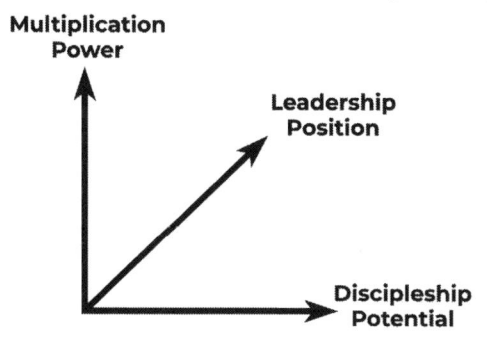

```
Multiplication
Power
    ↑
    |         Leadership
    |         Position
    |        ↗
    |       
    |      
    |                    Discipleship
    |_____→ Potential
```

Discipleship Potential

This is the 'transformational' aspect of the Discipleship Pipeline. This dimension defines how the Gospel causes a person's life to be completely altered through five distinct areas of emphasis: gospel fluency, secure identity, missional living, radical generosity and crucial conversations. A person with a large amount of Discipleship Potential will be able to consistently see those who they are leading experience growth in all 5 Discipleship Emphases. Discipleship Potential is referred to in terms of the depth of understanding, lived experience and ability to see others experience the areas of discipleship emphasis.

Multiplication Power

This is the 'influence' aspect of the Discipleship Pipeline. Multiplication Power is effectively a measure of how consistently and effectively a leader can mobilize people to head in a particular direction. Critically, a person can be a very effective influencer without holding a formal Leadership Position. Similarly, what a person is able to multiply is not necessarily connected to their effectiveness at doing so. A leader can be a very effective multiplier of very poor attributes.

Multiplication Power is referred to numerically as an indicator of how many degrees of leadership separation they are able to consistently and demonstrably have an influence across. The mark of a leader with significant multiplication power is a person who can influence those with whom they have no direct contact, by empowering others to hold the reigns of leadership. We call those living out this concept 'N+2' leaders, meaning they can reach two degrees of separation. This powerful and organization-changing idea will be discussed in detail below.

Leadership Position

This is the 'positional' aspect of the Discipleship Pipeline. This defines the specific role, responsibilities and expectations associated with a person in relation to the church. It defines clearly who they are discipling and who is discipling them. Leadership Position, in the Discipleship Pipeline, is the dimension that clearly defines the specific area a person is responsible for. The Leadership Position is the formal leadership role that a person may hold.

The overarching objective across these three dimensions is to create a system to maximize multiplication of the gospel to as many people as possible. When it functions properly, every person is empowered to both be discipled and to disciple others.

Considering postmodern culture's general distaste for systems and structures, it can be easy to view the Discipleship Pipeline as some sort of corporate ladder, but this could not be further from the truth! This is of utmost importance: the Discipleship Pipeline is not a hierarchy where people are trying to attain the top rungs of the organizational ladder. Rather, it is a means of consistently seeing people grow as disciples and ensuring that those with Leadership Positions are those who have a history of consistent and healthy multiplication. The Discipleship Pipeline is primarily a relational structure, not a hierarchical structure. It does not assign value to an individual based on a certain position they hold: rather, it describes how each person can uniquely contribute to the whole.

Discipleship Potential

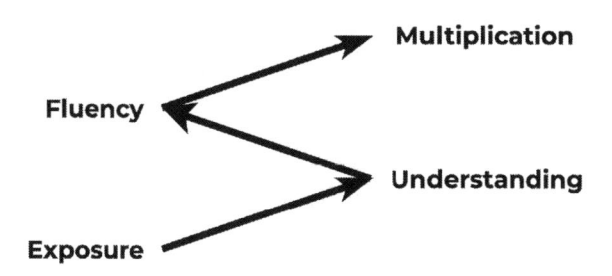

Multiplication

Fluency

Understanding

Exposure

Multiplication Power

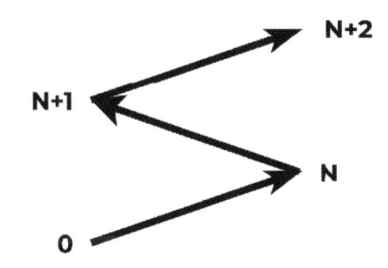

N+2

N+1

N

0

Leadership Position

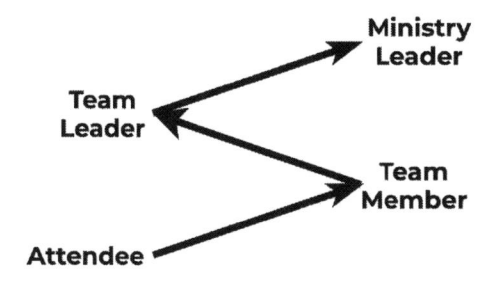

Ministry Leader

Team Leader

Team Member

Attendee

Summary

The three dimensions of the Discipleship Pipeline are intended to work together. They provide us with the content, culture and systems for multiplying discipleship. As each person is integrated into the Discipleship Pipeline, the desire is to see them growing consistently in all three dimensions. The goal is to see a demonstrated Multiplication Power and Discipleship Potential that is ahead or at least in line with someone's Leadership Position.

The coming sections outline each of these three dimensions in detail. It is important to remember that none of these dimensions are designed to be isolated. Discipleship Potential is deeply intertwined with Multiplication Power and is deployed through Leadership Position. For clarity, it is easier to discuss the three separately, but in practice, none can exist without the others.

Part 2

Discipleship Potential

5

What Is Discipleship?

In the framework, we speak of Discipleship Potential as the capacity for people to effectively and consistently create an environment for discipleship. If we are aiming to multiply, what precisely is the objective, aim or purpose of multiplication? If discipleship is the primary means of seeing multiplication happen, what then constitutes discipleship? We can talk a great deal about discipleship, but if we are not precise in our definitions, it can become a catch-all term that we use for all Christian activity.

The Great Commission to make disciple-making disciples, as found in Matthew 28:16-20, is undoubtedly among one of the most well known and often cited verses from scripture. However, if we are not careful, we can think of discipleship as building larger church services, attracting more people to come to our events or providing care to Christians. If we are not careful, we can mistake discipleship with the products that the church produces. The command to go and make disciples is not a command to grow the attendance base of the church. It is so much deeper. It is so much more beautiful.

Discipleship As Worship

Fundamentally, discipleship, and by natural extension, multiplication, is about God getting the glory that he deserves.[10] Discipleship is about worship. At first glance that appears to be a self-explanatory statement. However, it is profound as it means that when we speak of discipleship, we are talking about a process that is ultimately about Jesus, not about us. Our thinking about discipleship often places our maturity or formation as the primary goal. In reality, unless the primary goal is the glorification of God, then we will not produce meaningful disciples. Until we correctly understand the principle that discipleship is ultimately about God's glorification, we will struggle to be effective in seeing ourselves walk as multiplying disciples.

The fact that discipleship, and indeed all Christian life, is about worship is central to a proper and robust understanding of the Gospel. As we will discuss in detail later, we receive new life, freedom and purpose by receiving the grace of Jesus. We are invited to receive life and life to the full by participation in the life of Jesus (John 10:10). While it is true that we receive a tremendous gift by accepting the life Jesus has, it can cause us to think that discipleship is about us. Emphatically stated, discipleship is entirely a means by which we glorify God. Discipleship IS worship.

To fully understand the fact that discipleship is worship, we must examine Jesus' own life and the ultimate purpose of his mission. At a basic level, discipleship is following Jesus, which means that whatever Jesus' objective is must become our objective.

Isaiah 49 is one of the most important messianic scriptures in the Old Testament, as Isaiah paints a picture of who Jesus is hundreds of years before his life. In painting a picture of the 'suffering servant,' God states, through Isaiah, that his ultimate purpose in Jesus was that he would be glorified. [11]

Isaiah 49:3

You are my servant, Israel, in whom I will be glorified.

God's ultimate objective in the Gospel was that he would receive glory. Jesus' life was, ultimately, crucially, not just about us; it was about God getting the glory that is rightfully his. Jesus restates this himself just before he heads to the cross in John 17:

John 17:1

Father, the hour has come. Glorify your Son so that the Son may glorify you

Jesus came and died so that God would be glorified! The entire Gospel narrative is ultimately about restoring God to his place of worship in humanity. The Gospel is not about us; discipleship is not about us; the church is not about us; it's all about him!

We may be tempted to be offended by this concept as we may pridefully think, "Who does God think he is to desire worship?" The answer is that he is God! God has the right and the authority to demand worship. Instead of doing so, he has invited us to do so out of a free choice in response to his self-sacrificial love.

The principle of discipleship as worship is essential because it forms the basis of our heart for discipleship by shifting our attention off of ourselves and onto the Father. It is also a practical building block since the journey of discipleship will undoubtedly be uncomfortable, painful and difficult, as Jesus himself has promised (Luke 14:26-28). The call to discipleship is ultimately a call to die to ourselves and to live a life of worship.

Luke 14:27

Whoever does not bear his own cross and come after me cannot be my disciple.

Many of the disciples, and the second generation disciples, suffered and even died for their faith (1 Peter 1:6, Acts 7:60). How were they able to do this? Because they knew it was not about them. If we think that discipleship, and by extension multiplication and the church as a whole, is about us we will never be able to walk the road of discipleship that Jesus has called us to; it is simply too costly.

Much of our resistance to discipleship, or complaints about how it is functioning in our lives, can be traced as a refusal to live a life of sacrificial worship. Discipleship is an invitation to properly position our lives at the throne of God in surrender and declare, *"My life is no longer mine — use it for your glory."*

Naturally, the process of disciple-making is also, crucially, about God's glorification. The emphasis on multiplication in discipleship is an invitation to worship! Evangelism is an act of worship. When we properly understand this, we will no longer resist evangelism as an unfortunate Christian duty. Instead, evangelism will be the natural, joyful result of us desiring to live lives of worship.

The church, when properly understood, is the vehicle through which God has chosen to see people know who he is by revealing Jesus to them (Ephesians 3:10). We do not exist to multiply our name, branding, style or structures. All of the structures in this book, such as the Leadership Position aspects of the Discipleship Pipeline, are a tool for creating an environment to accomplish the real goal, worship of God!

1 Peter 4:11

If anyone speaks, let it be as one who speaks God's words; if anyone serves, let it be from the strength God provides, so that God may be glorified through Jesus Christ in everything. To him be the glory and the power forever and ever. Amen

All of this talk of glorification has an unbelievable, even shocking, implication. Through discipleship, we not only get to give glory to God, a supreme privilege in itself, we are also glorified in the process ourselves!

Romans 8:17

We suffer with him so that we may also be glorified with him.

Think about that for a moment: by living lives of sacrificial discipleship, we get to give glory and also be recipients of it! The supreme grace of God is that we get to receive his glory! He gives glory to us so that we can return the glory to him.

If the glorification of God is the objective of discipleship, then how do we do that? How is God glorified in our discipleship? If discipleship is about worship, how do we worship in our discipleship? In other words, what exactly is discipleship?

Discipleship is to follow and be transformed by Jesus. However, for many of us, that's where it stops in our thinking. We tend to think of discipleship as an individual, private pursuit. In reality, this couldn't be further from the truth. Discipleship is a fundamentally relational process whereby we are invited to follow Jesus and are doing the same with others. It results in a total transformation in every aspect of our lives: relationships, family, career, finance, identity and, of course, worldview. Discipleship transformation inevitably results in this radical change multiplied into other people. Such a transformation is internal and external to who we are. We call these the inner-life and outer-life components of discipleship.[12]

> **2 Thessalonians 1:11-12**
>
> *In view of this, we always pray for you that our God will make you worthy of his calling, and by his power fulfill your every desire to do good and your work produced by faith, so that the name of our Lord Jesus will be glorified by you, and you by him, according to the grace of our God and the Lord Jesus Christ.*

2 Thessalonians 1:11-12 paints a picture of discipleship as living a life worthy of his calling and producing good work through faith so that Jesus will be glorified. This short verse has painted for us a robust and holistic picture of discipleship by emphasizing that the goal of the Christian life, discipleship, is worship and is comprised of an 'inner-life' and 'outer-life' dimension as shown in the diagram below.

A Holistic Picture of Discipleship

- Glory to God (Worship)
- Inner Life (Sanctification)
- Outer Life (Multiplication)

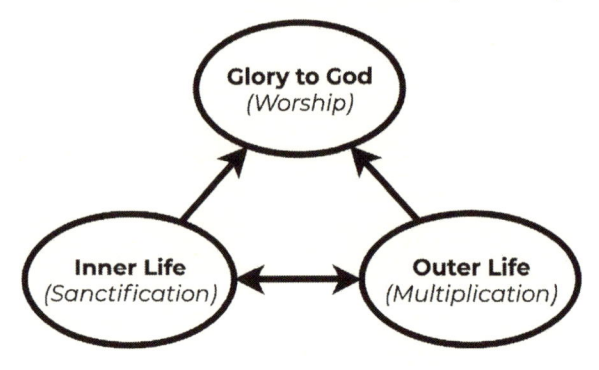

Inner-Life — Sanctification

By 'inner-life,' we are referring to the process of becoming more like Jesus in our thoughts, words, and actions. We recognize that all believers have dimensions of their lives that need transformation. There needs to be a continual process of identifying and repenting from sin. In its place, we learn to value and pursue the things of Jesus. We do not just focus on what we see externally, but we seek to see people experience a total heart transformation (Ezekiel 36:26). The process of personal transformation is what we broadly call "sanctification" in theological terms, and it ultimately produces eternal life.

> **Romans 6:22 [ESV]**
>
> *But now that you have been set free from sin and have become slaves of God, the fruit you get leads to sanctification and its end, eternal life.*

As disciples, we are transformed to live as people no longer enslaved to sin, but walking as people whose purpose is to glorify God. The sanctification process is a means by which we are slowly moulded more and more into the person of Jesus, as revealed in the scriptures.

Inner-life transformation is a deep uprooting of our soul. The process is often challenging, even painful, as we are matured into the likeness of Jesus (James 1:4). Inner-life transformation requires that we both know what Jesus is like and begin to look more like him in our lives. As we will discover further on, this maturation is deeply challenging.

One important aspect of inner-life transformation is learning to walk in security and harmony with the Spirit of God. Jesus invites us in John 15 to abide in him, meaning to find our security and hope in him. Inner-life discipleship, although challenging, is supremely life-giving, in part because we learn that our security, confidence and identity is in him. When we are grounded and abiding in Jesus, we can withstand any challenge or obstacle and need not have any fear. As we learn to have a secure inner-life we can live tremendously sacrificially without fear of burn-out, exhaustion, poverty or weakness because Jesus sustains us. A secure inner-life is the most stable, secure and peaceful life imaginable — even in an insecure, unstable and chaotic environment! The Apostle Paul emphatically makes the statement from prison in Philippians 4:12 that regardless of the situation, he has learned to be content. Similarly, David writes in Psalm 27:1 that the Lord is his light and his salvation and as a result he lives without fear.

It should be clear that inner-life transformation is a deeper issue than character formation. While character is an important consideration when raising a disciple, a person can have a robust character without necessarily having experienced the transformation that only the Gospel can bring. The Gospel is not a set of morals to which we have a subscription. The Gospel is news about an event: the death and resurrection of Jesus. The Gospel, and our invitation to become participants in its proclamation, is way more than a mere idea to which we declare adherence. This 'Good News' causes every aspect of our lives to be re-imagined in light of this tremendously good news.

Outer-Life — Multiplication

The second dimension is what we refer to as 'outer-life.' It is the work that is referred to in 2 Thessalonians 1 or the fruit referred to in John 15.

John 15:8

My Father is glorified by this: that you produce much fruit and prove to be my disciples.

By the 'outer life' of discipleship, we are referring to the reality that every believer is called to be a disciple-making disciple, or in other words, an ambassador for Jesus. Inner-life is the sanctification component of discipleship; outer-life is the multiplication component of discipleship. Discipleship multiplication is an integral part of discipleship. It is not a component reserved for the elite but a requirement for everyone who calls themselves a follower of Jesus. The calling to multiply disciples must not be restricted to the leadership of the church, but it has to involve everyone! Every person in the church must understand their role as simultaneously being discipled and being a disciple-maker in their own right. Growing in discipleship is equal parts personal, internal transformation (inner-life), and sharing and teaching others to do likewise (outer-life).

We can equate discipleship with internal personal transformation. It is undoubtedly true that internal transformation is an integral and essential component of discipleship. However, unless we subsequently multiply that personal transformation into other disciples, we have not unlocked the true potential of discipleship.

Outer-life is not the second step of discipleship; it is an indivisible, and integral, component of it. There is no inner-life transformation without outer-life multiplication. Scripture states it so clearly that without multiplication in our discipleship, our faith is dead (James 3:26).

> **James 3:26**
> *For just as the body without the spirit is dead, so also faith without works is dead.*

We must come to understand that being released to multiply in our discipleship is not an advanced concept but part of the definition of discipleship. Disciples multiply to other disciples. Disciples who do not multiply are not disciples. As Jesus himself states, we prove we are disciples by bearing fruit (John 15:8). It may sound harsh but it is simply the teaching and invitation of Jesus.

Summary

By combining the three components of discipleship, worship — sanctification — and multiplication, we have the following definition of discipleship:

> ***Glorifying God by following and being transformed by Jesus while inviting, modelling, training and empowering others to do likewise.***

When we speak of Discipleship Emphases we are placing equal emphasis on inner-life transformation for the individual and outer-life transformation so that they can effectively multiply their discipleship into others.

Before we can discuss the actual process of multiplying discipleship as outlined as inviting, modelling, training and empowering, we must first be clear about what sort of transformation is taking place. What does this multiplication movement look like and what shape does discipleship take?

Discipleship Emphases

There is tremendous and glorious potential in a definition of discipleship as "Glorifying God by following and being transformed by Jesus while inviting, modelling, training and empowering others to do likewise." Such a vision of discipleship is a tremendously effective and efficient process of multiplying a person's character into other people. The discipleship process will result in multiplication of whatever is in a person, both good and bad. Discipleship is life-on-life transfer from one person to another. Whatever is in that person will be reproduced into the people they are discipling. At first this process is slow but as it speeds up, the multiplied impact is massive as every person in the network is mobilized to strengthen and expand the network. This fast-moving, relational model of training people to fall in love with Jesus and teach others to do the same has the potential to be simultaneously fast-moving and healthy because it moves at the speed of relationships — when relationships are healthy, discipleship is healthy.

Consequently, by its nature, large scale discipleship is challenging to control because it is a distributed relational system. By this, we mean that discipleship scales rapidly and spreads widely, often in unlikely and unpredictable ways! It's very difficult to create an environment where everyone is simultaneously teacher and student. As a result, often a fear of multiplication of bad or incomplete character can result in centralizing the discipleship processes around a few professionals or experienced disciples. The desire to only have a few people doing discipleship is understandable; it is easy to be afraid of what people will multiply. We must clearly state, this is not what Jesus has commanded us to do. He has sent us to send others; we must invite everyone to the call to be discipled and to disciple others.

For this reason, it is important to be clear on what we are seeking to emphasize in the discipleship process. We must use wisdom to help make the Gospel accessible to all by mobilizing all people (Colossians 1:27-28).

Colossians 1:27-28

God wanted to make known among the Gentiles the glorious wealth of this mystery, which is Christ in you, the hope of glory. We proclaim him, warning and teaching everyone with all wisdom, so that we may present everyone mature in Christ.

What are the aspects of following and being transformed by Jesus that we desire to see multiplied into others? We have come up with five areas of Discipleship Emphases to help create clarity to answer the question: "What is it that we want to see multiplied in other people?" We call these the 5 Discipleship Emphases, which are:

Gospel Fluency

Our relationship to, and understanding of, the Gospel and our ability to multiply it into others.

It is in gospel fluency that our foundational theology, and resulting transformation, of the Trinity, creation, sin, repentance, church, the Kingdom of God, the new creation and scripture are found.

Secure Identity

The reception of Jesus as Lord and the formation in us as children, servants and ambassadors of God.

It is in secure identity that we begin to put into practice Jesus as Lord and are made fully alive in him. When we learn to live with Jesus as Lord, we are transformed into children, servants and ambassadors for the Kingdom of Jesus. Many of our habits and behaviours, good or bad, flow from our identity.

Missional Living

An integrated life of surrender to Jesus, where we live to maximize our impact for the Kingdom of Jesus.

Missional living is the dimension that addresses the purpose and structure of our lives. A fully missional life will result in intentional and integrated decisions, in the context of our Church family, to maximize our kingdom impact. To be specific, these are built around the everyday practices of putting church at the centre, intentional proximity, open and hospitable homes, sacrificial living, spiritual hunger and a nurturing a passion for the lost.

Radical Generosity

The giving of our time, talents and treasures in light of the radical generosity of God who gave his Son first.

It is in radical generosity that our gospel fluency, secure identity and missional living are expressed in the joyful and eager giving of our time, talents and treasures to others to bless them and further the name of Jesus.

Crucial Conversations

The ability to enter into intentional, and often tricky, discipleship conversations about what Jesus is doing in our life or another's.

Crucial conversations provide the ability to be challenged and to challenge others in their discipleship. Many discipleship issues arise from disciples who struggle to receive teaching and training or, on the other hand, struggle to give it to others. A disciple can live a rich Christian life but ultimately find themselves missing opportunities to be an effective multiplier due to needed growth in this emphasis.

Summary

There are other ways that we could break down the various aspects of being transformed by Jesus. However, the five areas outlined above are broad enough to provide coverage to the all-encompassing scope of discipleship, while simultaneously being sufficiently specific to encourage clear thinking and action in answering the question: "What do we multiply?"

6

Gospel Fluency

Gospel fluency is the foundation of discipleship. It is the cornerstone that all the other Discipleship Emphases are built upon. Gospel fluency is the area of discipleship that captures our awareness and comprehension of what Jesus has done, and our ability to communicate that hope to others. At the most basic level, gospel fluency starts with the foundational truths of what Jesus has accomplished as revealed in scripture.

However, gospel fluency is more than mere intellectual assent to the narrative of the scriptures. Gospel fluency refers to the total life transformation in light of the Good News of Jesus. To be fluent in the Gospel is to have our entire worldview re-shaped in light of the Gospel. Such a complete transformation would, of course, include a reasonable understanding of theology and scripture but must be extended to a life lived in light of those truths.

Our way of gaining understanding and knowledge is very influenced by the Greek conception of knowledge, which is primarily rationalistic and objective. While this type of knowledge is important and helpful, our knowing the Gospel must move from 'head' to 'heart.' In contrast, we are invited to a Hebrew influenced conception of knowledge. Rather than standing back and observing from a distance, we are invited to know the Gospel by engaging with it on a personal level, wrestling with the practical implications of it and finally putting it into practice in our day-today lives. Our understanding of the gospel must be not simply intellectual, but also practical and relational.[13]

Gospel fluency is about surrendering control of our lives in light of the incredible Good News of Jesus. It is an invitation to a radical life of total transformation, sanctification and mission! In order for us to accept the invitation to this radical life, the Holy Spirit must be working in our lives in two critical ways.

Colossians 1:9-10

We are asking that you may be filled with the knowledge of his will in all wisdom and spiritual understanding, so that you may walk worthy of the Lord, fully pleasing to him: bearing fruit in every good work and growing in the knowledge of God.

First, as Colossians 1:9-10 illustrates, the knowledge and understanding of the Gospel is a process that is spirit-lead and spirit-empowered. Second, the Holy Spirit will work to see Godly knowledge and wisdom manifest in the way that we live. The Holy Spirit works to develop gospel fluency in both our inner life ("knowledge") and outer life ("good work"). This is God's incredible grace: that he would send the Holy Spirit to help us understand who he is and what he has done and then empower us to live in light of that knowledge!

From Transactional to Missional

What then is the Gospel? At the centre of the Gospel is the Good News of the death and resurrection of Jesus. This is the defining event of the Gospel, our lives and even all of history. Everything centres on this work of Jesus. This miraculous event should change and inform the way we see our world, including our relationships, every aspect of our lives, all of creation and especially who God is. Gospel fluency is allowing the work of Jesus to be the lens through which we view our whole world.

For many people, the Gospel has been communicated in largely transactional, individualistic terms. By transactional we mean that the Gospel is often communicated something like: "each of us owed a debt to God, Jesus paid that debt and now we are ok." In this thinking, once the transaction is complete there is little for us to do other than continue on our way, confident in the knowledge that we are 'saved' or 'going to heaven' despite no evident relationship with God or desire to participate in this saving work in humanity. In a transactional view of the Gospel, the emphasis remains on the one-time work of Jesus, not his ongoing work in creation.

By individualistic, we mean that the Gospel is often communicated such that it only concerns our individual relationship with God, with minimal consideration given to our role as co-labourers with Christ or to the fact that God has a deep concern for groups and nations of people, as clearly evidenced in the entirety of the Old Testament.

While there is truth in a transactional individualistic view of the Gospel, hopefully we can see how it falls woefully short of the glorious grace that we are invited into in the Gospel. In a transactional view of the Gospel, inner life and outer life of discipleship will always feel awkward and at-odds since there is nothing in the transactional model that requires the outer-life component.

Through Jesus' death and resurrection, we are invited to a new life with him. We are dead without Jesus, but by his grace, we are made fully alive. The Good News of Jesus is not simply our debts being paid, but that we are invited to a new life of mission. A life dedicated to inviting others to be raised from death to life by the work of Jesus!

Ephesians 2:4-5 [ESV]

But God, being rich in mercy, because of the great love with which he loved us, even when we were dead in our trespasses, made us alive together with Christ—by grace, you have been saved

We, by our effort, cannot raise ourselves to life. We are utterly lost without Jesus. However, in Jesus, we are raised from death to life. Not just life but life to the fullest! The Gospel is both that we are made fully alive and that we are also called to invite others to be made fully alive!

Our thinking must shift from a narrow, transactional, individualistic view of the Gospel to a missional view of the Gospel. In a missional view of the Gospel, we primarily think of the Gospel as an invitation to a relationship with God and participation in his mission. In a missional view of the Gospel, we are invited to partner with what God is doing in the world.

The Gospel is news about how the Father sent the Son into the world so that we could be reconciled to him, and how in turn the Son sent the Holy Spirit so that we can be people of mission. The sending continues when each one of us receives the grace of Jesus to a restored relationship with God and the invitation to join his saving work in humanity. To be fully alive is to live a life in harmony with the creator of the universe and to live a life marked by fruitfulness — to be disciple-making disciples. The former is the work of Jesus on this earth, and the latter is the work of the Holy Spirit in our lives. The Good News is incomplete without the empowerment of the Holy Spirit engaging us on mission!

In a transactional view of the Gospel, the focus is on ourselves. In a missional view of the Gospel, the focus is on others. The Gospel is missional; therefore, our reception of the Gospel must also be missional. We cannot receive the Gospel without also receiving the call of the Gospel to see others invited to it — they are inseparable!

There are many important components to gospel fluency, but we must continually return to this basic building block: that we were dead in our sin, but by the grace of Jesus, we are invited to a new life of mission and joy.

Gospel Fluency Moorings

Gospel fluency is not about being the smartest theologian in the room, though some followers of Jesus may be specifically wired and gifted to gain expertise in the nuances of theology. Nonetheless, it is crucial that we are discipling others to grow in knowledge and wisdom derived from a clear understanding of the scriptures. We cannot multiply what we do not understand! It is not enough to merely have encountered the Gospel. Our discipleship process must result in an understanding of the Gospel that can be multiplied and discipled into other believers.

Gospel fluency is a process both enabled and led by the Holy Spirit, but that does not mean we can abdicate the responsibility of asking questions, gaining knowledge and learning to communicate the Gospel effectively. The Spirit is inviting us into a process that he leads, and we get to partner with him in it. We must be able to clearly speak about who God is and who we are. We need a firm, secure and well-formed theology, keeping in mind that proper theological formation will result in both clear thinking and bold living.

As we engage people from many different backgrounds, it is important that we can clearly define what we believe and why we live the way we do. There are so many ideas, concepts and perspectives that we can easily become confused regarding what is true. To ensure we are not blown about by the winds and waves of life (Ephesians 4:14), we must establish some core beliefs that can act as a foundation or mooring. Just as a mooring keeps a boat from drifting off to sea, strong theological moorings will help us not be led astray.

To help provide clarity, we have developed nine gospel fluency moorings that will help us grow as disciple-making disciples without going off track or getting distracted. Through the power of the Holy Spirit and in the context of the church community, these moorings will help us live our lives on mission in the world without becoming confused about what we believe.

With the exception of placing the Trinity at the centre, these moorings are not arranged in order of importance; instead, we should think of them all as equally critical in helping us walk as disciple-making disciples. If any of these were to be uprooted then our entire framework to communicate and live the Gospel may be at risk of drifting.

Gospel Fluency Moorings

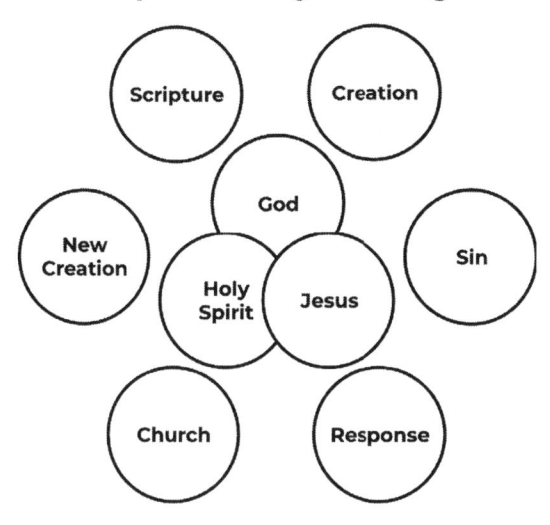

Diagram showing interconnected circles: Scripture, Creation, New Creation, God, Sin, Holy Spirit, Jesus, Church, Response

These moorings are designed to encapsulate the grand narrative of scripture. For a concise, one-paged, narrative version of the moorings see *Appendix A: The Story of Scripture*.

God

We believe in God, who is love and is the creator and sustainer of all things. He exists in perfect harmony as three persons in one (we call it the Trinity). The Father, Son and Holy Spirit: a perfect, loving and glorious relationship. There is one God who is sovereign over all creation, and all things exist for his glory. He is all-knowing, all-powerful and all-deserving of praise (Genesis 1:1, 2 Corinthians 13:13-14, Isaiah 43:7).

God is not like anything else — all metaphors or descriptions fail to entirely capture the magnitude of his glory. This is important because it means that we must humbly acknowledge that while God has revealed himself to us, we will never be able to fully comprehend the fullness of his glory.

There are two important applications of this mooring in the context of discipleship. First, we must continually point people to the supremacy of God over all. We are invited to humble ourselves before him and worship him because he is worthy of all. We worship him because of who he is! As Proverbs 9:10 says, "The fear of the Lord is the beginning of wisdom." Everything begins by acknowledging who God is.

The second aspect of this mooring is that it reminds us that God is relational in nature — the Trinity is a perfectly harmonious relationship. The relationship between Father, Son and Holy Spirit has been described by C.S. Lewis as an intimate dance involving each member of the Trinity — what a beautiful relational picture.[14] The fact that God is relational is important because it means that he desires a relationship with his creation; although he is sovereign and supreme he is knowable! Expressed as love, God's nature is one of invitation to participate in his joy. God's sovereignty is not a cause for separation from him: our sin is. His sovereignty is the basis for security in a relationship with him since he is unchanging in his love for us (Exodus 3:14).

Creation

Out of God's relational nature flows his creativity. The world around us was created by God, which means that it has a beginning. Distinct among his creation, God made you and I: humanity. We were created for relationship with God: to love and know him, each other, and ourselves. In our pursuit of this, we were meant to be creative and adventurous. We were created in the image of God as his ambassadors on this earth. Therefore, we are meant to reflect his very nature. God's nature is creative, so our nature is to be creative. God's nature is relational, so our nature is relational.

In creating humanity, God has invited us into relationship and partnership with him. We were made to join the purposes of God from the very beginning of time. When we speak of multiplication, it is an invitation to re-engage our created purpose (Genesis 1:26-28, Matthew 28:19)!

Creation is good and valuable. The world around us does not always view creation this way. Oftentimes, we view creation with dread or disdain when in fact it is beautiful. Humanity has dignity and value. How many people do not know that? How many people do not know that they have intrinsic and glorious worth? This is a beautiful truth that we need to proclaim!

It is from this basic starting point that creation is good and that people have dignity and worth that we build the imperative of Everyone Sent to Multiply Everything. Everyone has value and everyone is invited to participate in the work of God in creation. The Apostolic Imperative is merely an affirmation of the fact of the worth and purpose of every person.

From a discipleship standpoint in the 21st century, the necessity of the creation mooring is especially important. Many in our culture tend to view the emotional, intellectual, personal or spiritual as a greater reality than the created world. Consequently, we can tend to view creation as a tool to bend to our individual will or emotions as we see fit. This is nothing less than a violation of the created order and a travesty in our stewardship of creation. We must, as Romans 1:19-20 states, look to creation to understand God's nature and purposes.[15]

Consequently, living fully alive in Christ is to see alignment and harmony between the physical, emotional and spiritual aspects of who we are. As such, the value of creation applies to diverse areas such as sexuality, work, stewardship of the world and protecting the vulnerable. Part of raising disciples is inviting them to honour the created order. God has declared that creation is good, and we are both a part of that good creation and tasked with caring for it.

Sin

While we were created for relationship with God, we have ultimately rejected it and opted to establish ourselves as gods in our own right. Our selfishness and pride have resulted in death to creation. In choosing to reject a relationship with the author of life, we also find ourselves separated from the sustainer of life. As a result, we have a broken relationship with each other and the world around us. This rejection of a relationship with God is the root of what the Scriptures call sin, and within ourselves, there is no solution.

The sinfulness of humanity can be a challenging truth to wrestle with. We have to acknowledge the bad news in order to have full access to the Good News. We are enemies of God; we have offended his glory and cut ourselves off from him. It is difficult to overstate the depth of our sin or the effects of our rebellion to God. We are sinners in desperate need of a saviour (Romans 5:10).

There are different paradigms for explaining the nature of sin. It is a legal problem; we have broken God's commands. It is a relational problem; we have rejected a relationship with God. It is a spiritual problem; we have been ensnared by the enemy, Satan. It is a health problem; we have a disease that infects us and has stolen life. Regardless of the paradigm used, sin is clearly a serious issue! It should also be clear that sin is not just a behavioural issue, though it certainly reflects in our behaviour. In fact, our sin is so deep that scripture says that even our righteousness, our very best behaviour, is as filthy rags to God; even our very best efforts are tainted (Isaiah 64:6).

In short: we are not good people who Jesus makes a bit better. We are dead in our sin — utterly and completely hopeless apart from the grace of Jesus (Romans 6:23). Theologian N.T. Wright puts it this way, *"humans were made to function in particular ways, with worship of the creator as the central feature, and those who turn away from worship — that is the whole human race, without a single exception — are thereby opting to seek life where it is not to be found, which is another way of saying that they are courting their own decay and death."*[16]

Most people consider themselves to be 'good,' people. However, when asked to define what they mean by 'good,' a robust definition is not forthcoming. We are not the standard of goodness, God's holiness is (Leviticus 20:26). In comparison to that holiness, we are found wanting. This has the implication that we cannot define what sin is — God has the final word on that. Oftentimes, we think we are good because we have set the standard of goodness ourselves; we have self-determined truth. This self-determining of truth is a supreme act of self-deception where we do not acknowledge the reality of our condition, nor deal seriously with the challenges presented by the obvious brokenness in the world around us. In essence, if none of us are the problem, why is the world such a broken and messed up place?

Sin has not only fractured our relationship with our creator God, but also with one another. As we establish ourselves as our own gods and define good and truth for ourselves, we are naturally put in competition with each other. In seeking what is good or best for ourselves, the inevitable consequence is that we do that which is not best (and often damaging or disastrous) for those around us. From the very onset of sin in this world, this fractured relationship with one another has been evident as a consequence of sin (Genesis 3:12-16).

We must surrender to God as the sovereign ruler and authority in creation to determine what is good, right and pure. It is not up to us. In fact, as the book of Judges teaches us by connecting the refrain, *"In those days there was no king in Israel; everyone did whatever seemed right to him,"* to the destructive behaviour of the Israelites (Judges 21:25). When it is up to us to determine what is true, it will always result in tremendous harm.

Jesus

Jesus is the central figure around which the entirety of scripture, indeed history, revolves. From the lens of gospel fluency and discipleship, there are a few specific things to highlight:

The Incarnation

Jesus is God: as John 1 so emphatically states, he is the total, perfect and complete revelation of who God is. In Jesus' incarnation, he demonstrated what God is like. Not just in the actions of Jesus — though God's character was emphatically revealed in the actions of Jesus — but in the very act of coming, he demonstrates his deep love for us. Incarnation literally means 'with flesh on.' Jesus humbled himself by graciously entering our world and adopting the posture of the servant. We do not have to wonder what God is like; we merely need to look at Jesus as revealed in the scriptures.

Jesus' life was without sin, totally completely and entirely in alignment with the rest of the Trinity. While the Trinity is certainly something of a mystery, so too is the nature of Jesus as fully God and fully man. Nonetheless, we are compelled by the witness of his life and his death and resurrection, the testimony of the scriptures and the affirmations of the church to hold to this glorious mystery (Philippians 2:5-11).

Historical

It should go without saying that Jesus is not an idea but a real man who lived in the first-century Roman colony of Judea. Jesus was Jewish, the culmination of the promises of God that began in Genesis and were continually reaffirmed to the people of Israel. Jesus was a real man, born of a virgin into a humble home. Jesus' historicity is of paramount importance. Jesus' life came to a brutal, gruesome and horrific end in a Roman crucifixion, the result of an unjust verdict from a proud and angry mob (Acts 13:28-32). He, however, did not stay dead. He rose from the dead 3 days later. He rose from the dead! This is a historical statement, not a religious statement. If Jesus rose from the dead, then everything changes. Without the death and resurrection of Jesus as a historical fact, we have absolutely nothing to stand on. Jesus' death and resurrection is not a metaphor, myth or symbol. Rather, the resurrection is a fact that stands on very solid ground.[17] As Wright states, *"In terms of the kind of proof which historians normally accept, the case we have presented that the tomb plus appearances is what generated early Christian belief, is as watertight as one is likely to find."*[18]

New Kingdom

In his birth, death and resurrection, Jesus ushered in a whole new humanity. He came to bring about the Kingdom of God (Matthew 4:17). He was establishing that God, rather than rejecting humanity, had come to redeem it and be the King, once and for all. In doing so, he broke the curse of sin and death, conquered the powers of darkness and paid the debt that we owe to God. It is very difficult to summarize the work of Jesus in a simple statement because he has indeed accomplished so much!

Grace

At the heart of God revealed in Jesus is grace and truth. There was nothing we could have done to restore relationship with God, but

Jesus' grace made a way. This is paramount; we could not have saved ourselves, but Jesus saved us. We were saved from a position where there was absolutely nothing that we could do to save ourselves.

Model

Jesus is our model; we continually strive to be like him. Our modelling of Jesus includes the specific details of his sacrificial life: his intimacy with the Father, his care for the vulnerable, his bold teaching, his obedience to the will of the Father and his example as a disciple-maker. Our following of Jesus also includes obedience to his teachings such as loving your enemies and praying for those who persecute us (Matthew 5:1-11). Our modelling does not end there; we are also called to model the missional nature of Jesus' life — to live as sent people who give without expecting anything in return and who walk humbly and sacrificially so that the world around us can be restored to a relationship with God.

Response

The Gospel invites a response from us, as the crowds in Acts 2:37-38 understood. While God has acted and his grace has been freely given to us, we must respond; we must receive it. Our response to the grace of Jesus is expressed both in our inner life and outer life. First, our response begins in the inner life as we believe in our hearts that Jesus is Lord and affirm with our lips that God raised him from the dead.

Romans 10:9

If you declare with your mouth, "Jesus is Lord," and believe in your heart that God raised him from the dead, you will be saved.

We receive the new life that he has to offer and we give our lives over to him. At this point, we become recipients of his forgiveness and grace. As we are instructed in Romans 5:17, we must receive God's gift of grace. He has already offered it, so we do not need to ask for it, we merely need to receive it. Our response will include a serious repentance in our lives; we must turn from our ways and begin to chase wholeheartedly after the things of Jesus, forsaking all else and only desiring to see him glorified in us.

Second, we respond by living missional lives ourselves. As Jesus' grace was extended to us, we get the joy of extending his grace to others. Part of our response to the Gospel is our participation in seeing others know it as well. The Gospel compels us to be people who will bear the Gospel with our lives to those who have not yet heard it. Our confession of Jesus as Lord results in a reconfiguration of our entire lives around his purposes and his mission. The living of a missional life, the response to the Gospel, is not an optional, nice-to-have component of the Gospel; it is an integral mooring of it. As recipients of the Good News we respond by subsequently proclaiming it to others.

Our response is symbolized and celebrated in the two sacraments of Baptism and Communion as Jesus has directly and expressly commanded us in Matthew 28:16 and Luke 22:19. In communion, we celebrate the work of Jesus on the cross, and in Baptism, we celebrate our participation and reception of that work.

Holy Spirit

The Holy Spirit, as the third person of the Trinity, plays a critical role in establishing our gospel fluency. The Holy Spirit is fully God in the same emphatic sense that Jesus is fully God: Father, Son and Spirit all co-equal in the Trinity. The Holy Spirit is not greater or lesser than any other member of the Trinity but rather is equal in every way.

Seal

The believer is filled with the Holy Spirit at the point of accepting Jesus as Lord. The Holy Spirit serves as a mark or a seal on our salvation (Ephesians 1:13-14). We belong to God, and the enemy has no claim on us. The promised eternal life that Jesus offers us is confirmed in us by the Holy Spirit. The seal of the Holy Spirit also gives us authority, that would otherwise be beyond our reach, as we conduct ourselves as representatives of the King.

Wisdom / Counsellor / Comforter

Jesus introduces in John 14:25-26 that the Holy Spirit will come to comfort and guide the disciples. We are never alone because the Holy Spirit is with us, comforting and guiding us. Forming gospel fluency is ultimately a work of the Holy Spirit. The Gospel is foolishness apart from the work of the Holy Spirit softening our hearts to understand it. We must continually invite the Holy Spirit to work in our lives and in the lives of those we wish to reach so that they will know and respond to the grace of Jesus.

Power

There is a separate and distinct empowering of the Holy Spirit where each believer is specifically empowered for the purposes of building and serving the church (1 Corinthians 12:1-11, Romans 12:5-8, Ephesians 4:11-13). The Holy Spirit gives a supernatural capacity to believers to glorify God, edify the church and see people know the name of Jesus. This can be expressed in prophecy, healing, words of knowledge, tongues or other supernatural spiritual activities. The supernatural move of the Holy Spirit is a natural and normal part of the New Testament and it should be a natural and normal part of our gospel fluency — not just in theory but in practice. It is important that the power of the Holy Spirit is intrinsically tied to mission and always points to Jesus. The Holy Spirit does not grant this power, or 'gifts,' for the church to get a next level or more interesting church service — it is to send the church on mission!

For many people, the supernatural move of the Holy Spirit can be intimidating because it is unfamiliar, and many of us are not used to spiritual things. However, the Holy Spirit always moves in a way that is peaceful, kind and gentle (Galatians 5:22-33). We do not need to be afraid of the Holy Spirit; instead, we should eagerly ask him to move in our lives and the lives of those we are discipling.

Church

Responding to the Gospel and the reception of the Holy Spirit was never intended to be an isolated experience. All discipleship happens in the context of a relationship with other disciples. It is the collection of relationships, empowered by the Holy Spirit that we call the church. The church is not an optional component of the Gospel, it is an integral component. We cannot follow God alone; we need each other. The church has the job of contextualizing this glorious grace of Jesus so that every tribe, culture, tongue and nation can know and have the opportunity to respond to it.

In following Jesus, we must find ourselves walking as a family with a body of local believers (Acts 2:42-48). Of course, walking in relationship with people is not always easy, but the job of forming gospel fluency is to remember that our participation in a local church is not optional; it is part of what it means to be a follower of Jesus. The church is a family that is committed to covenant relationship for the sake of the name of Jesus in their community. In a family, we do not need to earn our right to belong. Participation in a church family is not earned or given as a reward for performance; it is a joyful gift from Jesus to be invited to his family. On the other-hand, participation in a family does come with responsibilities. These responsibilities include the need to contribute, fulfill our unique role and responsibility and see Jesus glorified through us as a part of the broader family.

Church can certainly be painful as sinful people learn to walk according to the purposes of God. However, it is in our challenges that Jesus can be glorified as we learn to embody the Gospel in our church family. Part of maturity in Christ is learning to live this reality of covenant community.

Worship

Committing to one another is important because the objective of the church is ultimately, as with discipleship, to see God made known and glorified (Ephesians 3:10). As with discipleship, the objective of the church is the glorification and worship of the king. We must forsake our obsession with particular forms or formats of the church. Those forms more often than not exist to serve the believer and make them feel affirmed in their preferences. The church exists for the sake of the glory of God and to be a witness to him. The church is not about us!

Mission

The church exists for the sake of the mission of Christ, not for the sake of ourselves: "it should be understood that the church is the missionary community of disciples of the King."[19] By extension, the job of leadership in the church is to mobilize the church for mission (Ephesians 4:11), not to provide spiritual goods and services. There needs to be a radical shift in our expectations around leadership in churches being providers of religious services to instead being mobilizers of missionaries.

> *The Church exists for nothing else but to draw men into Christ, to make them little Christs. If they are not doing that then all the cathedrals, clergy, missions, sermons, even the Bible itself are simply a waste of time.* — C. S. Lewis[20]

Mercy & Justice

Another important responsibility of the church is to embody and reflect the heart of God in mercy and justice to the poor, vulnerable, downtrodden, orphaned, widowed, imprisoned and sick. The church must care for the orphan and the widow, the vulnerable and the oppressed (Matthew 5:1-16). However, the church is not a generic social services agency; it is a body of believers that points to the saving grace and love of the creator God who entered a broken world to redeem it.

Global Church

Lastly, the church is global and diverse. No particular local church has the corner on what it looks like to be the body of Christ. Each family of disciples has the responsibility to carefully discern how they can worship God, fulfill the mission of Jesus and bring mercy and justice in their specific unique context. The beautiful truth of the Gospel is that it is trans-cultural, meaning it can take on all sorts of forms while still being true. There is great beauty in our diversity.

New Creation

Scripture concludes with the glorious promise of the new creation. *"Therefore, if anyone is in Christ, the new creation has come: The old has gone, the new is here!"* (2 Corinthians 5:17). N.T. Wright helps broaden our horizons on this passage to see that Paul's vision is simultaneously individual renewal in Christ and a picture of a new creation for the whole cosmos! *"Paul is not just speaking of the individual creation as a new creation, though of course that is true as well, but of the entire renewal of the cosmos in which the Christian is invited to be a participant."*[21] Contrary to popular belief, the final destination for followers of Jesus is not heaven. Our final destination is that of the new creation where God lives in harmony with his creation as its rightful and revered King (2 Peter 3:13).

The fact that the new creation is our final destination is important because it affirms that creation is a good thing. In Genesis 1 and 2 we see that we were created for relationship and creativity — in the new creation we will get to live into that in eternity!

Jesus will return and usher in the new creation and with it the final judgement (Hebrews 9:28). One important component of this judgement is that not everyone will have responded by receiving the grace that Jesus has to offer. Those who have rejected the grace of Jesus will be forever separated from God; this is what we call Hell. The eternal separation from God for those who have not received the grace of Jesus is a reality that we must hold to. Jesus is the only way to salvation and there is no other way. Apart from receiving his grace we are totally and completely lost (Revelation 20:11-15).

Similarly to the Creation mooring, the new creation mooring has especially relevant discipleship applications in the 21st century. The new creation mooring speaks to eternal hope and justice. We are reminded that we always have hope for the future: namely, that one day Jesus will restore final justice to creation. We are not simply organic matter. We do not just return to the dust. Instead, we were created for eternal communion with the creator of the universe. No matter the brokenness of the world around us, we always have hope that Jesus will restore ultimate justice (Romans 8:22-24). As Newbigin writes, *"You cannot have hopeful and responsible action without some vision for a possible future."*[22] The new creation mooring supplies a profound and glorious vision of the future (Revelation 21:3-4)!

Scripture

From the beginning of scripture, we see that Jesus promised to bring about a solution to the problem of sin, as described above. In fact, all of scripture is pointing to Jesus in some way. Whether it is the law, the prophets, the New Testament or the Psalms, all of it is pointing to Jesus. It can take time and energy to learn to read scripture from this Christocentric perspective, but when we learn to read scripture from the lens of Jesus, we discover the incredible joy that resonates from every page of scripture.

The Old Testament is a broad narrative that reveals our desperate need for Jesus. The repeated rebellion, sin, unfaithfulness and failure of virtually every major character in the Old Testament serves to demonstrate our need for grace. However, God's character is revealed as gracious, merciful, faithful, loving and kind — especially in the face of sin! He is also shown to be righteous, just and true. The figures in the Old Testament are all pointing forward to Jesus — whether it is Noah, Abraham, Moses, Joshua, Rahab, Job, David or Isaiah.[23] The law and history of Israel, as Paul argues emphatically in Romans, exists to reveal and make way for Jesus to come. It is all about Jesus and it has always been about Jesus (Luke 24:44-45).

The Old Testament, and the New Testament for that matter, can be difficult to read, but it is all profitable and useful. All of scripture helps us understand who we are and who Jesus is. We must learn to be moulded by all of it. We should struggle with it, wrestle with it, allowing it to get inside us and call us to greater depths in Jesus.

Scripture is the final authority in our lives. Morality and ethics are not a free for all for each person to self-determine what is true. Instead, morality and ethics are anchored in scripture. At times, this will mean that there are statements that are uncomfortable, difficult or hard to accept. We need to use wisdom to properly understand these passages by the aid of the Holy Spirit. However, we must equally submit ourselves to scripture and allow God to challenge us and to change us. We must come to scripture willing to be changed by it. Our fundamental posture when approaching scripture must be one of humility before the Word of God (2 Timothy 3:16-17).

Crucially, however, this submission to the word is part of a broader discipleship community that is committed to being collectively transformed by the word. Lesslie Newbigin, the great missiologist and theologian, remarked on the need to be submitted to the word of God this way: *"The Bible functions as authority only within a community that is committed to faith and obedience and is embodying that commitment in an active discipleship that embraces the whole of life, public and private."*[24]

Without scripture, we have no mooring from which we can discern all other truths. Scripture is our ultimate plumb-line from which we can discern and understand who God is.

Formed by Scripture

Gospel fluency is the foundation for every facet of our lives: our beliefs, emotions, plans and even desires. The beginning of gospel fluency is Scripture. Scripture extends an invitation to us to be challenged, changed and formed by God and his word. Gospel fluency goes beyond just knowledge of scripture. We can have a great deal of knowledge of scripture without it actually changing our heart. Gospel fluency invites us to a deeper relationship with scripture, one that goes beyond a set of abstract truths and allows scripture to be transformational in our lives This means that what we believe to be true, what we desire in life and how we practically make decisions must find their home in scripture. A disciple cannot be formed into the way of Jesus without a dependency on, faith in and formation by the Word of God. Without scripture as an anchor, we will either become overwhelmed by the challenges, discouraged in the trials or swept into the currents of our culture, thus neutralizing any multiplication capacity. Martin Niemoller was a German pastor who stood up to the rise of Hitler in the 1930s and was eventually imprisoned for this faith. He wrote this of his dependence on the Word:

> *"What did this book mean to me during the long and weary years of solitary confinement and then for the last four years at Dachau [concentration camp]? The Word of God was simply everything to me — comfort and strength, guidance and hope, master of my days and companion of my nights, the bread which kept me from starvation and the water of life that refreshed my soul."* — Martin Niemoller[25]

Most of us are led by our emotions. As a consequence, our emotions can become the king of our lives — we do whatever feels emotionally the most true. However, our emotions are not the highest truth or even the most reliable source of information. Scripture is the only thing that can take that place in our lives. Instead, our emotions serve as a signal, like a dashboard indicator on our car, inviting us to turn to scripture to calibrate what we believe and feel. As the diagram below illustrates, we must not merely accept our emotions or let them make our decisions; rather, we must allow what scripture says to define truth, direct our desires and shape our decisions. How do we do that?

Our Reality Formed by Scripture

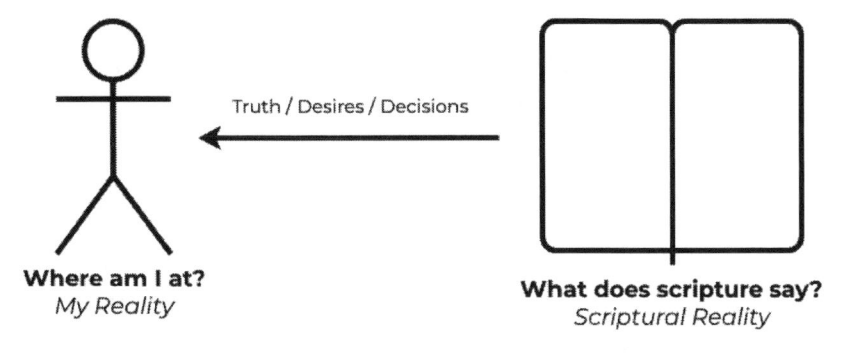

Truth / Desires / Decisions

Where am I at?
My Reality

What does scripture say?
Scriptural Reality

Defines Truth

We must first turn to scripture to define what is true. The invitation to have our reality defined by scripture applies emotionally, intellectually, morally and ethically. In the postmodern world we have elevated the individual, as a free moral agent, to the highest source of truth. The result of this is disastrous as our collective sense of what is true, right and good is effectively unhinged in the process. While postmodern thought has certainly brought with it a great deal of good, especially in helping to capture the importance and value for diversity and the need to contextualize the Gospel, we cannot accept or adopt an individualistic view of morality and truth. The book of Judges is a narrative account of what happens when people reject the authority of God in their lives; in short, chaos and pain ensues. As Newbigin quips, *"If there is nothing that is "good" in this universal sense, then in every conflict of interest the only argument that is not meaningless is 'this is what I want to do.'"*[26] We need an anchor, and that anchor is the word of God.

Psalm 119 is the longest Psalm in scripture and it is all about being shaped by God's word! Knowing and obeying the Word of God enables us to walk blameless lives (verse 1). Verses 25 and 32 invite us to discover life and to broaden our understanding. Verse 147 invites us to know the word as our source of hope. Verse 28 beautifully states that in our grief we can actually be strengthened by the word!

> **Psalm 119**
>
> *1 How happy are those whose way is blameless, who walk according to the Lord's instruction!*
> *28 I am weary from grief; strengthen me through your word.*
> *25 My life is down in the dust; give me life through your word.*
> *32 I pursue the way of your commands, for you broaden my understanding.*
> *147 I rise before dawn and cry out for help; I put my hope in your word.*

Oftentimes, there can be a difference between what we feel to be true and what Scripture declares to be true. These moments can be difficult, even painful, for us to navigate. However, we must allow ourselves to be challenged by the word and to have our lives moulded by it. Scripture defines and lays out a paradigm for discerning what sin is and how it functions. Moreover, scripture outlines what it means to be raised from death to life in Christ and what a life fully alive in the hope of Jesus looks like. So, we must allow our lives to be moulded by it! God's supreme love for us is the greatest truth and what is most real in this world. We must allow this great and glorious truth to establish deep roots in our soul in order for our lives to be transformed by it.

As we engage in discipleship, we must continually invite those we are discipling to return to the scriptures as the source of grace and truth. We must train our minds and hearts to yearn for and submit to scripture. Such an imperative is no small task and must be an intentional act of discipleship where we train and model those we are discipling to be formed by scripture.

Shapes Our Desires

As scripture begins to define what is true, right and good, it will also begin to inform the desires and longings of our soul. It is possible that scripture can actually change the things that we crave for in this world. Perhaps the greatest challenge in the life of the disciple is keeping our desires anchored in the hope of Jesus. There are so many options that we are presented with every day that if we are not anchored in the Word, we will simply desire that which affords us the most gratification in the most expedient fashion. However, we are not called to that which is gratifying to our carnal nature, nor are we called to that which is most expedient. In many cases, the life and work of discipleship is slow and the reward is delayed. Consequently, we must continually return to scripture to inform and shape our longings so that we are not blown off track. Philippians 2:13 beautifully says that God will give us the desire and the power to do what pleases him. Through God's word, we can see our desires moulded and shaped such that they will honour the Lord. C.S. Lewis masterfully describes this struggle of our desires:

> *That is why the real problem of the Christian life comes where people do not usually look for it. It comes the very moment you wake up each morning. All your wishes and hopes for the day rush at you like wild animals. And the first job each morning consists simply in shoving them all back; in listening to that other voice, taking that other point of view and letting that other, larger, stronger, quieter life come flowing in.* — C.S. Lewis[27]

The culture we find ourselves in is constantly vying and competing for our attention — and our money! We cannot fight the pressure of our culture on our own. It is not enough to simply force ourselves by the power of our will to be hungry for the things of God. Instead, we must continually go to scripture to inform our desires, to help create a longing for Jesus and his word. As we do that, the allure of fancy experiences or successes will fade as we begin to develop a deeper hunger for the values of Jesus: serving the poor and vulnerable, proclaiming the Gospel, worshiping the King and creating beautiful things. We will begin to see in us a genuine love for those we previously had never even considered. When the object of our affection is Jesus we will naturally find ourselves longing for that which will best draw us into relationship with him and afford him glory.

Again Psalm 119 invites us to treasure God's Word so that we might not desire sin (verse 11). It reminds us that our home is ultimately not this world, so we ought not capitulate to culture (verse 19), and it reminds us to delight in the Word and in so doing, be directed by it (verse 24).

Psalm 119

11 I have treasured your word in my heart so that I may not sin against you.
19 I am a resident alien on earth; do not hide your commands from me.
24 your decrees are my delight and my counsellors.

Part of discipleship is learning to have our desires become the desires of Jesus. We must genuinely and thoroughly desire to see the

Kingdom of God on earth as it is in heaven. Jesus' instruction to pray for his Kingdom was an instruction to see the purposes of God completely and totally formed in us. We must be willing to challenge those we are discipling when they begin to express desires for things that are not of Jesus. We must call them back to be formed by the Word before they drift into a general apathy towards the mission of Christ.

Directs our Decisions

As scripture lays the foundation of truth and shapes our desires, it must also direct our decisions. The Psalmist writes that his direction actually changed as a result of scripture (verse 59), and that scripture served as his guide on how to navigate the future (verse 105).

> **Psalm 119**
> *59 I thought about my ways and turned my steps back to your decrees.*
> *105 Your word is a lamp for my feet and a light on my path.*

While scripture informs what is true, and even directs our desires, it is when our decisions are actually shaped by scripture that the true power of the Word is unlocked. When what we believe, what we desire and what we do are all rooted in scripture there is tremendous joy.

Scripture calls us to love our enemies and pray for those who persecute us. When we actually start to love our enemies and forgive those who have hurt us, the power of scripture becomes real to us. It's not enough to agree with scripture; we must actually do what it says. However, the life that scripture invites us into is tremendously challenging. The call to forgiveness, mission, sacrifice, love and endurance that the Word extends to us is totally contrary to our human nature and is incredibly difficult.

Many disciples will complain, after hearing a sermon, that it was too basic for them. For example, a sermon on loving your neighbours has often been decried as "too simple." However, when that disciple is asked how they are loving their neighbours, they will struggle to come up with a clear answer. The problem was not the sermon but the willingness on the behalf of the disciple to actually do what Scripture says.

A mark of the mature Christian is that they can hear, read and study scripture on their own and allow the Holy Spirit to convict them in areas of their life that are not yet surrendered. Many Christians are rich in knowledge and poor in execution. They may agree with scripture but their actual decisions are hardly informed by it. The job of the discipler is to challenge those who they are discipling to be truly formed by scripture.

Part of being a multiplying disciple is to develop a missional framework for decision making. This means that the way we make decisions is informed by scripture with the goal being to maximize the glory of God in their lives. Our world offers many competing frameworks for making decisions, such as maximizing comfort, wealth, fame or experiences. We must invite the disciple to build a framework for decision making that forsakes comfort, wealth, fame or any other worldly venture and instead seeks to see decisions made with Jesus' glory as the goal. Such a missional proposition is only possible if our worldview is completely saturated with the words of scripture.

Practicing Gospel Fluency

The notion that gospel fluency involves truth, desires and decisions is of paramount importance. How do we practically allow scripture to take such a prominent place in our lives? What are the tools, methods and techniques that we can use to see scripture form what is true, our desires and our decisions?

When God gave his word to the Israelites, he gave them a set of commands in Deuteronomy 6 so that the nation would be formed by God's Word. These commands came to be known as *The Shema* and were often repeated as part of daily prayer by our Hebrew ancestors. From this command, we find three powerful actions that we can take towards this end: meditation, confession and repentance.

Deuteronomy 6:6-9

These words that I am giving you today are to be in your heart. Repeat them to your children. Talk about them when you sit in your house and when you walk along the road, when you lie down and when you get up. Bind them as a sign on your hand and let them be a symbol on your forehead. Write them on the doorposts of your house and on your city gates.

Meditation

6 These words that I am giving you today are to be in your heart.

The first tool is that of meditation. Biblical meditation is the process of filling our thoughts with the words of scripture, allowing scripture to be impressed upon our minds and hearts. Ajith Fernando, in his book *The Call to Joy and Pain*, calls this process "preaching to our heart."

> *"Because our heart is struggling with the situation, our mind preaches to the heart the truths we know from the Word.... We must learn to stop listening to our self-pitying conversation and start preaching the deeper realities to ourselves."* — Ajith Fernando[28]

Three practical tools to assist our meditation on scripture are that of memorization, devotions and praying scripture. First, we develop in ourselves, and others, the habit of memorizing scripture so that we can recall it throughout the day. We cannot effectively be formed by scripture, or disciple others, unless we have a robust knowledge of the word. Second, we must have the habit of turning daily to the scriptures in moments of quiet and calm. It is in our devotions that we intentionally create space to fill our thoughts with scripture and allow them to take root in us. To effectively meditate on scripture, we must remove distractions and allow all of our attention to centre on the word. Third, we can develop the practice of praying scripture over ourselves and others. For example, Psalm 51 contains beautiful truths about our sinfulness being met by the grace of God. As Romans 8 describes God's love for us, we should not just dwell on it but actually form it into our prayers.

Confession

> *7 Repeat them to your children. Talk about them when you sit in your house and when you walk along the road, when you lie down and when you get up.*

The formation of scripture in our lives is not an individual pursuit; rather, it is one that is done in the context of discipleship relationships and our broader church family. As we study and are convicted by scripture in our times of meditation or through the coaching of the person who is discipling us, we must reach a point where we are ready to confess that we need to change.

Confession comes from the Greek word *homologeo*, which literally means "to say the same thing." Biblical confession is not *just* about admitting or acknowledging sin. It is actually a process where we begin to declare that what scripture says is true! Confession is a process whereby we bring our thoughts and desires into alignment with scripture. When confessing sin, we acknowledge that we have offended God's holiness. However, as we study the scriptures describing God's love for us, we can also confess that over ourselves or others. As we confess God's love for us to another person, we begin to be moulded and shaped by it.

In confession, we begin to declare that which is true about God and about us. Confession is not a dull, dreary or depressing act. Rather, it is sublime in that, through confession, we begin to declare the freeing truth of God's word over our lives. Confession is one of the most life-giving and liberating things we can do.

It is for this reason that being formed by scripture is actually a matter of discipleship, not just individual faith. When we invite those we are discipling to confess the truth of scripture, we are doing some of the most important and powerful discipleship work we can do.

Repentance

> *8 Bind them as a sign on your hand and let them be a symbol on your forehead. 9 Write them on the doorposts of your house and on your city gates.*

Repentance is all about changing direction. When we repent, we are allowing scripture to serve as a directional guide for us. It is in the act of acknowledging that we need to change our behaviour and go a different direction that we unlock the real power of scripture. As with confession, repentance is about more than dealing with sin. Yes, much of repentance will have to do with sin and behaviour. But we should also repent when we have allowed ourselves to believe and act according to things that are untrue. For example, when we meditate on the truth that we are loved by God and confess that over ourselves as true, we must begin to act according to that truth — that is repentance. In repentance, our beliefs, words and actions find themselves in alignment.

Repentance should be a daily action taken by the disciple. We must daily call the people we are discipling to repent: to turn around and bring their actions into alignment with scripture. The daily decision to take specific actions to allow our lives to be moulded by scripture is a powerful act, but one that we must develop as a habit — both in ourselves and those we are discipling.

Finally, it must be clearly said, repentance flows from the fact that we are first loved by God. Our repentance is not an action taken to earn the love of God, rather it is an action taken because we already have the love of God!

Summary

The diagram below illustrates how the three actions of meditation, confession and repentance initiate a cycle whereby scripture can be formational in our desires, emotions and decisions.

Formed By Scripture Through Spiritual Practices

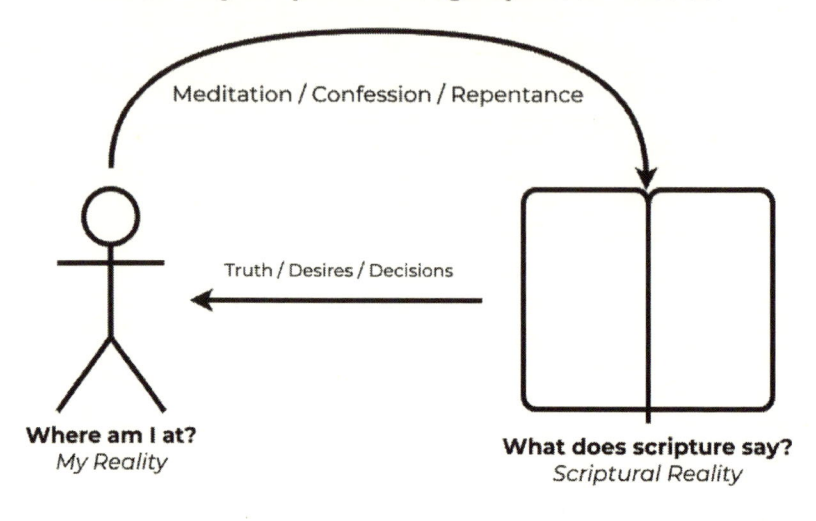

Meditation / Confession / Repentance

Truth / Desires / Decisions

Where am I at?
My Reality

What does scripture say?
Scriptural Reality

It should be apparent from this discussion that gospel fluency is so much deeper than knowledge! While knowledge is important, true gospel fluency is about the total transformation of our heart, mind and actions to align with the life-giving joy that is described in the scriptures. Through meditation, confession and repentance we can be truly and thoroughly formed by scripture.

This process requires that we engage in robust, accountable and genuine discipleship. As the 18th existential philosopher and theologian, Soren Kierkegaard, said of himself, *"I have wanted to make people aware and to admit that I find the New Testament very easy to understand, but thus far I have found it tremendously difficult to act literally upon what it so plainly says."*[29] The primary challenge in gospel fluency is one of being deeply formed in our actions, thoughts and beliefs, not just that of understanding it. The process of using meditation, confession and repentance to form our thinking and behaviour is easy to do in principle but exceedingly difficult to do on our own. Simple ideas may be easy to grasp but are difficult to implement. We must openly wrestle with the entire process and be faithful to the clear call of scripture with those we are discipling.

7

Secure Identity

A secure identity, in light of the glorious hope found in the gospel, is the second emphasis in developing Discipleship Potential. In speaking of secure identity, we aim to get to the heart of the question "who am I?" The answer to this question is foundational to informing our perspective of the role we play in the Kingdom of Jesus, and it profoundly influences our behaviour, relationships, vocation and virtually every other aspect of our lives. When we can clearly and confidently identify who we are, we become far more effective as multiplying disciples. The question is, who are we?

Jesus as Lord

The foundational starting place for discussing a secure identity is the Gospel itself. We start with who we are by first understanding and positioning ourselves in relationship to the Creator God of the universe. As the idiom goes, "There is a God, and it's not you." The Gospel tells us there is a God who cares profoundly about his creation. He is creative, involved, loving, kind and merciful. We cannot correctly understand who we are until we first surrender to who God is. The need to position ourselves in relationship to the Creator God is why Jesus says in John 3:16 that whoever believes in him will have eternal life and Paul says in Romans 10:9

that if we confess with our mouth that Jesus is Lord, we will be saved. The starting point for understanding who we are is understanding and surrendering to who God is. Everything about who we are is in response to who God is. This recognition of who Jesus is, and his rightful place as Lord of our lives, is perhaps one of the most significant barriers to people accepting the Gospel. To acknowledge who Jesus is, we must implicitly also recognize who we are in relation to him — a position that fundamentally requires that we surrender our rights and responsibilities — he is God and we are not!

It is absolutely crucial that we emphasize the necessity of Jesus as Lord, as our human propensity is to do precisely the opposite. Rather than allowing Jesus to be Lord over every area of our lives, we tend to manufacture God into our own image (Romans 1:21-23). Rather than allowing God to inform, direct and establish what is true, we instead build for ourselves an understanding of God that affirms who we already think we are. If we are angry, then God is angry. If we are vengeful, then God is vengeful. If we are greedy, then we imagine God affirming our greediness. If we are lustful, we look for God to affirm our lust. Our vision of God can end up as a reflection of us to such an extent that the God of the scriptures and our personal understanding of him are worlds apart. It might appear that this commentary belongs under gospel fluency, but it is placed here because only when Jesus is Lord can we truly be secure in who we are. Our security in Jesus is not possible so long as we continue to live as Lord of our lives. Only when Jesus informs who we are do we gain the footing for a bold and vibrant life. To say that this is counter to our nature is an understatement. In our pride and sin, we cling to our lives under the illusion that we are in control. However, nothing could be further from the truth. It is only in surrender to Jesus that we can indeed be secure, because it is only he who is truly in control (Matthew 10:39). Consequently, a secure identity without a proper understanding of Jesus' lordship is simply not possible. That is why Romans 1 goes on to describe the sheer and utter lostness in humanity that comes from a refusal to surrender. As the brilliant 20th century theologian, Karl Barth, remarks in his commentary on

Romans 1, *"When the frontier between God and Man, the last inexorable barrier and obstacle, is not closed, the barrier between what is normal and what is perverse is opened."* [30]

Fully Alive

To form a secure identity, we must first surrender to Jesus as Lord. It is through surrender to Jesus as Lord of our lives that we begin to experience a total transformation into who he created us to be. We find our new identity in Christ through acceptance of his gift of new life and complete surrender to him as Lord of our lives. The transformation that occurs through this acceptance and surrender is what it means to be fully alive in the hope of Jesus. As a result, understanding that we are 'fully alive' is the starting point for developing a secure identity. We have been raised from death to life by the grace of Jesus; our identity is one of resurrection. Without Jesus, we are not just bad, lost, orphaned or alone, we are dead. However, because of the grace of Jesus, we find ourselves fully alive.

This change in identity, from 'dead' to 'alive', leads to a transformation in both our inner life as well as our outer life. If we are now alive because of Jesus, then every aspect of our lives will align behind that reality. In general, our behaviour, lifestyle and decisions are a direct consequence of what we perceive our identity to be. In other words, behaviour and lifestyle decisions are an identity issue. As Colossians 3 puts it, our new identity is that of being alive in Christ, which means that we must "put to death" the things of this world. Our behaviour, or our misbehaviour, is directly related to the depth of our 'fully alive' identity in Jesus

Colossians 3:1,5

So if you have been raised with Christ, seek the things above... put to death what belongs to your earthly nature

Paul goes on in Colossians to highlight a host of different components of a life that is not fully alive: sexual immorality, idolatry, rage, anger, greed and so forth. Paul's invitation is great news because it means that the solution to the parts of our inner life which are unhealthy is to press more deeply into the things of Jesus, or as Paul says, to "set our eyes on things above."

Paul reiterates this with great precision in Romans 6:11: *"consider yourselves dead to sin and alive to God in Christ Jesus."* Paul's instruction that we should "consider ourselves alive" means that we must forge an identity, and an understanding of who we are, that is built upon the fact that we are fully alive in Jesus.

The transformation in being fully alive is not merely in our inner life or our behaviour, thoughts and actions. The transformation applies equally to our outer life, our ability to be disciple-making disciples. After Paul's instruction to put to death our sinful nature and put on our life in Christ, he commands the church to adopt a different way of living, filled with compassion, grace and love. His invitation to a fully alive identity culminates in the following multiplication-oriented command in verse 17:

Colossians 3:17

Whatever you do, in word or in deed, do everything in the name of the Lord Jesus, giving thanks to God the Father through him.

When we start to live fully alive, every aspect of our lives begins to be used and leveraged for the Glory of Jesus. It is from our transformed identities that we discover kingdom effectiveness, as Romans 6 highlights.

Romans 6:13

But as those who are alive from the dead, offer yourselves to God, and all the parts of yourselves to God as weapons for righteousness.

Weapons of righteousness is a powerful and vivid picture of a church on the offensive! When we have built our identity upon the fact that we are fully alive in Christ, we will inevitably see both inner-life and outer-life transformation. The offence here is not an offence of violence, but one of a weapon of truth. In Revelation 19:15, Jesus is depicted with a sword proceeding from his mouth as he overthrows the powers of darkness. It is the words of

Jesus, the truth proclaimed, that is his most powerful weapon. The weapon that Jesus wields is ultimately not a physical weapon, but a spiritual one: a weapon of truth. The dual-sided truth that we are dead in our sins, but because of the grace of Jesus, we have been declared righteous, is a powerful testimony on which we build our lives. Indeed, by the grace of Jesus, we have been raised from death to life, and the effect should be noticeable in such a way to the world around us that they desire to know Jesus as well. We do not need to live timid, afraid or ashamed, but rather we live as a people who have been assigned a glorious mission of seeing the world around us set free by the grace and goodness of Jesus. As we have been raised to life by Jesus, the testimony of our lives becomes a weapon to see others equally set free.

Secure Identities

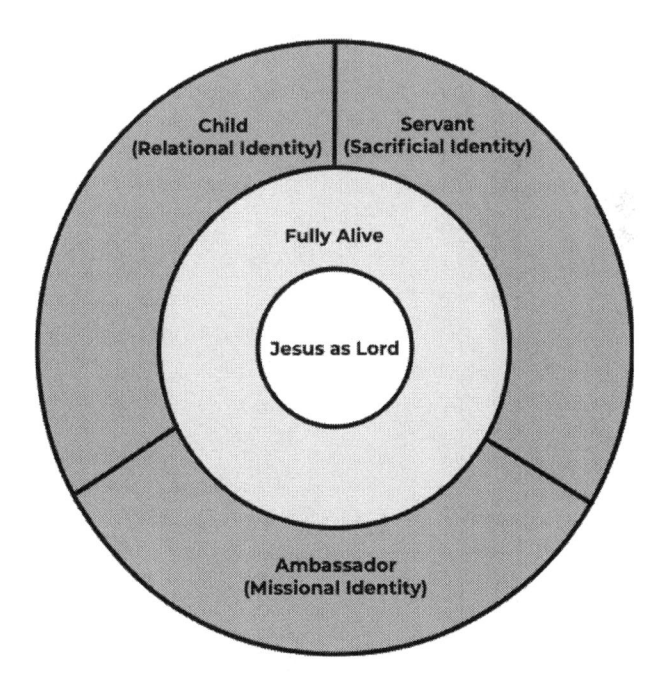

- Child (Relational Identity)
- Servant (Sacrificial Identity)
- Ambassador (Missional Identity)
- Fully Alive
- Jesus as Lord

With our identity securely built upon being fully alive in the hope of Jesus, we can turn our attention to several other essential identity markers that are integral to a secure identity in Christ. Specifically, that of being a child of God, an ambassador for the Kingdom of God and, lastly, a slave/servant of Jesus.

Child — Relational Identity

One of the most beautiful truths that we are invited into as we become fully alive is that we find ourselves adopted as sons and daughters of God. God initially chose a nation to himself in Abraham and the subsequent nation of Israel (see Genesis 12). However, God's ultimate purpose was that, through Abraham, someone would come that would see all people adopted into the family of God. The promises to Abraham ultimately culminated in the work of Jesus. It is through the work of Jesus that our adoption as sons and daughters was made possible (Galatians 4:4-6, 1 John 3:1). Jesus graciously made our inclusion in his family possible through his death and resurrection. Perhaps the most incredible aspect of our adoption is that it was a part of God's eternal plan!

> **Ephesians 1:5**
>
> *He predestined us to be adopted as sons through Jesus Christ for himself, according to the good pleasure of his will.*

When the writer of Ephesians describes how God predestined us to be adopted, it is a reference to God's ultimate purpose for humanity. His purpose, from before the creation of the world, was that we would be adopted as sons and daughters in Jesus. Our adoption was not an afterthought, or simply something that is nice to have. God created us to be sons and daughters through the blood of Jesus. Moreover, God delights in our adoption; it brings him joy when we turn to him. God is not satisfied or delighted in our performance; rather, he is delighted when we receive his gift of life in Jesus. His love for us is completely independent of our performance as it was ultimately Jesus who made it possible, not us.

> *But the Gospel transforms us so our self-understanding is no longer based on our performance in life. We are so evil and sinful and flawed that Jesus had to die for us. We were so lost that*

nothing less than the death of the divine Son of God could save us. But we are so loved and valued that he was willing to die for us. The Lord of the universe loved us enough to do that. So the Gospel humbles us into the dust and at the very same time exalts us to the heavens. We are sinners but completely loved and accepted in Christ at the same time. — Tim Keller[31]

Our adoption has two immediate applications, one to our inner life and one to our outer life. First, as sons and daughters, we are secure in the fact that there is nothing we can do to earn God's love and, by extension, nothing we can do to lose his love. Nothing in all creation can ever separate us from his love (Romans 8:39). Our security in God's love frees us from a performance-oriented relationship with God. We do not need to earn his love or his favour because he has already freely given it to us! In a culture where acceptance has a direct correlation to performance, this is a radical truth!

Many of us live with an attitude of lack or deficiency, and carry on our lives with the perception and thoughts that we are victims or defeated. While we may tragically be the victims of the sin of others and may suffer setbacks, our identity in Christ gives us the joy of a greater promise: we are secure in Jesus! In fact, all of the promises that the Lord gave to Abraham to be a blessing to the nations are ours in Christ (Galatians 3:14). As sons and daughters of God, we get to share in Jesus' glory. While this will likely involve trials and suffering, we can always remain firm and secure in the promise of Jesus' goodness (Romans 8:17).

Second, if God's love is free and utterly independent from what we have done, that kind of love will change the way we see and interact with others in the world around us. It is only natural that as we learn to be secure in the fact that God loves us as sons and daughters, we desire to see those in the world around us discover that kind of love as well. A person secure in the love of God will naturally lead those around them to be secure in the love of God. The fact that God desires to see those we are reaching adopted as sons and daughters is the driving force behind the "Everyone" in 'Everyone Sent to Multiply Everything.' When we learn to view people through a lens that allows us to see them not just 'fully alive' but also adopted as sons and daughters, we will inevitably learn to see them for the tremendous kingdom value that they actually have.

Our ability to live a life of mission, purpose and sacrifice is substantially amplified when we are secure and confident in the fact that we are loved. The outer life of our discipleship should naturally start to flourish as the security of our identity as sons and daughters of God establishes depth in our soul.

Secure in Church Family

The invitation to become sons and daughters is not an individual pursuit. When thinking about forming an identity, many of us tend to think of it as an individual pursuit. We tend to think of how we can be secure without any consideration of the broader community in which we find ourselves. Our self-centred, individualistic propensity for identity formation is nothing short of disastrous for the Kingdom of God and is one of the largest barriers for discipleship. We live in a world where faith is a largely private affair and where the role of community is discounted or ignored. It should be clear that if we are sons and daughters in Christ, then part of that identity is that we belong to the family of God! We are no longer alone on our journey but find ourselves as a part of a family as expressed in the form of a local church. If we are sons and daughters in Christ, then we are equally brothers and sisters in Christ! As Rosaria Butterfield writes in her book, *The Gospel Comes with a House Key*, *"We belong to each other because we share a heavenly Father. Our identity and our calling must emanate from God's image radiating in and through us."* [32]

The connection between the local church and our adoption as sons and daughters in Christ is essential. These theological concepts are intimately intertwined. That is why Paul writes in Galatians 3:28 that there is no longer Jew or Greek, slave or free, and male nor female but that we are all one in Christ as sons and daughters. Our call to be sons and daughters finds itself practically expressed in our 'oneness.' It is in the church family that our security in Christ finds a context to be realized. This concept is explicitly stated in Ephesians 2:19 *"So then you are no longer foreigners and strangers, but fellow citizens with the saints, and members of God's household..."*

When we submit to one another in the context of church family, we are actually reenacting the Gospel itself. Just as Christ died for us, we get the joy of laying down our lives for one another. Ephesians draws the parallels between Christ and his church and a husband and wife in marriage (Ephesians 5:15-33). Typically this passage is used to explain how a husband and wife walk in union and submission to one another and in so doing, reflect the Gospel. However, the starting point for the text is that we are called to submit to one another in the church. We are called to submit to a relationship of mutual sacrifice. It is in the church that we learn to love the unlovable, forgive the unforgivable and walk in unity despite hurt and pain — all things that Christ has done for us (Colossians 3:13)! We are not easily offended because we know that without Christ, we are offensive to God and therefore are dependent on his grace. As recipients of grace, we are eager to extend grace and in so doing, see Christ formed in us and others. It is in the church that we learn to receive Christ's love for us as we give it to, and receive it from, others. Without the application of the Gospel to our brothers and sisters in Christ, our true security in Christ will never be formed in us.

This principal was powerfully illustrated in third-century martyr Perpetua who was executed in a Roman gladiatorial ring alongside 5 others. What is notable is that the others were both slaves and free men. Two slaves, three free men and noblewomen were brutally martyred as family. Despite hailing from vastly different backgrounds and finding themselves in a very hopeless situation, they were full of joy as they prepared to die for their faith. Multiple times in the account of their death, they praise the Lord that they are together as brothers and sisters. The fact that they were totally secure as sons and daughters of Christ as they faced death is no doubt also connected to their intimate connection as brothers and sisters in the faith.

We cannot be secure as sons and daughters in Christ if we are not also committed to, and covenanted with, a particular family of believers where the truth of our adoption into Christ is a lived reality with a specific group of people. We tend to approach our church families with a largely individualistic consideration: "What is in it for my benefit?" "Do I like it?" "Was it entertaining?" These questions are utter nonsense if we have a view of the church as a family. No one goes to their family dinner with the thought, "I hope Dad brings good jokes today, and if he doesn't, I'm leaving."

For many people, their identity as sons and daughters remains underdeveloped because they have not been committed to a local church. When we learn to walk in community, we discover that we are loved regardless of our performance and are forgiven, even in our sin. God's love for us finds a distinct expression in the form of a local church, and it is a grievous thing that many people have not experienced it! In our discipleship, it is essential that as we lead others to be secure in Christ, we involve them in our local church family. Discipleship is designed to function in the context of the church. As Pete Grieg, the founder of the 24/7 prayer movement says,

> *"There is no place in the Christian community for the serial monogamy concept where each new friendship comes with a shelf-life. When a relationship gets awkward, we do not simply move on to another connection. Instead, we dare to go on a lifelong journey together through conflict and disappointment as well as seasons of mutual fascination and fun.... Our friendships survive seasons of vulnerability when people see our sin and somehow still choose our company."* — Pete Grieg [33]

Furthermore, our discipleship and evangelistic efficacy are directly connected to the degree of our security in the family. As Jesus himself said, it is our love for one another that demonstrates that we have received the love of Christ (John 13:35). The breaking down of racial, gender, age and socio-economic barriers is one of the primary works of the Holy Spirit and has been a part of nearly every major evangelistic movement in the last two millennia.

From a discipleship standpoint, there are several practical applications that we can call others to as they are formed as sons and daughters, brothers and sisters.

First, we must be committed to building our lives alongside one another (Hebrews 10:25). Rather than building our own individual kingdoms, we must ask the question of how we can mutually invest in and build up the church family as a whole. As we will discover, this is formational to both mission and identity. By building lives that are integrated with one another, where hospitality, community and openness are the norms, we can work to see Christ formed in one another. The commitment to the church runs far deeper than a commitment to attend a service. It is a commitment to walk alongside one another in the complex, messy and difficult moments of our lives. It means that we journey alongside with those we otherwise would never associate with, as a family. We open our homes and our hearts to vulnerable interactions where our security is ultimately in Jesus, so we do not fear the reactions of others.

Paul talks about how this is a painful process (Galatians 4:19) — so painful he analogizes it with childbirth. For this reason, we must also be submitted to one another (Ephesians 5:21). We must put others ahead of ourselves. Our desire must be to see Christ formed in those around us; a desire that runs so deep it causes anguish when we fail to see it occur. When we forsake our preferences for the benefit of the whole we are actually embodying Christ who gave up the glories of Heaven for our benefit. Laying our lives down for our brothers and sisters is perhaps one of the most Jesus-like things we can do, and as such is an essential component of being a son or daughter of Christ.

Lastly, at a deeper level, we also invite others to refine us in our brokenness and sin. Our identity in Christ is forged when we submit ourselves to correction and rebuke from our leaders (Hebrews 13:17). We do not submit to one another as those who are already perfect. Instead, we submit to each other knowing that we all equally need the grace of Jesus! A church family is not built on our individual holiness, but rather on the fact that together we are made holy by Jesus' holiness! We are not tolerant of sin; on the contrary, we deal with it seriously and directly. Crucially, however, our capacity to deal with sin in each other is predicated on the mutual commitment to the name of Jesus and the covenant of his family: the church. We correct each other because we know that we love each other as brothers and sisters. Our correction is not a pressure to belong; rather, because we already belong, it is an invitation to live whole and full in Jesus' goodness!

Ambassadors — Missional Identity

Jesus sent his disciples into the world as representatives of his Kingdom (John 17:18). His purpose in sending us into the world was so that others would hear about, and choose to accept, the message of Jesus (John 17:20). The Apostle Paul recognized that the fact that we are sent into the world with a mission is not so much a task that we have been asked to do as it is an identity that we step into when we become Jesus' followers. The word that Paul uses is "ambassador," which means that we are sent as representatives of a Kingdom; it is an identity statement, not a task statement.

> **2 Corinthians 5:20**
>
> *We are ambassadors for Christ, since God is making his appeal through us. We plead on Christ's behalf: "Be reconciled to God."*

The identity of an ambassador is one of great value and dignity. We have been invited to represent the Kingdom of God here on earth! We, as ambassadors, are emissaries of the king of the universe. A core part of Jesus' mission was to announce that the Kingdom of God had come. As Jesus himself demonstrated, the Kingdom of God is built on truth, grace, forgiveness and love. We, as recipients of his grace, are invited to represent that kingdom. This identity should give us great joy, confidence and security even in the face of great opposition. As ambassadors, we are secure no matter the situation in which we find ourselves, because we know that our King is sovereign on the throne.

> *Humanity's awesome dignity is found in its call to be the ambassador of God!* — Darrell Guder[34]

There are two immediate and essential applications to seeing the identity of an ambassador take root. First, being an ambassador means that our allegiance is always to Jesus, never to this world. An ambassador can take up residence in a culture that is foreign to them, but they are never subsumed into that culture. To a degree, no matter how long they reside in that culture, their first and primary responsibility will always be to the Kingdom that has commissioned them as an ambassador. Everything that an ambassador does in the foreign land is done in a manner that will strategically maximize their impact for the sending Kingdom. Likewise, for us as ambassadors, it means that we must arrange our lives in such a way that our allegiance and priority is always to strategically maximize impact for the Kingdom of Jesus. As ambassadors, we must resist the allure of success as defined by our culture. We must resist the false promises of comfort that are offered to us in our world and instead choose to do what is best for the Kingdom. The tension between our identity as an ambassador and the world around us will mean we will often feel somewhat "alien" in our culture, as Peter states.

1 Peter 2:11 [NASB]

Beloved, I urge you as aliens and strangers to abstain from fleshly lusts which wage war against the soul.

The sense of being alien to our culture does not mean that we are weird or isolated; it means that we live according to a fundamentally different value set. We must continually resist the temptation to be absorbed into the culture around us. We should look radically different in how we structure our lives, spend our money, pursue our careers, serve our cities and love our families. The value propositions of Jesus mandate that, as ambassadors, our relationships with every aspect of our lives be constructed on his value system, not the value system of the world.

As ambassadors, our allegiance must always remain with Jesus, which is an inner-life aspect of our discipleship. However, the identity of an ambassador is about living strategically on mission so that people will hear about Jesus. The purpose of an ambassador is to represent the kingdom, not passively, but actively. It means intentionally advocating for and introducing others to the way of Jesus. Paul's use of the word "plead" in the above verse in 2 Corinthians 5 is powerful. Pleading is an intentional, almost desperate, verb that indicates a sense of urgency and importance to the work. A fully formed identity as an ambassador should create a profound sense of urgency for us to see those around us know about Jesus. Multiplication is an inevitable product of the effective ambassador; we are inviting people into the Kingdom of Jesus and, in turn, sending them out as ambassadors in their own right.

A disciple that has a well-developed identity as an ambassador will have clear evidence in their lives of a life built upon a fundamentally different value system. Additionally, they will have a clear and demonstrated history of multiplication effectiveness stemming from their work.

Servants & Slaves — Sacrificial Identity

The crucial final identity marker that we can experience a thriving inner and outer life on is that of a slave or a servant. The identity of a servant or slave may be the most conceptually challenging of the identity statements. Jesus directly calls us to it in Matthew 20, and Paul reiterates this invitation in Romans 6.

Matthew 20:26-28

Instead, whoever wants to become great among you must be your servant, and whoever wants to be first must be your slave— just as the Son of Man did not come to be served, but to serve, and to give his life as a ransom for many.

Romans 6:22

But now, since you have been set free from sin and have become enslaved to God, you have your fruit, which results in sanctification—and the outcome is eternal life!

We serve others because we are called to become servants by the Gospel. The Gospel is news about how God became man so that he could serve us. The creator God of the universe became the servant of his creation that had completely and utterly rejected him. We, in turn, are invited to live as servants ourselves. We are, first and foremost, servants of Christ. As Paul brilliantly points out in Romans 6, we are all ultimately enslaved to the things that we obey. In this sense, freedom is a myth; we are all playing the role of slave to the things that rule our lives. For many, this may be career, family, money, success, comfort or experiences. When we allow those things to enslave us, we are committing the sin of idolatry: permitting something other than God to take the primary place in our lives. For others, a direct habitual sin may be that which enslaves them. However, make no mistake, both the active sins and passive sins in our life that have our attention in place of Jesus are ultimately going to enslave us.

The fact that we are "slaves to the things we obey," to use the words of Paul, is why understanding that we are first enslaved to Christ is of utter paramount importance. To be enslaved to Christ is to establish him as the right, true and good Lord of our lives. To be his servant is to give him the authority, which he rightly deserves, to direct, steer and mould our lives. He has the power and the authority to give in great abundance or to take away as he wishes. Why is this such good news? It is good news because when we submit our lives to Jesus as Lord and adopt the posture of a servant, the process of sanctification begins to do the work of producing life within us (Romans 6:22). Because we have released the tight grip of control on our lives and released it to him who is infinitely more capable, we can receive the fullness of life that he has to offer.

Just as adopting the posture of a servant changes the way we relate to Jesus and build our lives, so too are our relationships transformed by this identity shift. Often when we serve, we can do so out of a sense of obligation, eagerness or even a desire to see change happen in the world. However, there is a deeper motivation for serving in the life of a Christian: identity. We do not serve simply because it is something good to do. We serve because we are a people who have adopted the identity of a servant. As our identity shifts to become that of a servant, serving becomes a natural extension of who we are; serving becomes a way of life.

Serving others can quickly feel like a task done in addition to the rest of our life. However, we are not called to serve others as an add-on to the lives that we live. We do not give "serving hours" or participate in "community service projects" in an effort to please Jesus. Such a compartmentalized understanding of serving does not flow from the identity of a servant; it is not deep enough. We are called to serve others because it is who we are. Every moment of every day we are called to live into the posture and identity of the servant. The transformation of our identity into a servant means that we must build our lives to maximize our ability to serve and bless others, even ahead of our own need for comfort or ease.

Identity through Adversity

Many Christians know about their supposed identity in Christ. However, that identity is often a theoretical concept rather than a deeply rooted and formational belief. They know they ought to act, live and walk in confidence as sons and daughters; yet for many, this does not describe their daily reality. When they run into challenges or doubt what is true about themselves, admonishing them with the Word can feel like piling shame on their unbelief. As disciple-making disciples, we work to create specific church families where we can learn to live as sons and daughters, servants and ambassadors by being brothers and sisters in Christ. It is from within the church family that we can see secure identities in Christ formed. How do we practically help people learn to walk out their identity, especially through the trials and valleys that life inevitably brings?

Scripture gives us a solution that is as shocking as it is counter-cultural. The authors of the New Testament describe a rubric of adversity, trials, suffering and discipline as the means by which we develop secure identities and robust Christ-like characters. These challenges that come up help us refine our identity as fully alive children, ambassadors and slaves.

In Christ, we are set free from slavery to sin and raised from death to life. However, sin and brokenness still exist in us as we learn to yield to the sovereignty of Christ in us. Hebrews 12 teaches us that it is through discipline that our identity in Christ as sons and daughters is confirmed. By identifying sin and calling each other to repentance, we can simultaneously affirm dependence on Christ while urging each other to walk in our newfound freedom.

Hebrews 12:7-8,11

Endure hardship as discipline; God is treating you as his children. For what children are not disciplined by their father? If you are not disciplined — and everyone undergoes discipline — then you are not legitimate, not true sons and daughters at all. ... No discipline seems pleasant at the time, but painful. Later on, however, it produces a harvest of righteousness and peace for those who have been trained by it.

A life of continual and habitual sin will limit our formation as sons and daughters. Part of our mandate as disciple-making disciples is to call our brothers and sisters in Christ to radical holiness. The invitation to holiness can be painful as the private and shameful parts of our lives are brought into the light. As we confess our sins to one another and even suffer consequences associated with that sin, we are refined and established as more secure in Christ. We must disciple people to be disciplined in righteousness. If we wish to disciple people towards security as sons and daughters, we must be willing to confront their sin and call them to wholeness in Christ. The pain caused by discipline is only temporary and is never done to earn acceptance by God. Discipline is a reminder that we are already loved and received in Christ, even though we still sin. Discipline and rebuke strengthen and remind us of our security in Christ.

Consequently, we must not tolerate actions or words that are not reflective of Christ in our midst as they erode that identity. Our world flaunts and even brags about behaviour that is not honouring to Christ. Such flaunting of sin can include bragging about drunkenness, celebrating our gluttony, idolizing our possessions, tacitly endorsing violent and pornographic content, and sexual liberation. We must be disciplined in the pursuit of holy lives and be willing to be corrected when we miss the mark. When we call each other to a higher standard, we are reminding one another that we are sons and daughters of the King. Despite being painful, discipline and rebuke do not take away from our worth or security. Instead, they affirm it! That is why effective discipleship must involve both confronting the sin in those we are discipling and the humility to be challenged ourselves.

If discipline in righteousness affirms our identity as sons and daughters in Christ, then trials, challenges and adversity affirm our call to be servants and ambassadors. The culture around us teaches us that life is the most full, and we are the most alive, when everything is safe, secure and comfortable. There is nothing comfortable about the call to be an ambassador or servant apart from the security we have in Christ. We are conditioned to think that when something is uncomfortable it means that something is wrong. Many of us, for a good reason, fear being tired, poor, criticized or failing and so we live lives that are safe and secure in the comforts afforded us by our Western society. The call to discipleship is the exact opposite, as we give our lives for the benefit of others and the name of Jesus. This sacrificial way of life will surely involve trials and challenges. As disciples, we will often feel tired and weak, but we do not despair or conclude that our lives are imbalanced.

James 1:2-4

Consider it pure joy, my brothers and sisters, whenever you face trials of many kinds, because you know that the testing of your

> *faith produces perseverance. Let perseverance finish its work so that you may be mature and complete*

James teaches us that when we face all kinds of trials, we must consider it an opportunity to be made mature. We do not find the trial itself joy; instead, it is the knowledge that through the trial we will be brought into greater union with Christ. Harmony with Christ is certainly cause for great joy! If a trial is the means and the end is Christ, then let us embrace the means with great eagerness. What a tremendously liberating theology when we look at adversity as conquerors, not victims. As those who have been sent on a mission for Jesus, we can thrive amid trials knowing that it will cause us to be more reliant and dependent on Jesus.

For some, when they face trials, they despair and look for an easy way out. Others will double down on their efforts, grit their teeth and keep going. Both of these responses do not help forge a secure identity. Instead, we must allow the trial to strip away our fear of failure or discomfort, on the one hand, and self-reliance, on the other. We use adversity as an opportunity to cause us to look to Christ and depend on the power of the Holy Spirit.

It is very tempting to grumble, complain and fall into self-pity when things are challenging. We may be tempted to blame those around us for the challenges we are facing. When we take responsibility for the situation and choose an attitude of joy, our identity in Christ is strengthened. Trials, from a Biblical standpoint, are an opportunity for us to learn and deepen our security in Christ.

The call to be servants is by its very definition, sacrificial and uncomfortable. There is nothing natural to our human pride about washing the feet of those around us. As we practice the uncomfortable habits of servanthood, putting others ahead of ourselves, our pride and self-reliance are stripped away. By serving others, we shift the attention from ourselves to the intrinsic value and worth of others. Few things will help strengthen our security in Christ quite like thinking about ourselves less.

To be formed in Christ amid the trial, we must surround ourselves with those who encourage us to persevere in the way of Jesus. We must not seek out the voices that advocate for the route that will produce comfort and security. We must surround ourselves with those who encourage us to continue faithfully in the mission set in front of us.

Perseverance should bear the fruit of hope within us (Romans 5:3-5). The more we persevere, the more we should be joyful and hopeful in our ministry. If we find ourselves becoming resentful or embittered, we must stop and turn to Jesus. If we find ourselves lacking in joy, then we are very likely attempting to serve in our strength.

Lastly, the call to discipline and perseverance is ultimately a work of the Holy Spirit. If we seek to live as good disciple-making disciples in our own strength, we will be crushed into exhaustion or failure. We must continually invite the Holy Spirit to help us in our service.

8

Missional Living

Missional living is the third area of discipleship emphasis. Missional living, in the broadest sense, is the component of discipleship where we intentionally and strategically build our lives to maximize kingdom impact. If every person is called to be a disciple-making disciple, then our lives should be an integrated whole that sees as many people as possible discover the hope of Jesus through us.

We can misunderstand the nature of missional living as a sort of mere communal living or a derivative of a minimalistic worldview. Indeed, intentional community and a simple life are crucial ingredients in leading a productive missional life, but they are not an end in themselves. Missional living is all about mission: not our individual personal goals, but the great mission that Jesus has sent us on to see all people profess him as Lord and be baptized and sent to join the mission. The essential component of this process is discipleship. We are commanded to "go and make disciples." This discussion of missional living is about how we build lives that are effective in fulfilling the mission through intentional discipleship relationships.

Every follower of Jesus is called to be a missionary. When we speak of missional living, we are stating very clearly that to be a missionary is the normative call on all Jesus followers. To be a missionary is not a special call reserved for the spiritually elite. We are all missionaries for the Gospel; the only questions we need to be asking are where and how should we be maximizing our missional impact. The power of the Gospel is that it transforms every person into an agent of missional impact for the glory of Jesus. The Gospel is not just news about our spiritual transformation in Christ; it is equally an invitation for us to live a life of mission so that others can be made alive in the hope of Jesus.

What then does a missional life look like, how is it shaped and structured, and how do we maximize our kingdom impact? How do we live with Jesus as Lord?

As with secure identity and gospel fluency, the foundation of missional living is that Jesus is Lord. As our Lord, Jesus has the authority to command every component of our lives. There is no part of who we are or what we are doing that is beyond his reach or separated from his command. His Lordship includes our work, family, relationships, jobs, finances, where and how we live, and what sorts of goals we set for our lives. The Apostle Paul proudly illustrates the power of a healthy missional life as he describes his attitude towards his life, which notably included a great deal of hardship and suffering:

Philippians 4:11-13

I have learned to be content in whatever circumstances I find myself. I know both how to make do with little, and I know how to make do with a lot. In any and all circumstances I have learned the secret of being content—whether well fed or hungry, whether in abundance or in need. I am able to do all things through him who strengthens me.

His capacity to live a life of effective mission, especially when it was challenging, was directly connected to his surrendered and submitted posture towards Jesus (verse 13).

The surrender of our lives to Jesus leads us to an important principle of missional living: a missional life will not just be effective for seeing people know Jesus, it will also lead to us being satisfied and fulfilled in Jesus. To live missionally is not to form a vision for our lives; instead, we adopt Jesus' vision for our lives. It should be no surprise that when we adopt Jesus' vision for our lives, we become the most fully alive. As Paul says, *"For you died, and your life is now hidden with Christ in God"* (Colossians 3:1-4).

Practically, what does this submission to Jesus as Lord look like? More poignantly, what does it look like and how can we think of our lives in a way that maximizes kingdom impact? There are two keys that work together to unlock a missional life. Without these keys, trying to live on mission will likely feel like a set of tasks that are overwhelming. To be sure, a life of mission is sacrificial but is also profoundly satisfying! To this end, we must disciple people in a fashion that leads them to lead a life with increasing missional impact.

Simplicity

The first key is that of simplicity. Our lives are encumbered with all sorts of busy activities and commitments. Upward mobility, accompanied by increasingly complex and expensive lives, is the norm in the Western world. Does our ferocious appetite for more actually add anything meaningful to our lives? Certainly not! Do our busy lives lead to contentment, much less missionality? Absolutely not!

The writer of Ecclesiastes thousands of years ago recognized the futility of our human busyness and striving. He invites us to lead simple lives of faithfulness and focus on the things of God.

Ecclesiastes 12:12-13

Of making many books there is no end, and much study wearies the body. Now all has been heard; here is the conclusion of the matter: Fear God and keep his commandments, for this is the duty of all mankind.

It is so easy to get distracted with all the opportunities in the world around us. Many of them are even good and beautiful! How do we decide what to do? Through the prophet Micah, God invites us to live lives of justice, faithfulness and humility (Micah 6:8). We need to live unencumbered, simple, honest and focused lives in order to faithfully walk out the call to be a disciple-making disciple.

If we look at much of our busyness, we will discover that we spend a great deal of our time consuming. Moments spent consuming are the antithesis of simplicity. By definition, consumption means more and simplicity means less! A missional life will challenge our busyness and consumption. We cannot form the deep kind of relationships that discipleship requires if we are always busy pursuing our own interests or feeding ourselves. We must slow down and intentionally, and sacrificially, create room for the non-believer to know the believer.

The missional life will consist of significant time, energy, resources and effort invested into the things of God. It is a full life, but not a busy life. A busy life is filled with activities, responsibilities, hobbies and interests that are all competing for attention. We all have 24 hours to invest each day, and each person manages to spend all 24 of those hours every day. A busy life scatters those hours over many activities, many of which, if we are honest with ourselves, are self-serving. In a full life, we view those hours as a gift to be strategically invested. We may invest long hours and be tired or even exhausted at times as the Apostle Paul was (2 Corinthians 11:28). However, the investment is intentional and strategic rather than frantic and scattered.

2 Corinthians 11:28

I have laboured and toiled and have often gone without sleep; I have known hunger and thirst and have often gone without food; I have been cold and naked. Besides everything else, I face daily the pressure of my concern for all the churches.

The call to simplicity can be formed in us as disciples through two questions. First, we must ask, in what specific and measurable way will this decision increase our missional effectiveness? We must be honest with ourselves in this regard. The human heart can rationalize all kinds of things that are not of the heart of God. It's easy to justify an increased standard of living, or the need to carve out large amounts of leisure time. We live in a culture that idolizes vacations and "me time" under the guise of necessity. This chasing, however, is a recent invention and can lead us astray. Jesus never went on vacation, nor did Paul prioritize "me time." This is not to say that rest is inherently bad; however, so often it is the goal above all else. Further, when it really comes down to it, often we are not prioritizing rest in these moments, but consumption. In the missional life, we seek first the kingdom of God instead of chasing our momentary desires.

Second, we must ask, what are the potential negative missional consequences of this decision? For example, we may get a job that could legitimately open up new missional opportunities, but if it pulls us out of our discipleship relationships and church family then that is a very dangerous situation. We must stop and seriously reflect on our motivations for our decision making, and the consequences associated with them.

Integration

Often when we think of our lives, we think of the individual constituent parts of our lives and tend to isolate the different components from one another. In many cases, we may even seek to prevent the elements of our lives from touching one another.

An example of this compartmentalization concept is the popular phrase "work-life balance." While the intention of healthy, sustainable lives is commendable, the concept is dangerous. Work and life are not opposing forces or segments of our lives. When living missionally, instead of seeking to maximize "work-life balance," we instead seek to maximize "kingdom impact." The goal is to take all the components of our lives and see them integrated to be an effective Gospel witness.

In a compartmentalized view of our lives, the Gospel, church, and the mission of our lives are all merely single compartments. As a particular compartment grows it will naturally squeeze out some of the other compartments, as illustrated below. In a compartmentalized view of our lives, the Gospel/Church are always competing for attention. Such compartmentalization can, if not corrected, result in resentment towards the church, as we feel torn between serving the church and caring for ourselves. Given

110 | Discipleship Potential

enough time, this can ultimately lead to a life that is self-centred as we relegate the mission of God to the back-burner or let it become forgotten altogether. We are the most alive when we are committed to the mission of God; this call, however, will not always be easy (see Philippians 4, above).

A Non-Missional Life - No Integration

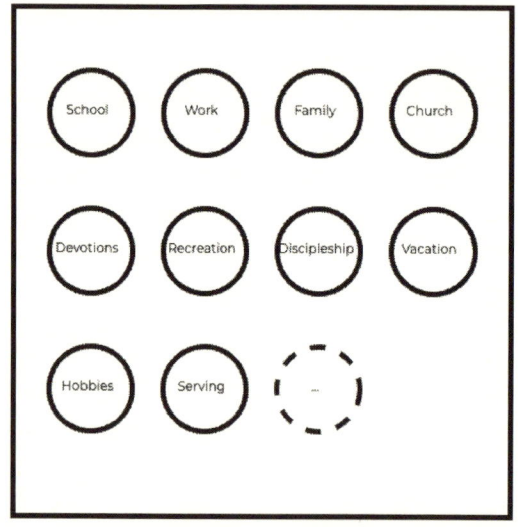

A non-missional life avoids integration. Lacks purpose and intentionality to maximize kingdom impact.

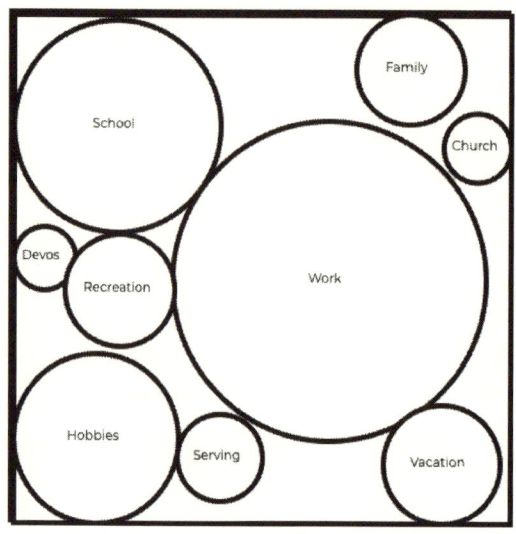

As things get "busy" discipleship/church relationships get squeezed out.

If compartmentalization is the opposite of missional living, then what is the alternative? The answer lies in living an integrated life where every component of our lives seeks to facilitate the common goal of maximizing kingdom impact. If we intentionally arrange every part of our lives such that they are all pointing towards the same goal, then instead of one area competing with another, they will all work together to facilitate the same purpose. Instead of "work and life" being opposing forces, our work and our play will both be leveraged to see people know Jesus.

James addresses the temptation to compartmentalize our lives such that our missional impact is ignored. Instead of compartmentalizing, which he calls evil, we are instructed to ask the question, *"What is the heart of God?"*

James 4:13-17

Come now, you who say, "Today or tomorrow we will travel to such and such a city and spend a year there and do business and make a profit." Yet you do not know what tomorrow will bring— what your life will be! For you are like vapour that appears for a little while, then vanishes. Instead, you should say, "If the Lord wills, we will live and do this or that." But as it is, you boast in your arrogance. All such boasting is evil. So it is sin to know the good and yet not do it.

This text highlights how easy it is to allow our plans to fall into the current of the broader culture around us or even the dreams within us. James calls us to pause our lives and seek to know the purposes of God in our lives. We can make plans that may be fruitful in the eyes of the world. We may be able to accomplish a great deal, but in the perspective of eternity, our plans do not amount to much. We must stop and seek the heart of God. The will of God is to see all nations and peoples brought to himself! So we need to structure our lives that way! James is instructing us to live integrated lives instead of compartmentalized ones.

A helpful illustration for understanding what an integrated life for mission looks like is that of a large river with several tributaries that are flowing into it. The central river of our lives exists to carry the Gospel. The tributaries are the various parts of our lives, all providing fuel for the movement of the Gospel. When we live missionally, every component of our lives is serving the same goal : Jesus' glory through the movement of the Gospel!

When we are not living missionally, the tributaries are cut off from the main river and result in standing and stagnant water. Stagnant water eventually grows scum and fails to support life. The image of the river is a powerful image in scripture. For example, Revelation 22 describes a river flowing from the throne of Jesus that brings multiplying life to everything around it. Similarly, Jesus promises in John 7 that when we come to him, he will produce living waters within us.

John 7:38

The one who believes in me, as the Scripture has said, will have streams of living water flow from deep within him.

A Missional Life - Integration

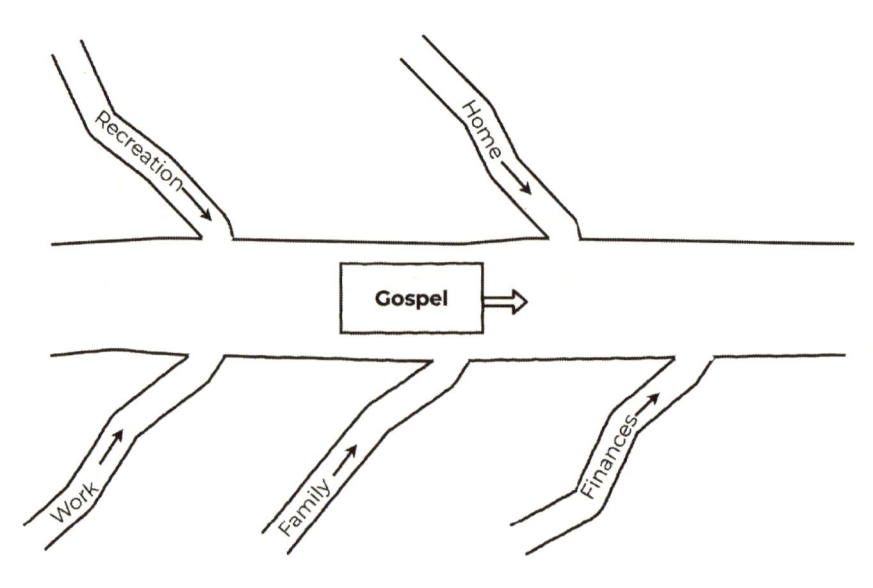

Tributaries contributing to an integrated life that carries the Gospel.

Notice that Jesus says that there will be streams — multiple sources of life within us that are all finding the source in Jesus. Are the components of your life all tributaries to a river or are they more like cut off stagnant ponds?

Seek First the Kingdom

Integrating every aspect of our lives so that people will know Jesus means that we must forsake the pursuit of our careers, hobbies or even family as ends in and of themselves. Instead, Jesus' glorification is the end towards which all things must point (Luke 9:26). These components of our lives are, of course, not harmful by themselves. In fact, they can be tremendously glorifying to Jesus, but they must not be the goal or the objective of our lives. To elevate any component of our lives ahead of the desire to glorify Jesus would amount to idolatry, pure and simple.

The call to such a radically integrated way of living is profoundly counter-cultural and challenging to adopt. Our cultural norms, the expectations of our culture for what a normal life looks like, are not congruent with a missional life. Jesus instructs us unambiguously to seek first his Kingdom above everything else (Matthew 6:33). His Kingdom must come before any other desire, hope or dream. For many people, missional living is viewed as another way of religious thinking that can be added to their lives.

Many of us fall into the temptation of putting career, security, or comfort first with the good intentions of thinking missionally once our life is arranged to our liking. This kind of delayed missionality will never produce a genuinely missional life. A missional life will always desire the Kingdom of God first, above all else. We must first seek to glorify God in our lives. Only when the Kingdom of God is the deepest yearning and longing of our soul are we liberated from the idolatrous pursuit of our self-interest.

Only when Jesus' mission is first, is our life free and whole. Jesus' commands to live a missional life are framed in broader teachings on worry and anxiety. A missional life is a life that is fully alive because it finds its home in Jesus. The call to sacrifice, openness, passion and vulnerability are all grounded in our own security in Christ. From this understanding of our security in

Christ and a desire to see him glorified, we can put the Kingdom before our doubts, fears and worries (Matthew 6:34). When we allow the people around us to place personal security, career, finances, fears, doubts and worries ahead of the Kingdom of God with the noble notion that we want them to be satisfied with their lives, we are actually allowing them to be ensnared by the lies of our culture (Proverbs 29:5-6). A missional life is a truly free life because it is a life with Jesus at the centre!

The high challenge of missional living is why gospel fluency and a secure identity are so crucial as discipleship building blocks. A call to missional living without an adequately formed gospel fluency and secure identity in Christ will be oppressive and unnatural. However, a missional life is the natural overflow of proper gospel fluency.

Everyday Practices

Having laid the groundwork with the importance of living an integrated life for missional impact, we must ask the question: what does it look like in practice? A great case study in what missional living looks like is found in Acts 2, shortly after the birth of the church. From it, we have identified six everyday practices that marked the missional church.

Acts 2:42-47

They devoted themselves to the apostles' teaching, to the fellowship, to the breaking of bread, and to prayer. Everyone was filled with awe, and many wonders and signs were being performed through the apostles. Now all the believers were together and held all things in common. They sold their possessions and property and distributed the proceeds to all, as any had need. Every day they devoted themselves to meeting together in the temple, and broke bread from house to house. They ate their food with joyful and sincere hearts, praising God and enjoying the favour of all the people. Every day the Lord added to their number those who were being saved.

Everyday Practice 1: Spiritual Hunger

> *42 They devoted themselves to the apostles' teaching, to the fellowship, to the breaking of bread, and to prayer. Everyone was filled with awe, and many wonders and signs were being performed through the apostles.*

There will be a lot of discussion on fellowship and breaking bread. However, before we can discuss those, we need to emphasize the necessity of spiritual hunger as exemplified in devotion to the apostles' teaching and prayer.

In a sense, spiritual hunger is the fuel that drives our missional lives. As we feed our appetite for more of God, we in turn begin to live missionally, which in turn causes us to be more spiritually hungry. Spiritual hunger is all about dependence on the Lord to do what we cannot — draw people to himself (John 6:44)! When we live on mission, we live as people who daily turn to the Lord in total and complete surrender. We surrender to be moulded by God in our inner-life to be sanctified and to invite the Lord to send us on mission in our outer-life through multiplication. As Charles Finney wrote, *"If Christians do not energetically awaken and if God does not pour out His Spirit, the world will laugh at the church."*[35]

Prayer

A missional life, by definition, is a life of bold faith. The church in Acts was utterly dependent on the work of the Holy Spirit in their midst. A missional church is ultimately sustained and supported by the work of God. We cannot live missionally without reliance on the work of God's grace and power. When we live missionally, we should be living with the faith that God will move in our midst and do what we cannot do.

Pete Greig, the founder of the 24/7 prayer movement, described the necessity of prayer in conjunction with mission this way:

> *When a vision is born in the pride of a prayer-less imagination, it is nothing more than a projection of the self. Self-projected vision is beamed indiscriminately onto the world by an inner drive*

> *to be larger than life in every conversation, in every context and in posterity too. Self projected vision is an empire building compulsion; it comes not to serve to be served.* — Pete Greig[36]

Prayer is a deeply missional activity. Any missional work that does not come from the place of prayer is almost certainly tainted with our pride and sin. It is due to the temptation to operate out of our pride that when Jesus taught us to pray, he instructed us to pray that the Lord's kingdom would come, that the Lord's will would be done, that what we see on earth would align with His purposes. Jesus instructed us to pray for the mission (Matthew 6:10)! It is through daily surrender before the Lord in prayer that the Lord's desires become ours.

This act of surrendering is a daily, recurring rhythm. When we take a step of faith to live on mission, we will often begin in a place of prayer but will then run in our own strength, hoping, in vain, that our spiritual high from months or years ago will carry us. Spiritual hunger and prayer must be a daily practice that occurs in private (Matthew 6:6) and in the community (Acts 4:24).

In a missional life, we daily bring the needs, hopes and dreams of the entire discipleship movement before the Lord. Out of that place of awareness of their dependence on God, they are sent on mission. The pattern that we see in Acts is very clear: the disciples prayed, experienced God, and were sent on mission. A missional life, empowered by the Holy Spirit, starts with prayer!

Submitting to Teaching

With the foundation laid in prayer, a key part of healthy spiritual hunger is the willingness to be corrected by the teaching of the church. As the apostles lead the way, the church began to put into action what they were being taught. The willingness to actually live what they were taught required that the church had the humility to change how they were thinking to reflect Jesus better.

As a result, missional living requires that we are submitted to the broader community and willing to allow God to use the church, particularly the leadership, to challenge our thinking and living. Again, this is a countercultural principle. We are typically conditioned to think very autonomously or individualistically. In a missional life, we learn to think communally and are submitted to one another.

This spiritual hunger, and willingness to grow and learn, were coupled to a supernatural move of God. A missional life is a supernatural life. The supernatural move of God is always connected to the missional impact of the church. A desire for the supernatural is never for our benefit or gratification. Rather, we must desire the move of God so that church family will be strengthened and non-believers will proclaim God's goodness. (1 Corinthians 14:12,25)

In this way, boldness to invite people to know Jesus must always be the overflow of a fervent, passionate, desperate and faithful public and private prayer life and time in the word.

Discipling Spiritual Hunger

Spiritual hunger is a discipleship issue because it is neither innate nor binary. It is not simply something that you are born, nor is it something that you have or not. Rather, spiritual hunger is something that we develop. Spiritual hunger requires that we come to Jesus, in humility, asking him to mould our hearts. We cultivate spiritual hunger by asking the Lord to soften our hearts so that we can clearly hear his voice. A soft heart is marked by one who can identify, by the work of the Holy Spirit, their sinful desires and their pride and ask the Lord to give them new desires and longings. Spiritual hunger is not cultivated in consuming more sermons, finding a better preacher or engaging in trendy worship. When we approach those things as if they exist for ourselves, we only fuel and satisfy our own narcissism. Spiritual hunger is cultivated in the place of surrender before Jesus.

Spiritual hunger is cultivated by coming before the Lord in prayer, and submitting to the power of his word in our times of quiet on our own, as well as through collective times with our missional family — the church. The church cultivates spiritual hunger in a two-fold process. Firstly, by calling people to a process of knowing and being transformed by Jesus; sanctification through prayer and the word. Secondly, the mandate of the church is to missionally mobilize people who have encountered Jesus. Spiritual hunger without a missional edge to it is not true spiritual hunger. Spiritually hungry people will yearn to be sent on mission so that others will know Jesus. In short, spiritual hunger and multiplication go hand in hand.

As disciple-makers, we must invite people to the transformational process of spending intentional, sacrificial time in prayer and the word, alone and in community, with an eye to both sanctification and multiplication.

Everyday Practice 2: Church at the Centre

> *42 They devoted themselves to the apostles' teaching, to the fellowship, to the breaking of bread, and to prayer...*
> *46 Every day they devoted themselves to meeting together in the temple, and broke bread from house to house.*

The first component of the early church's integrated life is that the church was at the centre of how they lived their lives. Missional living is always in the context of community. We cannot live missionally on our own. We are not lone-rangers or islands unto ourselves. Rather, we are invited to be committed to the body of Christ in the context of a local church. However, this goes far deeper than a mere once-a-week commitment. The church integrated their lives such that they were in constant contact with both one another, as well as unbelievers. Church was not a once a week "event" that they attended; instead, it was a family of believers that were on a mission together 24/7. Let us state clearly: to live missionally is to change our thinking about church from an event or building to a family committed to one another 24/7.

The church was their family. They were devoted to one another. They were committed to one another through thick and thin, even at significant personal cost. The church was not a relationship of convenience but one of mutual investments into one another and commitment to the cause of Christ. The commitment to one another as the body of Christ is what it means to be a covenant family. We are not family by our own blood; we are family by the blood of Christ who has invited us into a new family (1 Peter 2:9, Revelation 1:5-6).

We have limited relational capacity in our lives. There are only so many people who we can build meaningful relationships with at the same time. Discipleship relationships require significant time and energy invested in them, as do relationships with non-believers. By placing church at the centre of our lives, we seek to integrate all of our relationships into our church family relationships. By way of metaphor, our church family serves as the hub to which all the spokes that are our relationships connect. To do this properly will mean that from a critical outside perspective, it may appear that all we do is church. Placing church at the centre is not the norm in our culture. We tend to silo or isolate our relationships from one another. Our work, school, church, family and hobby relationships may never interact! By placing church at the centre, we seek to bring all of our primary day-to-day relationships together in our church family. This does not mean that we avoid relationships with non-believers — quite the opposite! Instead, we seek to integrate our lives so that our non-christian friends have regular interactions with our brothers and sisters in Christ.

Placing church at the centre is risky as we are opening our lives and ourselves up to the possibility of being hurt or wounded by those we are journeying with. Deep relationships and deep discipleship require the very real possibility of being hurt. To be truly known and truly loved we must open our lives up to one another and build lives where the good, the bad and the ugly are part of journeying towards Christ together.

Missional living with church at the centre is undoubtedly a fantastic context for a life of security in the context of community. However, how exactly is it missional? How does orienting our lives around church family increase missional impact?

1) People will know us by our love

Our witness in the context of church family is perhaps the most powerful witness that we have (John 13:35). When people see a missionally mobilized family of believers, it should be immediately apparent to those who look on from the outside. As Christians, our mission is to call people to be secure as sons and daughters in Christ. How much more effective is our witness when people can see that identity expressed in unity and harmony in a body (Psalm 133:1)? As the world becomes more and more self-focused and isolated, living in vulnerability with a church community becomes more attractive to those looking in from the outside. A loving community built on more than similar interests, personalities or lifestyles, but instead formed through the Holy Spirit, is both extremely confusing and profoundly attractive to those who have no context for such a community.

2) *Our witness of Jesus is collective rather than individual*

When we seek to introduce people to Jesus, our witness is incomplete and flawed. We point people to Jesus, but we do that as flawed and imperfect representatives. If the only witness that people have in their lives is us, then we are only introducing them to a small dimension of who Jesus is. Of course, an individual witness is still fantastic, and we must celebrate it. However, when we witness as individuals alongside our brothers and sisters in the faith, our impact is that much stronger. By placing church at the centre, the entire community can serve as a witness. When we are broken or fail, we can demonstrate to those who do not know Jesus that even in our weaknesses and brokenness, Jesus is still good. As the family of Christ rallies, they help people see a bigger and fuller picture of who Jesus is.

3) *The context for conversion is safe*

For many people, the invitation to follow Jesus is profoundly risky. Such a risk is especially true for those from backgrounds and cultures where the Gospel is not prominent. Accepting Jesus may mean that they could be disowned, or worse, by their families (Mark 10:28-31). If we are going to see people know Jesus when there is such a risk, we must provide a family that will support, encourage, uphold and resource those brothers and sisters.[37]

One important consideration when seeking to implement church at the centre is that we do not isolate ourselves in a bubble. The community itself must always be missional and oriented around that mission. We must remain vigilant and alert to the temptation to build insular communities where serious engagement with those who do not know Jesus are limited.

Everyday Practice 3: Intentional Proximity

John 1:14 [MSG]

The Word became flesh and blood, and moved into the neighbourhood.

The second everyday practice that we can see from an integration standpoint is that the early followers of Jesus were in intentional proximity with one another. When living missionally, our work, home, play and church family are all geographically near one another.

> 44 Now all the believers were together and held all things in common. They sold their possessions and property and distributed the proceeds to all, as any had need. Every day they devoted themselves to meeting together in the temple, and broke bread from house to house.

The above familial relationships are not possible without being physically close to one another. Furthermore, it is exceedingly difficult to integrate our work or school relationships into the pursuit of Jesus if they are not close to us. The daily contact exhibited by the disciples was critical. So often, our lives are fragmented geographically with the various components of our lives all in different places. Effective integration of the 'tributaries' of our lives requires that we actually connect all the pieces. This is illustrated in the diagram below.

The requirement for proximity may be one of the more challenging components for missional living in 21st Western culture, where large/long commutes to work or play are the norm. However, at a bare minimum, our church family and our living should be as close together as possible: ideally within walking distance of one another to maximize integration.

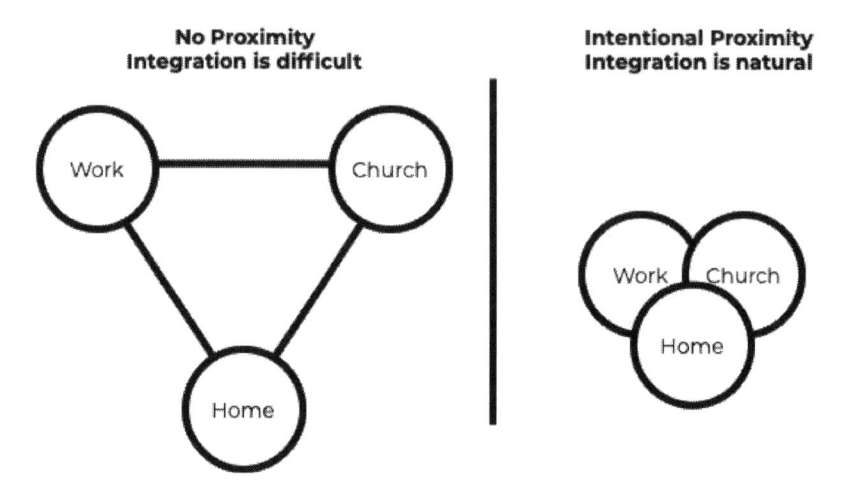

Intentional Proximity

No Proximity
Integration is difficult

- Work
- Church
- Home

Intentional Proximity
Integration is natural

- Work
- Church
- Home

Intentionality

What is "intentional" about intentional proximity? Intentional proximity means that we choose, deliberately, to place integration and missional living as crucial driving factors in deciding where and how we live. The default cultural norm is to either put our biological family or our career as primary driving factors; intentional proximity instead places missional efficacy as the primary factor.

Many disciples have good intentions of living missionally, but slowly over time, the temptation for upwards mobility, purchasing a house, getting a better house or prioritizing our career cause us to compromise where we live and thus compromise missionality.

In many cases, a person will get a job and immediately move because of the apparent logistical implications. We will often minimize our commute to work but increase our commute to our core relationships and missional church family. Why do we accept that in the church world? In missional living, glorifying Jesus and seeing people know him through our witness as Gospel proclaimers must be the motivating factor in our lives.

We must resist the cultural pressure to place career, comfort, luxury, trendiness or other worldly desires as determining factors of where we live. Instead, we must choose to value proximity with the people we love and the mission we are called to first. We must not trade relationships for the things of this world or treat church, discipleship and closeness as if they are dispensable or easily replaceable.

Healthier Rhythms & Spontaneity

One significant benefit of intentional proximity is that it enables a far more sustainable and healthy rhythm for discipleship. Intentional proximity minimizes commuting time, maximizes relational time and creates avenues for spontaneity in our relationships. Paul highlights this brilliantly in 1 Thessalonians.

> **1 Thessalonians 2:7-8**
>
> *Just as a nursing mother cares for her children, so we cared for you. Because we loved you so much, we were delighted to share with you not only the gospel of God but our lives as well.*

Paul lived so that those he was discipling had direct, local access to his life. When he was starting churches, he intentionally lived so that people would have access to him. He uses the compelling picture of a nursing mother to indicate the kind of close, dependent, ongoing and immediate access that discipleship and missional relationships require. As with a nursing mother, intentional proximity is essential for the health of the disciple and the discipler. Similarly, deliberate proximity creates opportunities for spontaneity in our relationships. We cannot form the kind of deep relationships that missional living requires if our relationships are always scheduled. Spontaneity, enabled by being close to one another, allows us to see people as they really are.

We will discuss the importance of intentional proximity in greater detail when we consider the three discipleship ingredients of time, proximity and vulnerability in Chapter 11.

Sharing proximity with one another is why communal living is a natural byproduct of missional living. If we are living missionally, then we will see dense pockets of community form around that mission. Would you be willing to move your house so that you could be close to those in the church? Are we willing to call those we are discipling to do likewise?

Everyday Practice 4: Open Home

> *46 Every day they devoted themselves to meeting together in the temple, and broke bread from house to house.*

Twice in Acts 2:42-47 it mentions that they "broke bread" (shared meals) together. The most mundane and yet profoundly impactful way to integrate our lives is the sharing of meals and the opening of our homes. In our culture, the home acts as a private refuge for a personal retreat. It is where we isolate ourselves from one another. However, in a missional life, the home becomes the gathering place for mission! The home is an essential tool of a missional life. It can be used to gather people, teach the Gospel, lead people to Jesus, pray together, process hurt together and celebrate wins.

The mission was not in addition to their life; no, the mission was their life! Following their example, every component of our lives becomes a tool that we can use to serve the cause of Jesus. Living missionally transforms the simple, daily tasks that we tend to see as irrelevant into tools used for Jesus' glory. Our possessions and homes, indeed our entire lives, do not belong to us. Yet for many disciples, there is a line that they have drawn, often around their homes, where Christ does not have total dominion and discipleship is excluded. A home may be a place for private spiritual refuge, but what if we were to view them from the perspective of multiplying discipleship and missional living?

Open Lives

In the framework of discipleship, missional living is perhaps the most controversial as it confronts the details and structure of our lives. There is no room for a faith where the details of our lives are exclusively a personal, private affair. Jesus' lordship of our lives does not allow us to segment off parts of our lives as irrelevant to the mission. All of our lives must be part of the mission to raise and send disciple-making disciples. Open homes are part of open lives. As disciple-makers, we must live with openness and vulnerability, allowing people to see our strengths as well as our weaknesses. An active Christian witness must include the ability for people to see who we really are, not just a refined projection of an idealistic Christ follower. When we invite people into our lives, especially the raw and messy parts, we are allowing them to see how the power of Jesus' grace works. Rosaria Butterfield masterfully makes a case for open homes and lives in her book *The Gospel Comes with a House Key*. With a theological depth and practical details, she builds the following case:

> *Radically ordinary hospitality begins when we remember that God uses us as living epistles and that the openness or inaccessibility of our homes and hearts stands between life and death, victory and defeat, and grace or shame for most people.* — Rosaria Butterfield[38]

One of Jesus' disciples, Simon, invited Jesus to heal his sick mother-in-law in her home. After a day of long ministry, late in the day, Jesus heads to her home and miraculously heals her. Immediately after being healed by Jesus, Simon's mother-in-law begins to serve Jesus and open her home up for the entire town to encounter Jesus (Mark 1:29-31). She takes her home, her place of refuge, and because of Jesus' grace, she transforms it into a refuge for others. Our homes are not our private castles where we hoard our treasures, but sanctuaries to which we welcome with open arms those who need to encounter the death-to-life transformation available to them in Jesus.

Each of us has people who we can uniquely reach and welcome into our lives. There are those whom no one else can reach other than us. When we think about our lives from a missional standpoint, our homes, apartments, dorms and student houses are tools that we can use to become a place of refuge for those in our world to come and encounter Jesus in a real, tangible and practical way. Homes are raw, messy and authentic and as a result, provide the perfect environment to expose people to the grace of Jesus — both those we are discipling and those who do not yet know Jesus. The home is perhaps one of the most natural ways to bring together those who know Jesus and those who do not.

Hospitality

Hospitality and opening our homes lie at the centre of an effectively integrated missional life. We eat meals many times a week; each of those is an opportunity to create community and live on mission by inviting people to join us at the table to share a meal. The liberating aspect of this is that an open home does not require a great deal of effort. We do not need to host to impress people; no, we invite people into our homes as part of the natural rhythm of our lives lived on mission. Practically, we are not just inviting others to our homes for specially prepared meals on our fancy china. Instead, we are inviting others into our messy homes for leftovers.

Open homes are about valuing and cherishing people. In many homes, the TV is at the centre of the house with the couches arranged to consume content. In an open home, we structure our homes around people to love. What if our homes were structured so that the couches faced each other? This suggestion is both metaphorical and literal. In building open homes, we trade our televisions for dinner tables. We arrange our couches so that we see each other's smiles and tears and break down the barriers that separate us. Addressing loneliness may be one of the oldest and deepest human needs. As Butterfield humorously states, *"Hospitality is necessary whether you have cat hair on the couch or not. People will die of chronic loneliness sooner than they will cat hair in the soup."*[39]

Open Homes are Costly

Open homes and open lives are profoundly costly to both our finances, schedules and our pride. On a practical level, we open our lives up with generosity. An open home is not a tit-for-tat relationship. An open home is one where we give generously without expecting anything in return. On a practical level, it costs money to host people. Part of discipleship in missional living is learning to view that cost as a kingdom investment that we are privileged to make.

Secondly, open homes are costly to our schedules. Appointments and schedules drive much of our lives. Of course, schedules and appointments are essential and necessary to create a sustainable routine. However, our lives can end up so over-scheduled that there is no room to provide the spontaneous and compassionate care that an open home requires. An open home means that we intentionally create time and space in our lives into which people can enter our lives. An open life means that we may have to sacrifice our preferred schedule, slow down and invest in someone in need. Discipleship is not always convenient or practical. The responsibility of a disciple-maker is to be willingly, eagerly and joyfully giving of themselves for others.

Lastly, an open home will cost us our pride. If we attempt to always be perfect and in control, we will either inevitably fail in that pursuit or exhaust ourselves in the process. An open home requires that we do not strive to impress or have everything in perfect order to uphold a false perception of who we are in others' minds.

Start Where You Are

The invitation to an open home can be intimidating and scary. We are discussing how the private, even intimate, moments of our lives are used for Jesus' glory. Instead of viewing this everyday practice as an insurmountable task, we should instead take it as an encouragement to start making small changes. We should start wherever we are and begin to take steps to intentionally and sacrificially open our lives up. The process will require some trial and error as we learn to open our lives and possessions up for the benefit of others. That's ok! Failure is not final in discipleship.

Every person's home situation is unique, and in some cases, the kind of openness described above may not be possible. We must ask, how we could foster an open home environment wherever we are. We must find ways that it can work rather than looking at all the reasons it is disruptive and challenging.

Everyday Practice 5: Sacrificial Living

45 They sold their possessions and property and distributed the proceeds to all, as any had need.

We tend to view our successes as belonging to us. However, in a missional life, our possessions are merely a tool to be used for the glory of Jesus. In church circles, we regularly teach that our possessions are not our own. However, we must contextualize this teaching in light of the broader call to live a missional life. Without applying missional thinking to our possessions, we can give intellectual assent to the idea that our possessions belong to Jesus but live in exactly the same manner as if they didn't. In missional thinking, our possessions are tools to advance the mission.

In the economy of God, our temporary possessions are transformed into tools that can build something of eternal value. It is a beautiful and wonderful privilege that we can use what we have for the glory of God. When we start to think this way, it goes far beyond the basics of tithing 10%; it is a matter of building our lives to have the greatest possible kingdom impact.

Such strategic thinking may mean that we purchase a cheaper house, drive less expensive cars or take transit, or eat more economical food so that we can leverage our resources for the Kingdom. It may mean we do not go on as many vacations. It may mean that we do not take the promotion that we have worked hard to earn as it will consume more time.

At first glance, limiting our experiences or possessions sounds restrictive; but in fact, it is tremendously liberating. We are trading the temporary for the eternal in these moments. We are rejecting the lies of our culture that new experiences and better possessions are the key to a fulfilled life, and instead choosing to find our satisfaction in Jesus.

It may also mean that we work extra hard at work to gain the bonus so that we can invest it into the kingdom. In either case, we do not labour for our benefit; we labour for the benefit of others and the name of Jesus. In missional living, the driving motivation for what we do with our possessions is maximizing kingdom impact, not personal success or comfort. The temptations of worldliness can so easily hijack our attention, and we must continually return to Paul's words: *Set your minds on things above, not on earthly things* (Colossians 3:2).

Following Paul's instruction to set our minds on Christ in Colossians 3, he highlights earthly tendencies that derail that effort: impurity, lust, evil desires and greed. Notably, he specifies that greed is a form of idolatry. We can identify the idols in our lives by evaluating what, should we lose it, would result in discontentment in our lives (Philippians 4:12). When our contentment, satisfaction and joy is found in Jesus, and in inviting others to know him, we no longer require more to be satisfied. By giving up what we have so that others can know Jesus, we are declaring that Jesus is in fact our King and we are not beholden to the idol of material success. Sacrificial living means that we create three types of space in our lives: financial, emotional and calendar.

Financial Space

Part of living sacrificially is to create financial margin in our lives so that we have the financial resources to bless others. Sacrificial living is not the same principle as radical generosity. Sacrificial living is about structuring and building our lives so that as many people as possible will find hope in the Gospel. Radical generosity is about learning to give our time, talents and treasure to advance the kingdom. Sacrificial living is about structuring and designing our lives to have less, whereas radical generosity is about giving to be a blessing. Consequently, sacrificial living lays the groundwork on which we can build radical generosity.

In an entirely practical sense, consumer debt is the death knell of sacrificial living. Debt is the practice of stealing from our future missionality to pay for our present greed. Sacrificial living is the practice of investing in our future missionality by giving up our present desires.

Part of creating financial space is to intentionally live with less so that we do not have to spend all of our energy trying to financially sustain a standard of living or pursue greater possessions. Creating financial space means that we consider the cost of our possessions, homes, jobs and careers to our missionality.

Mental and Emotional Space

The text in Acts 2 highlights that the church gave *"as they had need."* Being aware of others' needs is actually a part of sacrificial living. By default, we tend to think about ourselves, our wants, interests and hobbies. We are easily consumed with all sorts of mental or emotional addictions that limit our ability to serve and love others. These addictions include social media, television, sports and so forth. These things are not inherently evil, but we can very quickly become obsessed with them such that they consume an unhealthy amount of our mental and emotional capacity. Part of creating mental and emotional space means that we can be sensitive to others' needs. We structure our lives so that we intentionally have space to think about others instead of ourselves.

Calendar Space

Lastly, part of sacrificial living is to live simple, humble lives where we live to serve others. It means that we do not busy ourselves furthering our own interests, passions, careers and hobbies all the time. Instead, we structure our lives so that there is space for the needs of others. Physical space, of course, will fall into this category through the previous principals of intentional proximity and open home.

Everyday Practice 6: Passion for the Lost

> *47 Every day the Lord added to their number those who were being saved.*

The final statement that described the church is that it was regularly seeing people discover the saving grace of Jesus. The final statement here about the church is not anecdotal to the description of the church; rather, it is the end towards which everything else was pointing. The church passionately exists to see people know

Jesus. They engaged their world with the Gospel and were regularly and consistently engaging people who did not yet know Jesus ("in the temple courts").

This final everyday practice of a missional life is of paramount importance. A missional life is all about seeing people know Jesus! The church was passionate about seeing people discover the hope of Jesus. They understood, at a very fundamental level, that the church does not exist to create a community, but rather, the church exists to see the dead brought to life! Although, as discussed above, the community is an essential component of effectively living that mission, it is not the objective in and of itself.

The desire to see the lost know Jesus means that we must be regularly in contact with people who do not know Jesus. Our proximity with the church is a tool that allows us to invite those who do not know Jesus into contact with those who do. Our open home is a tool to welcome people who do not know Jesus into our lives so they can meet him. Our sacrificial living is a tool to demonstrate our profound freedom from consumerism and selfishness and invite people to the life of joyful generosity in Christ.

In a missional life, absolutely every component of our lives exists to see people know Jesus. We do not live our lives for ourselves; we live our lives so that people will know Jesus. We must resist the desire to create insulated Christian communities. We must be in the world, actively engaging it and proclaiming the simple Gospel message: that in Christ, we can be raised from death in sin to new life, by the grace of Jesus. Missional living and Gospel multiplication go hand-in-hand; they are inseparable. We know we are effectively living missionally if we are multiplying new disciples of Jesus, who, in turn, are multiplying new disciples of Jesus.

What does passion for the lost look like? Jesus powerfully invites us to a life of passionate pursuit of those who are lost in Luke 15, using the three parables of the lost sheep, the lost coin and the lost son. In the parable of the lost sheep, Jesus emphasizes the values of reaching a single lost person weighed against the security of the masses. Passion for the lost means that instead of remaining in the safety of a Christian bubble, we are compelled to go and see just a single person come to know Jesus. The community must exist for the sake of the mission, not the mission for the community.

In the parable of the lost coin, the woman who has lost a coin carefully and intentionally rearranges her life to find the lost coin. She takes responsibility and invests time, energy and resources to see the coin found. Passion for the lost means an intentional, dedicated and concerted effort to see people know Jesus. Passion is not accidental. It requires us to rearrange the furniture of our lives to see lost people found, to use the metaphor of the parable.

In the parable of the lost son, passion for the lost is exhibited through the humility to receive people into the kingdom as brothers and sisters. Despite the lost son's rebellion, sin and harm he caused to others, he was received as a son by his father. His reception as a son is crucial because it means that lost people are not less than those of us who have found Jesus — they are those who may be invited to the kingdom as brothers and sisters. We must be vigilant to the subtle pride that can arise to think that somehow those of us who have found Jesus are more valued, inherently holy or naturally righteous because of that. We were all lost before we found Jesus. Consequently, our position towards the lost arises from compassion, love and kindness. We desire the lost to be found because we have ourselves been found, and we know the life that is found in Jesus.

Weaved through the narratives of all three parables is the picture of rejoicing and celebration at the finding of a soul. Passion for the lost is expressed as joy when those who are found discover the hope of Jesus. It is no mere accident or fluke that people are resurrected to a new life in Christ. It is a profound and glorious testament to the goodness and loving-kindness of a God who sought us out, died for us, saved us and has invited us to be home in his presence.

9

Radical Generosity

The fourth area of discipleship emphasis is radical generosity. Radical generosity is the component of discipleship where we begin to actively and intentionally reflect the Gospel into every aspect of our lives. Radical generosity is the natural extension of gospel fluency, secure identity and missional living. When we think of the word generosity, we tend to think of finances or resources. While that is an essential component, true generosity is about so much more than just our finances and includes our time and talents as well.

Reflecting the Gospel

Radical generosity, at its core, is an invitation to embody the nature of the Gospel by giving away that which is precious to us. The Gospel is the news about how God entered into the world that had utterly rejected him, and freely and intentionally gave of himself to see us restored to life and relationship with him (Ephesians 5:25; Philippians 2:7). God is an outrageously, radically generous God, who loves to give of himself to bless his creation. The invitation to radical generosity then is nothing short of an invitation to embody the character of Jesus.

Our generosity starts with gratitude, or worship, in response to the Gospel. When we see that the Gospel is about how God gave himself, we cannot help but respond in worship. From that place of worship, we will want to see others also discover the hope of Jesus, and see our own lives transformed so that we live with missional generosity as the following diagram illustrates.

Radical Generosity Cycle

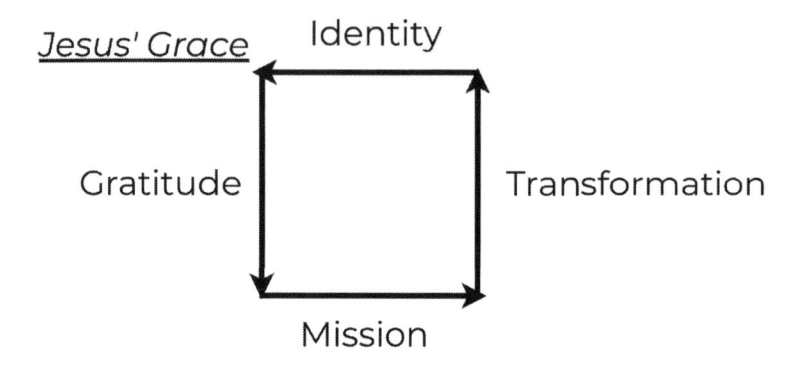

```
         Jesus' Grace    Identity
                    ↖  ↑  ↗
                       │
            Gratitude  │  Transformation
                       │
                    ↙  ↓  ↘
                      Mission
```

Our giving, in response to the Gospel, will naturally begin to transform us, which in turn leads us back to building a secure identity in Jesus. In other words, when we are generous, it naturally reinforces our understanding of the Gospel, our identity in Christ and the effectiveness of the mission of our lives.

Generosity, especially financially, gets to the heart of who we are and is one of the hardest areas to yield lordship to Jesus. Jesus places tremendous emphasis on financial generosity, because he recognizes how intertwined our souls can be with giving. Why does he speak about money so often? The answer is simple: your finances are a reflection of your heart (Matt 6:21). Jesus desires authority over your whole heart, and if you are not willing to trust him with your finances, then he cannot have his way in your life. The fact that our attitude with money is a direct reflection of our attitude towards Jesus is a simple, inescapable fact of the Christian life. Here are just a few instances where Jesus addresses generosity:

> Matthew 6:21; Matthew 6:24; Luke 3:14; Matthew 19:21; Matthew 21:12-13; Luke 12:33; Matthew 6:1-4; Matthew 12:41-44; Luke 14:28; Luke 16:13-15; Matthew 13:22; Matthew 13:44;

Matthew 17:24-27; Mark 10:17-27; Mark 11: 15-18; Luke 10:29-37

In one particularly powerful encounter in Mark 10, Jesus engages a rich man who is yearning to discover the abundant life of God. He asks Jesus what he must do to achieve it, and Jesus responds by instructing him to give everything he has away. Jesus is inviting us to discover a profound principle: when we cling to our lives, financial or otherwise, it is a sickness that robs us of our life. The antidote for this sickness is simple: radical, unqualified generosity.

When we speak of radical generosity it is important to define exactly what we mean by 'radical'. Generosity, of course, exists across the entire human experience. There are people who do not know Jesus who are very generous. However, radical generosity is generosity that is shaped and influenced by the gospel in at least seven specific ways.

1) Costly

Firstly, the generosity exhibited in the Gospel is profoundly costly. As Philippians 2:8 says, Jesus emptied himself, giving up everything to enter our world and suffer and die for us. 1 John 4:9 highlights that the Father gave that which was the most precious to him: his only Son. Radical generosity is not stingy, piecemeal or safe generosity. It is costly and often risky. Radical generosity will cost us; it will mean that we will have to give up that which is precious to us. However, part of radical generosity is that we give without fear because we know that God is our ultimate provider.

2) Independent of Past Performance

Secondly, radical generosity is independent of past performance. While we were still sinners, Christ died for us (Romans 5:8; Colossians 1:21)! God's radical generosity towards us was in spite of the fact that we had done absolutely nothing to earn it. We found ourselves as enemies of God, yet he chose to restore relationship proactively. A generosity that is attached to performance is not generosity; it is just payment.[40]

3) Given Freely

Thirdly, radical generosity is given freely, without strings attached. When Jesus commissioned the disciples for ministry he said to them, *"Freely you have received; freely give"* (Matthew 10:8). In Luke 6:35, Jesus affirms that we should give without expecting anything in return. In his address to the Athenians, Paul affirms that we could never repay God for his generosity (Acts 17:25), yet God gave himself anyway. When we give, we do not give so that we can get in return. Rather, we give freely because we have already freely received. This is equally true when we give to God as when we give to those around us. Just as we do not tithe or give to God in order to receive a blessing, likewise we do not give to those around us in order to receive anything in return.

4) Intentional

Fourthly, it is intentional. Radical generosity is not random or without wisdom. Listen to how Paul describes the wisdom of God in the Gospel:

> **Ephesians 1:7-9**
>
> *In him we have redemption through his blood, the forgiveness of our trespasses, according to the riches of his grace that he richly poured out on us with all wisdom and understanding. He made known to us the mystery of his will, according to his good pleasure that he purposed in Christ*

Not only was the Gospel tremendously costly, free and without strings, it was also wise and preplanned! Radical generosity will be generosity that seeks to maximize its impact. One word of caution: the wisdom when dispensing radical generosity will not be the wisdom of the world but must be patterned after the wisdom of God, as revealed in the previous three aspects. This also means that we do not simply wait around for opportunities to be generous or for significant needs to pop up. Instead, we must actively and intentionally seek out avenues to practice radical generosity in the world around us.

5) *Joyful*

Fifthly, radical generosity is joyful! We are called to give with a joyful and eager heart in 2 Corinthians 9:7. Radical generosity is the natural and joyful overflow of people who have encountered the radical generosity of God! Giving of ourselves is a privilege and should bring us joy. In fact, Hebrews 12:2 states that it was joy that motivated Jesus to sacrifice himself on the cross for us. The result of the sacrifice of Jesus was joy for Jesus! Radical generosity that is modelled after Jesus produces joy in us. Notice that this is the opposite of pride, bitterness or arrogance that would result from selfish "generosity." Holy Spirit led generosity will always produce the fruit of joy in our hearts (Acts 2:46)

6) *Requires all of us*

Sixthly, radical generosity requires all of us. Often the question is asked, "Where do we start when implementing radical generosity?" The answer is simple, yet demanding: we start with all of our lives. We must give all of ourselves to the cause of Christ. If Jesus is Lord, and his mission is our mission, then our entire life must be given to that cause.

> **1 Corinthians 9:19,22-23**
> *Although I am free from all and not anyone's slave, I have made myself a slave to everyone, in order to win more people… I have become all things to all people, so that I may by every possible means save some. Now I do all this because of the gospel, so that I may share in the blessings.*

In this way, radical generosity is the natural extension of missional living. In being invited to give our lives, we are invited to exhaust our lives for the benefit of others that they may know Jesus (Philippians 2:17). Radical generosity is indeed quite radical in that we are being invited to give all of ourselves to the cause of Christ — not just a part of ourselves or portion of our lives. There is no better way that we can spend our lives. We are called to lower ourselves so that we can lift others up. In doing so, we adopt the posture of a servant or slave so that we see them raised to life. The Gospel invites us to give all of our lives for the benefit of others. To restate this clearly: we do not live our lives to benefit ourselves. We live our lives for the cause of Christ and the service of others (Matthew 20:27-28).

7) *Invitation to Partnership*

Lastly, the invitation to radical generosity is directly connected to and expressed as an invitation to partner with the mission of God in this world. In this way, our generosity is an active partnership as we invest into what God is doing in the world.

> **2 Corinthians 9:11-12**
>
> *You will be enriched in every way to be generous in every way, which through us will produce thanksgiving to God. For the ministry of this service is not only supplying the needs of the saints but is also overflowing in many thanksgivings to God.*

In both the Old and the New Testament, financial giving served the purpose of supporting, sustaining and advancing what God was doing through his people. God is always moving, and when he moves it is always through people. Through financial giving, we are given the privilege of partnering with what God is doing in our church, our city and our nation.

God's desire to use disciples to build his church can be seen in 2 Corinthians 9, as Paul invites the church to continue the mission of the local church by "supplying the needs of the saints." In Numbers 18, the Levites also depended on the contributions of the people to facilitate worship in the tabernacle. The people of God have always been called to invest in the broader things that God is doing in the world, with our time, talents and treasures. It is a supreme joy that we, the people of God, are always invited to the opportunity to partner with the mission of God through our radical generosity.

Giving to the Kingdom of God is very different from giving to a charitable cause, because we are invited to practice it in the context of our church family. We are not just throwing our gifts over the fence and hoping for the best. Rather, we give with radical generosity as participants and co-labourers. We give as a part of a much bigger whole, not as a disconnected investor who is relationally disinterested in the outcomes. The call to radical generosity is part of a broader call to be an active participant in the purpose of the Kingdom. Giving is just one component of the beautiful truth that we are called to be a contributor to the kingdom of God.

Radical generosity is practiced in three different domains of our lives: time, talents and treasures.

Time

The first area of our lives with which we can be radically generous is our time. If Jesus is Lord of all of our lives, then the application of that is that Jesus is Lord over all of our time. All time is Jesus' time. Every second we have is a gift from him, and we have a responsibility to steward that gift of time effectively. Just as missional living is about the integration of every aspect of our lives to advance the Gospel, radical generosity with our time is about learning to see that Jesus is Lord over all of our time. As a result, we give our time to him and do not hoard it for ourselves. Our time is one of the most precious gifts that we can give away. We only have a limited quantity of it, and once it is spent, we cannot get any more. It is a very limited resource, which is why it can be so hard to give it away.

Radical generosity with our time is giving our time away to benefit others ahead of ourselves. One of the primary ways we can give our time away is in the act of serving others as Jesus commands us in Matthew 20:27. Serving others, putting their needs ahead of ours, is one of the best ways that we can be generous. However, serving others will require that we give time regularly. The act of serving cannot be a one-off or occasional activity but must be an intentional, costly, freely given gift for the benefit of others.

Radical generosity with our time is about so much more than merely adding volunteerism to our already hectic lives. As mentioned above, radical generosity is intentional. As such, being generous with our time requires that we intentionally build our lives so that we can be as generous with our time as possible. We may not be as gifted as others or have as many resources, but every single person has time that they can be generous with. We are all allocated the same 24 hours per day. What would it look like if we desired to be as generous as possible with the time we have been given?

We often approach generosity with a fear that if we give away that which is precious, we won't have enough. One of the primary areas where this occurs is in our time; we can eagerly hoard it for ourselves as if it was ours. As the Gospel transforms us and we adopt the identity of a servant, the desire to give our time away will build in us, and it will become as natural as breathing. It is true that radical generosity with our time may mean that we have less time for ourselves or our preferred activities. However, as we learn to give, our desires will change, as Psalm 90:12 highlights.

Psalm 90:12

Teach us to number our days carefully so that we may develop wisdom in our hearts.

We can contextualize the need to be generous with our time in the local church as the instruction in Galatians summarizes. For this reason, we encourage people to serve the church and join in the mission by giving their time. The invitation to give our time will likely mean that we have to surrender our schedules to Jesus and allow him to bless us with the time resources we need to accomplish all that he has entrusted us.

Galatians 6:10

Therefore, as we have opportunity, let us work for the good of all, especially for those who belong to the household of faith.

The invitation to radical generosity in our teams means that we need to rethink what it means to "work for the church." Churches have historically been operated by professional clergy. However, with all of the above comments regarding missional living and radical generosity, it should be abundantly clear that we all work for the church. We may or may not be paid to do so, but that is of relatively minor consequence. The real question we should be asking is not one of pay but one of structure: *"How can I structure my life so that I can generously invest it in the purposes of the kingdom?"*

Talents and Gifts

The second component of radical generosity is generosity with our talents and spiritual gifts. Jesus has given every single disciple natural and supernatural gifts. However, these gifts are not for our benefit; they are for the benefit of the mission of the church and the name of Jesus.

Our natural gifts are given to us so that we can serve others, not ourselves. When it comes to our talents, we should be eager to give our best to the glory of God. Often we will give Jesus what is left after we have first leveraged our talents for ourselves. What would it look like if we gave our best to the cause of Christ? Jesus has given us specific natural gifts so that we can use them to serve the mission of God, not just ourselves!

> **1 Peter 4:10**
>
> *Based on the gift they have received, everyone should use it to serve others, as good managers of the varied grace of God.*

For our individual talents, we get the privilege and the joy of asking how we can use them to further the mission of Jesus. So often, talented and gifted Christians are sidelined from active ministry because their gifts don't fit a stereotypical mould of what church ministry "should" look like. In reality, the church should have all the diversity in gifting that we see more broadly, because we are made up of all people! What would it look like to take the things we are most gifted at and most passionate about, and to surrender them to Jesus with an attitude that said, *"These are yours, use them for your glory?"*

Radical generosity with our gifts means that we don't expect or desire recognition for our giving. We do not seek praise. Radical generosity means that the primary object in our giving of gifts is to be a blessing, rather than accruing spiritual credit.

Just as we should be generous with our natural talents, we likewise need to practice radical generosity with our spiritual gifts. Scripture is abundantly clear that the Holy Spirit supernaturally empowers every believer in a specific way:

1 Corinthians 12:7

A manifestation of the Spirit is given to each person for the common good

The phrase "to each person" means precisely what it says; everyone has been given a gift. The generosity of our God extends past the Gospel of Jesus to the invitation and empowerment to join him in his mission! However, the temptation is to think that these talents and gifts give us a special heightened spiritual pedigree. Such an attitude is categorically false. The gifts the Spirit has given us have absolutely nothing to do with us, and they certainly do not exist for our benefit. We are given gifts, as the above scripture clearly states, "For the common good." Said another way, we have been given a spiritual gift so that we can freely and generously give it away — so that we can bless and build up the body of Christ! Paul briefly highlights this in 1 Corinthians 12:7-11 and Romans 12:6-8.

1 Corinthians 12:7-11

To one is given a message of wisdom through the Spirit, to another, a message of knowledge by the same Spirit, to another, faith by the same Spirit, to another, gifts of healing by the one Spirit, to another, the performing of miracles, to another, prophecy, to another, distinguishing between spirits, to another, different kinds of tongues, to another, interpretation of tongues. One and the same Spirit is active in all these, distributing to each person as he wills.

Romans 12:6-8

According to the grace given to us, we have different gifts: If prophecy, use it according to the proportion of one's faith; if service, use it in service; if teaching, in teaching; if exhorting, in exhortation; giving, with generosity; leading, with diligence; showing mercy, with cheerfulness.

Spiritual and natural gifts are both a work of grace in our lives; they are radically generous gifts from a good and loving God that reflect his character and the Gospel itself. God has blessed us as an outworking of his grace, not as a reward for our work. The Holy Spirit gives them because our God is a generous God who loves to bless his people. Spiritual gifts are given to us with the same four properties of radical generosity that we highlighted above (costly, unearned, free and intentional). As a result, we should desire and use our spiritual gifts with a posture of radical generosity: eager to see the Lord bless us so that we can be a blessing to others.

Treasures

The final area of radical generosity is with our treasure or our finances. As mentioned above, finances represent a major thrust of Jesus' teaching. Jesus' emphasis is in large part because money is at the very heart of who we are (Matthew 6:21). Without question, there is a clear and compelling invitation to radical financial generosity painted in the scriptures. It is expanded from Jesus' teaching and reiterated by the Apostles in 2 Corinthians 9, 1 Timothy 6 and James 5. Radical Financial Generosity also has a significant emphasis in the narrative of the Old Testament. This includes Abraham (Genesis 12), the nation of Israel (Micah 3:10) and God's critiques of the pagan nations (Isaiah 47:8). God has made it abundantly clear that our financial blessing is ultimately not for ourselves. Instead, if we have been blessed financially, we have the joy and responsibility of giving it away.

> **1 Timothy 6:17-18**
>
> *Instruct those who are rich in the present age not to be arrogant or to set their hope on the uncertainty of wealth, but on God, who richly provides us with all things to enjoy. Instruct them to do what is good, to be rich in good works, to be generous and willing to share*

We may think that we do not have enough to be generous, but Jesus drives the important point home that all financial blessing, no matter how small, has been given so that we can bless others. The story of the poor widow giving everything she has in Luke 21:1-3 powerfully illustrates this point.

A joyful and eager heart should accompany our generosity (2 Corinthians 9:7). However, this should not mean that we need to wait until our heart is happy to give to begin the practice of giving. If that were the case, we would likely never learn to be radically generous. Instead, if our hearts are struggling with giving, we should pray that the Lord would provide us with a new heart! The very next verse in 2 Corinthians 9:8 highlights that our generosity is a reflection of the grace that we have received!

> **2 Corinthians 9:6-8**
>
> *The point is this: The person who sows sparingly will also reap sparingly, and the person who sows generously will also reap generously. Each person should do as he has decided in his heart —not reluctantly or out of compulsion, since God loves a cheerful giver. And God is able to make every grace overflow to you, so that in every way, always having everything you need.*

Our hearts yearn for all kinds of things, some of them useful and some of them selfish. Part of learning to live radically generous is training our hearts to seek after the things of God (Colossians 3:1-3). We must be intentional, and regularly submit our hearts to the words of Jesus and reject the temptations of the world. Every day we are bombarded with thousands of messages that we need more, deserve more and should get more. It is no wonder we continually feel as though we lack! We must counteract our culture by daily saturating our minds with the values of the kingdom: in Christ, we have everything we need; in Christ we are rich, and our satisfaction is Jesus, not consumption. We need to train our minds and our hearts to reject worldliness and instead pursue pleasure in the love of the Father (1 John 2:15-17).

> **1 John 2:15-17**
>
> *Do not love the world or the things in the world. If anyone loves the world, the love of the Father is not in him. For everything in the world—the lust of the flesh, the lust of the eyes, and the pride in one's possessions—is not from the Father, but is from the world. And the world with its lust is passing away, but the one who does the will of God remains forever.*

As our hearts are increasingly satisfied in Christ and moulded after him, we will naturally begin to see the fruit of regular radical generosity in our lives. In this way, being radically generous with our finances will break the hold of anxiety about our finances. When we are discipling people, and we encounter those who are anxious about financial provision, we can often anticipate an associated underdeveloped habit of generosity. The best way to invite people to discover freedom from anxiety about their finances is to invite them into the habit of regular, consistent giving.

That is why giving must be a consistent and frequent part of our lives. Throughout scripture, this was often referred to as the tithe or first-fruits (Exodus 23:19). Radical generosity does not give from our leftovers; it is intentional and proactive. As with our time and talents, we are invited to give away the very best of our treasures.

> **Proverbs 3:9**
>
> *Honour the LORD with your wealth and with the best part of everything you produce.*

Tithing, which Jesus himself affirmed in Luke 11:42, is often referred to as giving 10% of our income. However, this is likely a low estimate based on the Old Testament patterns around tithing.

10% is not the goal, but rather it serves as a good starting point to practice generosity. The New Testament does not prescribe a particular quantity that we should give away, because all of it ultimately belongs to Jesus and exists for his glory. As a result, the goal is not to give away 10%. The goal is to give away as much as possible to see as many people as possible come to know the goodness and grace of Jesus.

Muscle Practice

Radical generosity is a discipleship emphasis that takes practice to develop. Like a physical muscle, we must routinely and regularly exercise it to see it grow. To develop radical generosity, we need to start by structuring our time and finances so that we are positioned to give. Intentionally structuring our time and finances may mean putting aside activities or habits that are not productive for the kingdom, or developing a proper financial plan. We must remember that Radical generosity is intentional, and that means we must intentionally build and structure our lives so that we can give in a radically generous way.

10

Crucial Conversations

The final discipleship emphasis is crucial conversations. This is the discipleship emphasis which hones in on our ability to both lead and be led in relationships with people — especially on matters of faith and life. The conversations and relationships in question could be between believers or between believers and unbelievers. While it may sound strange at first that our relational and conversational ability would be a discipleship issue, it is absolutely critical to discipleship. In order to see consistent growth in discipleship and multiplication for the kingdom, it is essential that we can engage in discipleship conversations with substance, humility, conviction and boldness. Our relationship with Jesus is not a private issue; rather, our faith is always worked out publicly and in the context of our particular local church community (see missional living) in order to see others know Jesus. Without the ability to receive and lead discipleship discussions, the Gospel cannot propagate — either in us or in others. The Gospel, after all, is news about what has happened in Jesus, and news requires that someone proclaims it.

Our engagement in crucial conversations is a direct reflection of the depth of formation in the previous four Discipleship Emphases. As we grow in gospel fluency, secure identity, missional living and radical generosity, the conversations and relationships in our life will naturally begin to be shaped by them.

A crucial conversation is a conversation where we are either moving someone closer to an effective multiplying relationship with Jesus or one where we are the one being challenged to grow in our relationship with Jesus. Crucial conversations are a primary mechanism for both inner-life transformation and outer-life multiplication. On one hand, crucial conversations are the means by which the other Discipleship Emphases are formed in us, but they are also the means by which we multiply the Discipleship Emphases in others. Crucial conversations are where we are confronted, and confront others, about the gaps between our words about Jesus and our actions. One of the greatest threats to our faith is when our ability to talk about Jesus is not reflected in our actions. Jesus is very clear that hypocrisy, when our actions and words do not line up, is a great evil that we must not tolerate (see Matthew 23). This is why crucial conversations are such an important aspect of discipleship, as highlighted in Ephesians 4:15; without the ability to challenge and be challenged in our walk with Jesus, we cannot see people mature to fullness in Christ.

Ephesians 4:15

But speaking the truth in love, let us grow in every way into him who is the head—Christ.

Grace and Truth

The invitation to engage in crucial conversations is a direct reflection of Jesus' own life. As John 1:14 states, and Jesus' ministry repeatedly evidences, Jesus came in grace and truth. Grace, because Jesus did not have to come and we did not deserve the gift of his life, death and resurrection. Truth, because we needed to be called to repentance as sinners in desperate need of a saviour; we were dead people in need of resurrection.

John 1:14

The Word became flesh and dwelt among us. We observed his glory, the glory as the one and only Son from the Father, full of grace and truth.

The Gospel itself is simultaneously the most gracious message on earth and the most truthful. The Gospel takes the human condition of our sinfulness tremendously seriously. We are dead in our sin and there is absolutely nothing we can do ourselves to change that fact. This is the profound truth attested to by the Gospel and reaffirmed throughout the scriptures — especially in the narrative of the Old Testament. The narrative of the continual rebellion of Israel against the loving kindness of God demonstrates both our sinfulness and our desperate need for a saviour. However, the Gospel is also grace; we have been raised to life in Jesus because of his great love for us. This incredible duality of grace and truth is woven throughout the Bible.

Jesus' own ministry is equally characterized by an invitation to receive the Kingdom of God (grace), and his direct challenge to turn around when people were not headed in the right direction (truth/repentance). Jesus calls the disciples to follow him (grace) but he also calls people to repentance (truth). We can see this duality directly in Jesus calling the disciples in Matthew 4.

Matthew 4:17-19

From then on Jesus began to preach, "Repent, because the kingdom of heaven has come near." As he was walking along the Sea of Galilee, he saw two brothers, Simon, and his brother Andrew. They were casting a net into the sea—for they were fishermen. "Follow me," he told them, "and I will make you fish for people." Immediately they left their nets and followed him.

Another powerful example of Jesus inviting the disciples into deep relationship while also challenging them directly is found in Matthew 16. Jesus invites Peter to acknowledge who he is as the Messiah and subsequently celebrates Peter (Matthew 16:18). However, moments later, Jesus famously rebuked Peter for misunderstanding the impending crucifixion with the direct words, *"get behind me Satan"* (Matthew 16:20-23). It is a brilliant example of the grace and truth of Jesus being lived in a discipleship context.

Similarly, we must model this duality ourselves when being discipled and discipling others. We must invite people to a deeper relationship with Jesus while challenging them in the areas they are not submitting to Jesus. We must pattern all our discipleship conversations after Jesus' life of grace and truth, invitation and challenge. We must directly confront our sin, on the one hand, and ,on the other hand, consistently point to the forgiveness and grace of Jesus.

It may appear that grace and truth exist in tension with one another, as if grace comes at the expense of truth or truth at the expense of grace. We must note that Jesus came *full* of grace and truth. He was completely grace and he was completely truth. A proper discipleship relationship will include both in concert together; grace and truth exist in a supporting relationship with each other in healthy multiplying discipleship relationships.

It is worth emphasizing that while moral issues may play an important role in crucial conversations, they do not represent the totality of the content. We must resist the urge to fatally reduce the Gospel to a moral code in which the pious challenge and judge the sinner. The primary emphasis in our crucial conversations must be an invitation to embrace the fullness of the Gospel. In the same way that the Gospel sanctifies us and calls us to mission, crucial conversations are an invitation to personal transformation and a call to mission. Crucial conversations must speak to both inner and outer life. The second component of outer-life challenge is equally as important as the inner-life aspects of our crucial conversations. In crucial conversations, the primary objective is to lead people to embrace the goodness of Jesus and his call on their life.

There are two distinct types of crucial conversations. Crucial conversations between believers and crucial conversations with non-believers.

Crucial Conversations with Believers

There are two essential ingredients when we approach crucial conversations: humility and boldness. We require these ingredients on both the receiving side and the leading side of the conversation.

Receiving with Humility

Firstly, we need a significant degree of humility when being on the receiving end of a crucial conversation. One of the most important character traits in a discipleship relationship is that of teachability. When we are on the receiving end of a challenge to our character, the temptation is to immediately get defensive and assume the person challenging us is wrong. There are few things that can derail our own discipleship journey as quickly as a defensive and unteachable spirit. Our discipleship journey is going to require a deep unearthing of our souls in order to see them more conformed to the person of Jesus. By its very nature, this process of discipleship will be uncomfortable, and likely painful. While the Holy Spirit can, and regularly does, convict us directly through his leading and his Word, many of the direct challenges of our discipleship will occur in the context of a crucial conversation.

Humility is more than just receiving the challenge with eagerness and gratitude. Humility actually means that we will seek out the discipleship relationships knowing that we have work to do. Humility in crucial conversations requires that we not only graciously receive input into our lives, but also that we intentionally seek it out. Discipleship is a two-way street in which the disciple must open their life up, inviting input, and the discipler must speak boldly. However, without the foundation of a willing and teachable attitude, the discipleship process will be difficult to initiate. Peter commands the church to receive these challenges this way:

> **1 Peter 5:5**
>
> *All of you clothe yourselves with humility toward one another, because God resists the proud, but gives grace to the humble.*

God's grace is mediated in the context of mutual humility in relationships. Without the humility to be challenged, we cannot grow. The requirement for a large amount of humility highlights why commitment to the church family is so important. It is very natural to isolate ourselves from direct challenge in our lives — it can be very uncomfortable when people call us out! However, God designed our discipleship journey to occur in the context of the church and in relationship with one another, for the purpose of creating healthy opportunities for us to be challenged and called out.

> **Hebrews 13:17**
>
> *Obey your leaders and submit to them, since they keep watch over your souls as those who will give an account*

In the West, where individual autonomy is the ideal, the concept of submission towards one another is profoundly counter-cultural. Jesus' command against "judging one another" (Matthew 7:1-3) is often quoted. Jesus' command, however, must not be interpreted as an invitation to total moral relativism or the freedom to self-determine what is right or true. Jesus' command was a command against hypocrisy more than it was against judgement.

For example, in addressing a case of moral degradation in the Corinthian church, Paul clarifies that while he is not particularly concerned about the behaviour of those who are not followers of Jesus, he is deeply concerned that the church was becoming tolerant of things that were not of Jesus:

> **1 Corinthians 5:12**
>
> *For what business is it of mine to judge outsiders? Don't you judge those who are inside?*

As disciples, we must be willing to both receive and give the high call to live a life like Jesus.

Leading with Humility

Jesus' words about leading and speaking into each other's lives naturally leads us to the need for humility when speaking into someone's life. On the leading side of the conversation, we need the humility to listen to the person and take the time to earn their trust before we can speak. It is tempting to barge into a relationship without having taken the time to earn trust. Humility and patience are vital in these conversations in order for us to speak from a place of credibility.

We must take the time to understand why those we are discipling are making decisions the way they are. If we are not careful, a crucial conversation can become simple instructions for people to do what we do — as if our approach is the only valid approach. The objective in discipleship is not to produce clones of ourselves, but to see people made more like Jesus. When approaching a crucial conversation, we must take the time to evaluate the driving rationale behind the issue we wish to discuss. In many cases, there is more going on in that person's life than we realize. The basic building block of this requirement for humility is the process of asking probing questions about the person we are discipling. We must resist the urge to immediately share our perspective but first seek to understand the person and demonstrate that we are coming from a place of care and compassion.

Further, we cannot speak from a place of hypocrisy. Discipleship is about transformation and we cannot disciple people towards a transformation that we ourselves are not open to. Discipleship is not a process where we merely dispense information. Rather, discipleship is a process where we invite people to examine our own lives and thereby see Christ at work. For this reason, we must have the humility to recognize that we ourselves are imperfect disciples.

Leading with Boldness

The second necessary component in a crucial conversation is the need for the boldness to confront the issue at hand. Often our primary objective in a crucial conversation is to avoid hurting the other person's feelings. Many of us approach conversations with a general fear of conflict. However, hurt feelings or conflict by themselves are not problematic; in fact, they can even be essential to growth. Jesus was bold with his words, and certainly created conflict with them at times. Check out Matthew 23 to see how he addressed the leaders of the day. When we have taken the time to humbly listen and build trust over a long period of time, we can, and must, speak with clarity and boldness into the lives of the people we are discipling.

In our culture, we are often fearful of offending others. Such a fear can result in a timidity in our faith and will ultimately eliminate our discipleship effectiveness. We cannot see people move closer to Jesus if we are not willing to challenge them when they are moving in the wrong direction or not moving at all. The responsibility of the discipler in a disciple-making relationship is to engage in the difficult conversations that are needed to see someone develop gospel fluency, security identity, missional living, radical generosity and crucial conversations. All of the Discipleship Emphases are profoundly counter-cultural, and as a result, it is essential that we are continually pointing disciples back to the kingdom principles they represent. It is not enough to merely address sin or moral failure; rather, we must boldly call people to adopt the revolutionary and missional ways of living that the scriptures call us to.

Practically speaking, we will require boldness to speak into the sensitive areas of a person's life such as finances, relationships, job, family, career and identity. While we need to first examine our own heart and motives and ensure we are developing a clear theology and understanding of what we are boldly calling people to, if we are not willing to challenge someone in these areas, who will? Hebrews 12:11 clearly reminds us that sometimes the conversations, and discipline, will not be enjoyable, but in the long run, it produces tremendous fruit.

Hebrews 12:11

No discipline seems enjoyable at the time, but painful. Later on, however, it yields the peaceful fruit of righteousness to those who have been trained by it.

We may be afraid of consequences such as a tense relationship, lost team member or failed discipleship. However, when we do not engage the tough conversation, we will eventually fail as a discipler. The types of issues that require boldness in our conversations will not address themselves on their own. As a result, eventually the issue will grow until it causes a major issue or crisis. The moment we fail to do what we know we need to do, because we are afraid of the consequences, we are no longer actually leading or discipling that person. The person we are afraid to correct may even be indirectly leading us instead of the other way around. Summoning the humility and the boldness to address issues will, when done properly, often result in greater trust and a deeper relationship. Delaying the conversation will exacerbate the issue and if left too long, may even make it nearly impossible to correct. It is for these reasons that crucial conversations are a critical discipleship emphasis. Without them, the entire discipleship process would break down.

Further, unaddressed issues will have a communal effect on the multiplication effectiveness of the whole community. For example, unaddressed bitterness will have the effect of "defiling many" (Hebrews 12:17). Paul, in 1 Corinthians 5:13, instructs us to boldly address issues and where there is unrepentance, to remove the capacity for evil to propagate. In case the necessity for boldness in our discipleship has not been convincingly addressed yet, Jesus provides us with a process in Matthew 18:15-17 to confront issues head on, whereby we graciously, but firmly, escalate a discipleship or relational issue.

It must be stated that the source of the boldness is not our own wisdom or experience alone. Rather, our boldness must be rooted and derived from a clear understanding of scripture. Scripture alone must be the primary source of our wisdom and experience, which in turn provides a foundation for our boldness. Only when we have been transformed by the truths revealed in the scriptures can we properly speak into someone's life.

2 Timothy 3:16-17

All Scripture is God-breathed and is useful for teaching, rebuking, correcting and training in righteousness, so that the servant of God may be thoroughly equipped for every good work.

Radical Candor

We have discussed the juxtaposing principles of invitation and challenge, grace and truth, and humility and boldness in laying the groundwork for crucial conversations. Kim Scott, a former Google executive, developed a useful framework for helping managers in large organizations develop effectiveness in their leadership called *Radical Candor*. While this framework was not developed with the above discipleship context in mind, it is tremendously helpful in articulating the ideas. What follows is a brief summary and adaption of the framework for a discipleship context. [41]

Radical Candor Grid

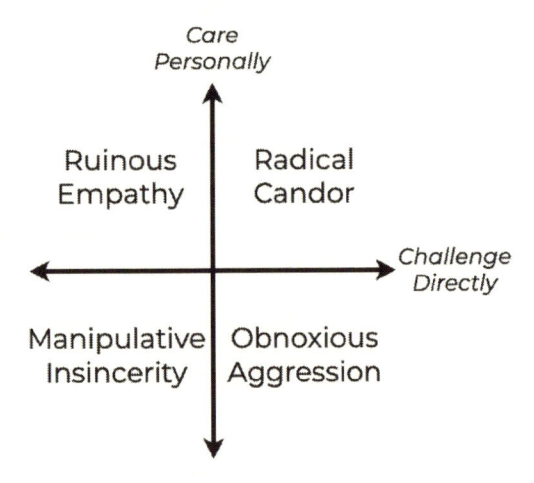

```
                    Care
                  Personally
                      ▲
                      │
      Ruinous         │     Radical
      Empathy         │     Candor
                      │
◄─────────────────────┼─────────────────────► Challenge
                      │                        Directly
                      │
    Manipulative      │   Obnoxious
    Insincerity       │   Aggression
                      │
                      ▼
```

The two primary ingredients in an effective discipleship relationship are 'caring personally' and 'challenging directly.' Put simply, 'caring personally' is the genuine care shown for another person that, over time, allows trust to build. 'Challenging directly' is the willingness to confront the issues at hand when they present themselves.

As shown above, when these two traits are functioning properly together, it is what Scott calls 'Radical Candor.' We sometimes call this 'family zone,' as it is should be characteristic of a healthy church family and would be similar to the tone of relationships described above with humility and boldness.

However, when either 'caring personally' or 'challenging directly' are not present, the results can be quite severe, even disastrous.

Firstly, where relationships are characterized by high care but low challenge, we find ourselves in 'Ruinous Empathy.' In this quadrant, we avoid crucial conversations out of fear of how it will go. The results of avoiding the conversation are often ruinous for the person we are avoiding. We harm them by allowing them to continue in a pattern of unhealthy thinking or behaviours that they may be unaware of. It may feel empathetic to avoid addressing an issue, but it is ultimately unkind and unempathetic because we hurt that person in the long term. It is typically our own insecurity and fear that causes our inaction, not genuine compassion or empathy.

Conversely, when relationships are characterized by high challenge but low care, we find ourselves in 'Obnoxious Aggression.' 'Obnoxious Aggression' is what occurs when we challenge a person directly but do not have the credibility or trust to do so. It can also be obnoxious because of the tone or delivery of the feedback. The results of obnoxious aggression are relationships that are tense and fractured. However, we would advocate that in many cases, we must move from 'Ruinous Empathy' to 'Obnoxious Aggression' in order to find our way to 'Radical Candor.' We may overstep the bounds and enter 'Obnoxious Aggression' when trying to engage in a candid conversation. However, when we do so with humility and allow room for feedback, we can mature into 'Radical Candor.'

Lastly, where relationships are characterized by low challenge and low care, we find ourselves in 'Manipulative Insincerity.' These are relationships that are passive-aggressive, self-serving and ultimately headed for disaster. Discipleship relationships do not exist for our benefit. If we are the one being discipled, we are being discipled for Jesus' glory so that we can better develop effectiveness as a multiplying disciple for Jesus. If we are the one doing the discipling, it is not for our interests but with the intent of maximizing Kingdom Impact. As a result, we cannot tolerate 'Manipulative Insincerity' of any kind, ever.

A particularly good example in scripture of 'Radical Candor' is found when the prophet Nathan confronts David for his sin with Bathsheba in 2 Samuel 12. He masterfully blends caring personally and challenging directly to see David repent from his sin and receive forgiveness.

Crucial Conversations with Non-Believers

The above discussion about crucial conversations with believers would also apply with non-believers. We, of course, must approach those relationships with humility and boldness. When considering a crucial conversation with a non-believer, we can break the process into four components: the messenger, the recipient, the message and the Spirit.

The Messenger

As we discussed in the section detailing gospel fluency, the Gospel is something that is known from both an intellectual and a relational standpoint. As a result, our discussion on communication of the Gospel must start with the messenger. Revelation 12:11 declares that it is our testimony that ultimately overcomes the enemy and will see people come to know Jesus.

> **Revelation 12:11**
>
> *They conquered him by the blood of the Lamb and by the word of their testimony; for they did not love their lives to the point of death.*

In other words, it is our lives and the story Jesus is telling through them, that leads to people knowing Jesus. Yet again, we can see the intersection of inner-life and outer-life aspects of discipleship. As our lives are transformed, the effectiveness of our testimony increases as well. As the Discipleship Emphases are formed in us, they will also be formed around us. A clear, bold and authentic testimony about what Jesus is doing in us will also see the world around us attracted to know Jesus. When we speak of the messenger, there are two components to highlight: integrity and authenticity.

Integrity

Oftentimes, those who do not know Jesus will highlight that the greatest critique they have of Christians is that of hypocrisy. This critique can cause us to be timid in our witness for fear that if we invite people to examine our lives they will not like what they see. If there is a glaring issue in our lives that we are aware of and have not addressed, that is a major issue for which we should immediately repent and seek accountability. However, this does not mean that we should be slow or timid to share the Gospel, but rather that we should be quick and eager to repent. We must continually submit ourselves to the way of Jesus and ensure that what we say we believe and what we actually do are in alignment. As followers of Jesus, our integrity is paramount. Our lives need to be blameless (Titus 1:6) and innocent (Matthew 10:16) and wise in our relationships (Colossians 4:5).

It is worth mentioning that perfection is not the issue; rather, integrity is. Our aim is to ensure that the way we live and the way we talk about Jesus are congruent. When we pridefully present ourselves as being "perfect" or "having all the answers," we are setting ourselves up for failure because we are never perfect or all-knowing. The problem arises when we act and communicate as if we are. This usually is expressed when we are more interested in being correct, winning debates and espousing our view, than we are in compassionately listening to and understanding the roadblocks to someone accepting Jesus. The goal is to help people see Jesus in us, not merely to communicate an idea. We point to ourselves, even in our own weaknesses, so that people can see Jesus in us. When we acknowledge that we are imperfect but communicate our joy and satisfaction in Jesus and thankfulness for his grace in spite of our imperfections, our witness can be amazingly effective. The invitation to integrity and humility in our communication means that even a brand-new believer who still has many areas that need to be refined can be an effective evangelist. While they are not yet perfect, they can joyfully point to the work that Jesus has done in them.

Simply put, our witness is built on Jesus' grace, not our perfection. Our behaviour only becomes an issue when our words and actions are not in alignment. The invitation to know Jesus is an invitation for sinners to receive grace. Our message is not primarily about convincing someone of information so much as it is inviting them to accept Jesus as King and join his Kingdom. That invitation will only make sense to the hearer when they can clearly see that Jesus is, in fact, our King and that the invitation is genuine.

Authenticity

Oftentimes, the greatest barrier to our ability to see people around us know Jesus, is our fear. If Jesus is transforming and forming us, the work will be immediately and naturally apparent to all those who see it — if we will let them see it! Many of us produce an "edited" version of our lives. Jesus may be working in us, prayer may be a natural part of our rhythms and living with bold faith may be our norm. However, often when we talk to those who do not know Jesus, our love of him and his work in our lives is edited out and removed from the conversation.

When we authentically and genuinely talk about our faith in a natural way, it is a powerful witness. We naturally talk about the things we are passionate about, so why do we edit Jesus out? Oftentimes, it is from a fear that we will be ridiculed, do not know the answers or have not developed a habit of talking about spiritual things. Each of those hesitations are indications of a need for deeper discipleship work in our life. However, those fears are best overcome by naturally beginning to flex our evangelistic muscles. When we naturally invite people into our lives and allow them to see and hear how Jesus is working, they will respond.

The Recipient

When we are engaging in conversations with non-believers, we must take the time to understand who we are talking to. When we are talking to someone about Jesus, there are both contextual and cultural issues, as well as individual issues that we must take into account.

Context

When we are communicating the Gospel to someone, we must take the time to understand their context: specifically, their worldview and culture. The Gospel will always be understood by people through the lens of the cultural context in which find themselves in.[42] The context could include things such as race or ethnicity, religion or economic position. Communicating the Gospel to a Hindu will take a very different form than communicating the Gospel to a Muslim or an Atheist. Similarly, we must humble ourselves and take the time to understand how others understand the world. In the same way that the Apostle Paul took time to understand the Greeks in Acts 17:16-34 or adjusted his own lifestyle to suit those he was trying to reach in 1 Corinthians 9:19-23, we must be culturally flexible and wise. The objective is not to export our view on culture, but to lead people to Jesus.

Individual

In addition to the broad cultural issues briefly mentioned above, there are also individual considerations to take into account. As we will discuss later, discipleship involves inviting people into our world and opening our lives up to them. However, it is not just about us; we must take the time to understand the unique story of each person we are engaging with the Gospel. They may have specific and unique objectives or hesitations in hearing about Jesus. Perhaps a past hurt or fear due to family pressures. Regardless, we must compassionately and graciously take the time to understand who we are trying to reach. Communicating the Gospel is a three-way exchange between us, the Holy Spirit and the person we are trying to reach. Too often, we are too quick to give our perspective, and not humble enough to understand the person we are talking to. A great tool is to ask probing and honest questions.

The Message

With all of the comments about ourselves and the recipient, we must turn to the message itself in engaging crucial conversations. We will briefly address the subjects of grace and truth, simplicity, and apologetics. 1 Peter 3:14-16 provides a helpful framework through which we can articulate the message.

> **1 Peter 3:14-16**
>
> *But even if you should suffer for righteousness, you are blessed. Do not fear what they fear or be intimidated, but in your hearts regard Christ the Lord as holy, ready at any time to give a defence to anyone who asks you for a reason for the hope that is in you. Yet do this with gentleness and respect, keeping a clear conscience, so that when you are accused, those who disparage your good conduct in Christ will be put to shame.*

Grace & Truth

As discussed under Gospel fluency, when we are introducing someone to faith, it is important that we communicate with both grace and truth. One the one hand, we compassionately and graciously invite people to respond to the Gospel, and on the other, we must help them see the reality of their sin. However, we must not compromise the message itself. We must, graciously but firmly, remain fixed on the moorings of our faith. It is not much help to communicate a Gospel to someone that is so watered down that it becomes basically useless. In our context, an authentic and honest communication of the truth of the Gospel is normally the most winsome. When we have taken the time to understand the context and the individual, we can boldly begin to lead them to Jesus in all of his glory. We must have the confidence to communicate our faith without the fear of rejection. Not everyone will respond positively to the message, but our job is not to win over everyone, but to faithfully bring the message of Jesus.

One important consideration in communicating the Gospel is that we do not need to focus on specific moral issues initially. Said another way, until Jesus is Lord of someone's life, we cannot expect them to live as if he was. Of course, following the commands of Jesus is the most life-giving way of life, but expecting someone to obey Jesus when he is not Lord of their life is nonsensical. As Paul highlights in 1 Corinthians 5:12, our job is not to morally judge those outside the church, but to lead them to the truth of the Gospel first. Moral issues are certainly important, both inside and outside the church, but in communicating the Gospel, it is important that we lead people to Jesus so that Jesus can do the work of sanctification in their lives when they receive him. Justification precedes sanctification every time. We are all sinners in need of a saviour, so focusing on a specific sin is beside the point when we are communicating the Gospel. This is something of a challenge because awareness of our sinfulness is important in leading someone to receive the grace of Jesus. This is why, as we will discuss below, the Holy Spirit is so important in the process. One helpful strategy is to ask genuine and empathetic questions about why someone is making the decisions they are, so that we can understand how to best articulate the Gospel so that it speaks to their specific story.

Simplicity

An important consideration when communicating the Gospel is that of simplicity. We can very quickly end up in all sorts of "theological weeds" and confuse both ourselves and them. The communication of the Gospel is not a primarily intellectual process, although our intellect must certainly be involved. If we are not careful, we can engage in fruitless discussion around interesting philosophical ideas without making any progress with the Gospel. When we are leading someone to Jesus, the objective is to look for those whose hearts are tender and receptive to the Gospel. That is not to say that we should not pray for and witness to those whose hearts are hard towards the Gospel. Rather, we should be aware of when someone is resistant to the message and distracting us with interesting conversations but has no real intention of engaging the message themselves.

Apologetics

Lastly, in communicating the message, we will need to have some awareness of apologetics. Apologetics is the discipline of well-reasoned arguments in defence of our faith. These could include scientific, historical, psychological or philosophical arguments. Many people will have legitimate questions about the veracity of the Gospel. It is important that we are familiar with the major arguments in defence of the faith in these major arenas. We do not need to know all of the answers, but we do need to know enough so that we can demonstrate that we have taken seriously the reliability of what we believe. If we have not even taken the time to ask if scripture is reliable, why should someone listen to us?

The specific apologetic strategies will be largely dependent on the people who we are talking to. It is important to have taken time to understand the context we are speaking into. One interesting anecdotal observation from recent years is that the highly rational, scientific and philosophical apologetic arguments developed in the 20th century appear not to hold as much sway as they used to. In their place, more psychological and personal arguments appear to be more impactful. The Gospel is not just truth in an abstract depersonalized sense; it is also true because it helps us make sense of the world in a more individualistic sense.

It is important to remember that while apologetics can be a powerful evangelistic tool, very few people have ever been argued into a relationship with Jesus. The goal of apologetics is not to win arguments and prove to others that we are right. Instead, it is a tool to both show that we have taken our faith seriously and bring light into any legitimate questions that someone may have on their journey to a relationship with Christ.

The incredible news is that the Gospel can speak truth into any darkness. Our job is to understand how to do that into each context that we engage with.

The Spirit

The final, and perhaps most important, component of crucial conversations with non-believers is the role of the Holy Spirit: specifically, in empowering and preparing us to communicate the message as well as softening the others' hearts to receive it.

Prayer

Prayer is the starting point for all of our interactions in our faith, but especially in communicating the Gospel. Ultimately our battle is a spiritual one that is fought on a spiritual playing field.

> **Ephesians 6:12**
>
> *For our struggle is not against flesh and blood, but against the rulers, against the authorities, against the cosmic powers of this darkness, against evil, spiritual forces in the heavens.*

So how do we pray? We pray for ourselves that we would be bold, gracious and true. But we also pray that the message will be received and that hearts will be ready to receive it. In Exodus 7:3 and Ezekiel 36:27, God demonstrates that he can actually soften, or harden, hearts towards him so that his purposes can be fulfilled.

We must continually be in prayer to see the Holy Spirit prepare the hearts of those we are communicating to and equip us to articulate clearly his message of Life. Inviting people to know Jesus can be both scary and vulnerable, so we must rely on the Holy Spirit to do the work, not just our own strength. We must draw our boldness, courage and wisdom from him and trust that he is moving in others to prepare them to receive the message.

> **Ephesians 6:18-20**
>
> *Pray at all times in the Spirit with every prayer and request, and stay alert with all perseverance and intercession for all the saints. Pray also for me, that the message may be given to me when I open my mouth to make known with boldness the mystery of the gospel. For this I am an ambassador in chains. Pray that I might be bold enough to speak about it as I should.*

We must routinely be praying that our efforts will be effective because the Holy Spirit is moving to achieve his purposes in them.

We cannot save anyone by ourselves, and we must ask the Holy Spirit to move so that his purposes can be fulfilled. The saving grace of Jesus is a miracle. That our hard hearts can be humbled such that we can understand and receive the Gospel is a miracle on par with the miracles of the New Testament. Why? Because apart from a move of God in us, we cannot possibly fathom his grace (1 Corinthians 1:18-20).

Power & Authority

Lastly, in our conversations with those who do not know Jesus, we must walk with power and authority. When Jesus sends out the disciples in Luke 10 he gives them power and authority. Throughout the book of Acts, supernatural work accompanied the disciples. We should both expect and ask for God to move supernaturally.

Why is this under crucial conversations? Because we should, from the testimony of the New Testament, expect God to move supernaturally in the lives of non-believers so that they can see the power of God and respond. Think about how different our conversations introducing people to Jesus proceed when they are accompanied by the demonstrable work of God in their lives. Our world is craving answers to the situations and challenges they find themselves in. What if we were to speak with power and authority, flowing from the Holy Spirit, into those situations the same as Peter did in Acts 3:6: *"But Peter said, 'I don't have silver or gold, but what I do have, I give you: In the name of Jesus Christ of Nazareth, get up and walk!'"*

Crucial Conversations & Disciple Emphases

What exactly is the content that would come up in a crucial conversation? The previous Discipleship Emphases provide us with a helpful framework for thinking about what types of conversations we may engage in. It can be difficult to know where to start in a crucial conversation; what follows are some suggestions of how we can think about using the Discipleship Emphases to open up a meaningful dialogue.

Gospel Fluency

The most crucial conversations of all are those concerning who God is. Our crucial conversations must keep people anchored and formed by the exclusive and beautiful truth of Jesus while simultaneously ensuring that their eyes remain fixed on his Mission to the world. We need to engage in intentional discipleship conversations with people to ensure that their understanding of the Gospel is not just intellectual but transformational. Similarly, our conversations must tackle more than personal, inner-life transformation. We must engage people such that they are forming a heart for the lost and a desire to see them found in Jesus. This desire must subsequently translate into evangelistic action. With intentional discipleship, the ability to communicate the Gospel coherently, accurately and persuasively should be properly developed.

Secure Identity

It is under secure identity that many of our character issues will arise. As previously discussed, our propensity for sin often arises out of an insufficient formation of who we are in Christ. As mentioned, the foundational building block of our identity in Christ is our acceptance of the Lordship of Jesus over every area of our lives. Consequently, crucial conversations in some of the deepest parts of our soul reside in this area. For example, conversations around pride, sexuality, addiction, character deficiencies, selfish ambitions, lust and so forth will all flow out of who we are in Christ. The objective in all of these is to see the disciple not just abandoning the way of sin but also being transformed such that their fulfillment is found in Christ and Christ alone. While many behavioural issues will arise out of the discussion around identity, we do not merely call people to acknowledge and apologize for their sin, we call them to repent. To repent is to turn around — to go a new direction. It is critical that our conversations around forming a person's identity does not end with identifying the areas of sin. We need to go far deeper than sin identification; we must invite people to see who they are in Christ. It is the discovery of who they are in him that will truly set them free.

Missional Living

The way of Jesus is beautiful and life-changing, but it is also very difficult and requires continuing course corrections as we build our lives. The forces of culture can easily distract a disciple from living an integrated, missional life that maximizes impact for Jesus. Crucial conversations in missional living will tackle the decision making processes that people are using to build their lives. A conversation may open up what could be very private issues such as housing decisions, workplace or family structures, or even investments into specific hobbies. We encourage people to intentionally structure their lives so that they are moving the Gospel into unreached places. These conversations will almost always include some degree of sacrifice, and must be navigated within the context of a healthy discipleship relationship. Every facet of our lives comes under the authority of Jesus, and it is in our missional living that we must be challenged and challenge others to think about the mission of Jesus as their very first priority instead of as just an afterthought.

Radical Generosity

A particularly sensitive area for discipleship conversations is that of radical generosity. It is in this area that we will open up the questions of time, talents and treasures. The discipler has the responsibility to call people to invest their whole lives for the kingdom. We must boldly and confidently call people to give their time, talents and treasures so that others will know Jesus. The greatest invitation we can make is to see people explicitly participate in the mission of God. The crucial conversations around generosity are an invitation for people to live lives that are reflective of Jesus. We need not fear asking people to reallocate their time or resources to serve the Church. When we lead people to live in a way that is radically generous, we are leading them to a more full life. The invitation to kingdom generosity is in fact a gift we are giving people; we are giving people the gift of participation in the move of God in our world. In Mark 1:16-20, Jesus calls his first disciples to give up both their livelihoods as well as their entire way of life. Yet, while the disciples gave up everything they had, they received something much more valuable in return: a relationship with Jesus and an invitation to participate in his Mission alongside him. As disciple-making disciples, we have the opportunity to extend the same invitation to others to give up their whole lives for Christ. While it may be sensitive, we must shift our thinking such that in every discipleship relationship, the potentially taboo subject of generosity is transformed into a beautiful invitation to life.

Crucial Conversations

Engaging in crucial conversations about crucial conversations is itself a crucial conversation. In discipleship relationships, it is important that we empower those we are discipling to develop the skill of discussing their faith, both with fellow believers and unbelievers. The discipleship conversations may involve their own response to difficult conversations you have had with them or a proud or unteachable attitude. For example, you may address an issue of radical generosity at one point and be met with pride, which in turn will create the gateway to have a conversation about being teachable. Similarly, many people will misstep in their crucial conversations. They may be too timid or too harsh, and growing in their ability to engage crucial conversations will require intentional and sustained coaching. Lastly, many people struggle to engage in a substantive conversation about their faith with nonbelievers. A crucial conversation may be needed to encourage a disciple to engage the world around them in their faith, along with follow-up conversations to continue to calibrate their thinking and approach.

11

The Work of Discipleship

The 5 Discipleship Potential Emphases provide clarity around the content and shape of discipleship, but how does discipleship actually happen? Discipleship is not a process of angelic revelation, nor is it primarily concerned with gaining knowledge. How then does discipleship as a process actually operate? Simply, discipleship is a relational process, not a didactic one. Through relationships with other believers, we grow in our relationship with the Triune God. There are three absolutely critical relational ingredients and four necessary steps that we must see in action in all discipleship relationships. The three ingredients are time, proximity and vulnerability. The four steps of the discipleship process are inviting, modelling, training and empowering.

Three Relational Ingredients

When we observe Jesus' ministry, there is a clear pattern of three unmistakable ingredients in the relationships that Jesus formed with his disciples. These ingredients are essential in the discipleship process. Oftentimes, we are looking for a quick fix in discipleship; a silver-bullet program or system that will result in everyone immediately becoming a passionate sold-out follower of Jesus. However, as Jesus' own ministry illustrates, there is no way to short-circuit the process. These ingredients are indispensable and cannot be replaced by great preaching, good reading or even effective counselling, as important and effective as those things are! It bears saying again; great preaching or reading excellent books is not a substitute for discipleship.

Time Together

In our day to day lives, almost everything is reduced to a transaction. We pay for a service and we immediately receive what we have requested. A tendency towards transactional thinking combined with a propensity to pursue instant gratification can result in a very flawed approach to discipleship. We must resist the urge to reduce discipleship to a transactional affair. Similarly, we must allow any and all desires to see immediate results to die. Discipleship requires time, typically several years of investment into those we are discipling to see fruit begin to form.

Discipleship requires that we invest over a period of time. This might sound obvious, but in a world where instant and immediate results are normative, it bears repeating. A discipleship relationship is not a casual acquaintance with which we share pearls of wisdom when the timing is suitable, nor is it reduced to occasional coffees. Discipleship is an intentional commitment to invest relationally in another through thick and thin. This means that discipleship is not an action taken in response to a person's specific need at one point in time — a mentoring or counselling relationship would be more appropriate for that. Discipleship is not about fixing a person's issues or dealing with the way they have dropped the ball or sinned most recently. If this is what our discipleship primarily looks like, then it is an indication that something is wrong in our discipleship process. A discipleship relationship is continually pointing people to Jesus so that they can, in turn, do the same for others. In a discipleship relationship, our primary job is to see people living lives in light of the Gospel. It is not a reactive relationship to a particular need, though poignant needs will arise. Discipleship is a process where a person is moved from wherever they are to a greater relationship with Jesus and multiplication for his name. As a result, this takes time.

This investment of time means that discipleship is a risky process because we do not know in advance if it will produce fruit. Sometimes, we pour significant time and effort into a discipleship relationship that does not end positively. Jesus himself had one of his 12 disciples betray him despite the years of time and energy poured into that discipleship relationship. An extended pattern of failed discipleship relationships, however, can be indicative that personal growth may be needed. When we examine how Multiplication Power operates, we will be better equipped to identify our own biases in determining where to invest time and what sorts of characteristics have a higher likelihood of producing a multiplying disciple from our investment of time.

It is worth noting, however, that although discipleship takes time, this does not reduce the urgency or the need to see our discipleship bear fruit.

Proximity to Each Other

The second ingredient of discipleship is that it requires proximity. This means that we are "in each other's world." Discipleship requires that our lives are intertwined. Jesus' ministry was one of intentional engagement with the people around him. Those Jesus was discipling were intimately involved in each other's lives. They ate together, travelled together, worked together and even shared living quarters.

We like to use the phrase "up in each other's business." Discipleship is a means by which we are so involved in each other's lives that there is ample opportunity to observe both the positive and negative in the actions and words of one another. Proximity means that we cannot hide who we are; there are no masks or pretend Christians in these relationships.

It is worth noting that this kind of relationship is only possible by the grace of Jesus. The friction that can result in this type of situation requires that we demonstrate supernatural grace and love towards one another. Perhaps this is part of the reason why John writes so emphatically to love one another as believers in 1 John.

As mentioned earlier, discipleship is not a reactive process to issues in people's lives. In order to see our discipleship be intentional and consistent, we need to be engaged in the regular lives of those we are discipling. We need to see who they are at their best *and* their worst. More importantly, we need to see who they are in the day-to-day moments. It is in the normal everyday moments that we can best see discipleship happen.

This is actually a liberating and powerfully freeing aspect of discipleship. It means that discipleship functions best when it is integrated into the natural rhythms of our lives. It is not a burden to be added to our lives, but a process to be interwoven into every aspect of them. This is why Jesus says in Matthew 11:28-29 that his burden is light and that those who come to him will receive rest. Discipleship is not a program to be added, but an invitation to live a life where the natural ebb-and-flow of our life results in people knowing Jesus. It may be sacrificial, yes, but not burdensome.

If the natural rhythm of our life is not amenable to effective discipleship, then we have no alternative but to change the rhythm of our lives to allow that to happen. Jesus has given us a command to make disciples; if the setup of our life is not helping that happen then we need to change the setup of our life. This may mean changes in where we work, where we live, where and how we are engaged in a church family, or even how we spend our money. This simple ingredient of proximity is closely linked to missional living; we cannot live missionally without having proximity to the people Jesus has placed in our lives to disciple.

This ingredient is particularly important to see new believers come to put their faith in Jesus. Evangelism and discipleship are not distinct practices but intimately and irrevocably intertwined. In order to see people know Jesus, we must be in proximity to people who do not know Jesus! This may sound like a truism, but it requires intentional effort to prevent ourselves from forming cloistered, isolated Christian bubbles. It is critical that we intentionally invest time and live in proximity with people who do not yet know Jesus so that they can hear about him from our lives *and* our lips!

Vulnerability

The final ingredient is that of intentional vulnerability on both sides of discipleship relationship. As we will discuss in more detail below, discipleship is a process by which another person observes Christ in us and imitates it. Discipleship requires that our lives are opened to one another. Again, from observing Jesus' ministry, he was profoundly vulnerable with his disciples. They saw him weep at the death of friends and show fear in the face of death. The Gospel writers go out of their way to highlight Jesus' 'humanity — exhaustion, weariness, fear and grief. The fact that they could write about this means that Jesus had been vulnerable enough to allow them to see him at his weakest!

Time and proximity do not automatically produce vulnerability. There are people with whom we spend a great deal of time and proximity but whom we may not really know; often co-workers or fellow students would fall into this category. It is through vulnerability that our lives are opened up and the transformational work of Jesus is ultimately revealed to the person we are discipling. Vulnerability is about inviting a person into more than a transactional relationship but a relationship of intimacy.

The fact that vulnerability is a key ingredient for growing in Discipleship Potential is liberating because it means that healthy discipleship relationships do not require us to be strong, perfect or to have all the answers all the time. In fact, it is in our weaknesses, fears, doubts and concerns that the person we are discipling can see who we really are and the degree to which Christ is moving in us.

The fear can exist that if we are vulnerable then our credibility to be a discipler could be lost. Perhaps if there is a hidden sin or hypocrisy then this fear is justified. However, this would indicate that there is a pretty severe breakdown in our own discipleship and sanctification. In this case, it is important that we be vulnerable and proactive in raising this issue with the person who is discipling us.

However, when hidden sin and hypocrisy are not particular concerns, this line of thinking is indicative of a misunderstanding of the nature of discipleship. Discipleship is a process where we open our lives for people to see how Christ moves in us and may also move in them. As our lives are opened, Christ moves through our lives to transform theirs. The supreme joy of discipleship is that it is not about us but about what Jesus is doing. This means that our vulnerability, especially in our weaknesses, is a powerful tool in the hands of the Holy Spirit.

The Apostle Paul drove this point on vulnerability home in that he would not just be vulnerable in his weaknesses, he would boast in them!

2 Corinthians 12:9-10

Therefore, I will most gladly boast all the more about my weaknesses, so that Christ's power may reside in me. So I take pleasure in weaknesses, insults, hardships, persecutions, and in difficulties, for the sake of Christ. For when I am weak, then I am strong.

The question could be fairly raised about appropriate and responsible degrees of vulnerability. If the Leadership Position aspect of the Leadership Pipeline is properly functioning then it helps to organize people into a structure where people can clearly answer the question "who cares for me" and "who do I care for?" We are not vulnerable with all people equally. With wisdom, we open our lives to those with whom we are entering a discipleship relationship.

It is worth mentioning that if there is very close proximity and a high degree of vulnerability then the amount of time required can certainly be shortened, as illustrated in Jesus' own ministry. In a mere three, years he was able to raise incredible leaders who, when empowered by the Spirit, would initiate the birth of the Church. This is why high-proximity situations such as sharing a house or travelling together, and high-vulnerability situations such as processing grief or confessing habitual sin, can be so powerful in moving a discipleship relationship forward.

It is for this reason that we are fundamentally limited in the number of people who we can adequately disciple. Discipleship is clearly an intensive process. We can only share time, proximity and vulnerability with a limited set of people. While this may seem to hinder discipleship, it actually reveals the true power of a discipleship movement! Discipleship cannot happen effectively when it is centralized around a single person; it has to be multiplied into the entire body of Christ! Jesus could have elected to leverage a growth-by-addition model in saving the world by attracting greater and greater numbers to himself. Instead, he chose to involve every follower in the process. Discipleship by nature cannot be built around a single person but must be multiplied through the entire body of believers.

It is also clear that discipleship is not "in addition" to the life of a believer; it is their life! If we try to add discipleship as a program or initiative, it will quickly become overwhelming and fail. Discipleship is our life; we are disciples. "Disciple" is an identity, not an activity. All of life is discipleship. It is for this reason that the invitation to this radical multiplying force of discipleship is not a burden but in fact, an invitation to experience, as Jesus said, life and life to the full. (John 10:10)

Four Steps: IMTE

How then does discipleship actually happen? How do we mix these 3 ingredients — what is the recipe, so to speak? How do we intentionally and proactively engage with people in a way that leads them to be made alive in Christ and subsequently to see others also made alive in Christ? How do we disciple people in a way that consistently and reliably results in a multiplication of disciples? The Apostle Paul paints a picture for us of how this can work with four distinct steps.

> **Philippians 3:17**
>
> *Join in imitating me, brothers and sisters, and pay careful attention to those who live according to the example you have in us.*

Paul introduces four steps in this short verse: inviting, modelling, training and empowering (IMTE). As we will demonstrate, the four steps are not isolated to this single verse but were demonstrated and woven into the very nature of discipleship from the start of Jesus' ministry. All four steps are critical to effective discipleship.

Inviting

Paul starts by extending an invitation to "join in." Discipleship starts with an invitation. "Follow me" (Matthew 4:19a) were the first words that Jesus spoke to the disciples. This invitation went far deeper than an invitation to a relationship. It was an invitation to a life of mission: "and I will make you fish for people" (Matthew 4:19b). Discipleship is not the same as an invitation to friendship, though friendship will certainly result from it! Discipleship is an invitation to join us in experiencing life in Christ so that they can do the same to those in their world.

We are fundamentally inviting people into relationship, to come and "do life" with us. "Come be with me" is the basic essence of the invite or, as Paul says, "join in." We are inviting people to ourselves and in doing so, inviting them to know Jesus. This is not an invitation to an event or a program, but an invitation to be in proximity to us. Invitation to a leadership position or to a Simple Church Huddle may be part of the environment that they are invited into, but discipleship is first and foremost an invitation into relationship. Jesus invited people to follow him and be in a relationship with him.

This simple starting point may expose that we have work to do in our own discipleship journey. We cannot invite people to do life with us with the intent that they will see Jesus if Jesus is not being formed in us. However, the fact that we have work to do is not an excuse to procrastinate in inviting people into a discipleship relationship. All of us have work to do, so this can never disqualify us from the call to disciple others. It is not about whether you have work to do or not, it is about whether you are allowing Jesus to do that work. A resistance to the transforming power of Jesus, in other words, a refusal of his Lordship, is the only thing that can disqualify you from the call to disciple. This invitation is not for the mature or advanced, but in fact to all people.

This crucial step of discipleship is often the easiest but the scariest at the same time. Oftentimes, extending an invitation means exposing ourselves to vulnerability. We may be rejected, we may feel under-equipped or afraid of failure. However, as previously discussed, discipleship is ultimately the work of the Holy Spirit. While we are inviting people to come to be with us, we are ultimately inviting them not to ourselves but to join in what Christ is doing through us. When we extend an invitation, we do so with a profound reliance on the Holy Spirit to work in that person, such that, through us, Christ will be formed in them. As a result, we would encourage everyone to simply begin to invite people into discipleship. The starting point of this is laying the groundwork in prayer. "Lord, who can I invite to know you or be in a relationship with you?"

It is also worth mentioning that this invitation is applied to all areas. Extending invitations is not restricted to non-believers. We are constantly inviting people to come to be with us. *Every day* the prayer is "who can I invite to be with me in this mission that Jesus has called me to?" That may mean inviting someone to take a step towards increased leadership responsibility, it may mean inviting them to stretch themselves in a way that they are not sure they can do, or an invitation to take a leap of faith. It is through invitations that we both initiate and maintain momentum in the discipleship process.

Modelling

As Paul says, "Join in imitating me." Discipleship is an invitation for people to come and observe our lives and copy them. It is in this step that the tremendous potential impact of discipleship lies. We call the discipleship dimension of the Discipleship Pipeline "Discipleship Potential," because it is evaluating how much potential people have to invite people to observe Christ in their life. A person's Discipleship Potential is directly connected to the degree to which Christ is observed in their lives.

When Paul invites the church to imitate him, it is an invitation to observe all of his life. In 1 Corinthians 10:31-11:1 he invites the churches to imitate him in matters as simple as eating and drinking and illustrates how everything he does reflects and points people to Jesus.

1 Corinthians 10:31-11:1

So, whether you eat or drink, or whatever you do, do everything for the glory of God. Give no offence to Jews or Greeks or the church of God, just as I also try to please everyone in everything, not seeking my own benefit, but the benefit of many, so that they may be saved. Imitate me as I imitate Christ. [1]

Similarly, when Jesus called the disciples to follow him, it was an invitation to an intentional and transparent community. There is no divide between the sacred and the secular in this aspect of discipleship. We are inviting people to examine every dimension of our lives so that they can observe a desire, willingness and obedience to see Jesus as Lord.

The temptation in discipleship is to restrict our modelling of Christ to formal "discipleship moments," to invite people to model after us in only the restricted areas to which we give them access. The true power of discipleship lies in vulnerably opening our lives up so that people can see how Jesus is living in us. As a result of this step in discipleship, the question that must be continually asked is: "is this aspect of my life reflecting Jesus, and do I want those I am discipling to copy it?"

On the surface, the concept of modelling is simple enough, but it requires profound humility, personal awareness and a life formed by the truths of scripture. Modelling is an invitation for people to make copies of our life. As a result, there is a significant responsibility to ask the question "is my life reflective of the image of Christ?" Humility is required as we must allow the Holy Spirit through, the power of scripture, to cause us to shift the substance and patterns of our lives to better reflect the call of the Gospel. As we do this, we should identify aspects of our lives that need to be adjusted so that the impact of being copied is effective in advancing the Gospel. This means that we have to look at the Discipleship Emphases and ask "are these ingrained in my patterns of living?" Are we living as ambassadors, servants, sons and daughters, and ministers of the Gospel?

If we are not careful, the invitation to discipleship can result in us replicating the patterns of the world instead of the Kingdom of

Jesus. We are constantly being "discipled" by the world around us and have to be careful to identify the ways in which our lives are modelled after the prevalent decision making processes of our culture, typically called social norms. For example, one social norm is to prioritize career advancement over faithfulness to the Kingdom. We will easily move cities for a job. That would be socially acceptable, even praiseworthy. However, would we, with greater intentionality, move somewhere that is strategic for the church? Often we, largely unintentionally, model through our lives and decisions that career is more important than Kingdom. The subtle ways our lives are modelled after worldly culture instead of Kingdom culture requires that we are continually returning to scripture with humility to allow the way we are living to be turned upside down.

> **1 Peter 1:13-14**
>
> *Therefore, with your minds ready for action, be sober-minded and set your hope completely on the grace to be brought to you at the revelation of Jesus Christ. As obedient children, do not be conformed to the desires of your former ignorance.*

When we invite people to model after us, we have to ask ourselves, have we set our hope and patterned our lives completely after the grace of Jesus? As we repeatedly ask this question and are refined by the Holy Spirit, the potential Kingdom impact of people modelling after us — or rather, Christ in us — increases tremendously. The "private" details of our lives are no longer entirely private. Through discipleship, we invite people to examine our lives, discover the way of Jesus and subsequently model themselves after what they see.

Training

Paul subsequently invites the church to "pay careful attention," indicating intentional learning and transmission of practices, knowledge, attitudes and techniques for producing followers of Jesus through our discipleship efforts. We call this aspect of discipleship "training." Training is the step where we pass along the important tools and information to help people thrive in their journey with Jesus and to be able to pass along wisdom and understanding to others.

In the process of producing multiplying disciples of Jesus, it is important that they are equipped with a high-quality, transmittable and doctrinally sound understanding of the Gospel. While the Gospel is profoundly simple in one sense, it is also tremendously deep. A lifetime of study would not unearth all the riches that it contains. Formulating a solid foundation of gospel fluency in each person we disciple is critical for them to produce disciples themselves.

There are three fatal errors that we can make when considering this step of discipleship. First, we run the risk of thinking that training is merely information transmission. Information is important of course, but it is only a starting point. Part of the training is to see that information moves from 'head' to 'heart' in the people we are discipling. This is accomplished through vulnerability.

There is a tremendous cost to following Jesus, as Jesus himself reminds us in Matthew 16:24 that the cost of following him is, in fact, an invitation to adopt an execution device. *"When Christ calls a man he bids him, come and die"* [43] as the famous theologian, Dietrich Bonhoeffer, famously said in his work *The Cost of Discipleship*. We are training people in the way of dying to themselves and living instead with the ambition of making the Gospel known (2 Corinthians 5:20). This clearly extends far beyond information transmission; rather, it is training people for a life of discipleship. As Ignatius of Antioch wrote in the second century:

> *"Now I begin to be a disciple. Let fire and the cross; the crowds of wild beasts; let tearings, breaking and dislocations of bones; let cutting of members; let shatterings of the whole body; and let all the dreadful tortures of the devil come upon me; only let me get to Jesus Christ. All the pleasures of the world, and all the kingdoms of this earth, shall profit me nothing. It is better for me to die on behalf of Jesus Christ than to reign of all the ends of the earth."* — Ignatius of Antioch[44]

For Ignatius, training in discipleship was a training in dying to ourselves that Christ might be glorified. For this reason, our training should not be restricted merely to knowledge formation, but equally to spiritual formation and character development. Are our disciples being formed into the image of Christ in every aspect of their lives? This training in discipleship is profoundly formational and can be painful at times. In our discipleship training, lives are entirely reoriented around the Gospel and seeing others discover it also. We must resist the desire for discipleship to be an easy or comfortable process for both the discipler and the one being discipled. We must confront, with grace and love but also truth, those we are discipling. At times, as directly as Jesus does in Matthew 16:23. He confronts Peter and calls him out for not seeing the things of Jesus. At other times, he confronts more gently, but even so he is still firm, as seen in his interaction with the woman at the well in John 4. In either case Jesus is working to see a truth formed deeply in a person.

Participating in a training course, working through a curriculum or listening to a podcast may be supplemental to the discipleship process. They may be helpful in providing fuel for discussion and activation for the disciple. However, as powerful as these tools are, they do not serve as the basis of discipleship. The basis of our discipleship must be an invitation to share time, proximity and vulnerability with us and, in so doing, open our lives so that as Christ is formed in us he will also be formed in those we are discipling.

The second potential pitfall in the discipleship process is when we restrict discipleship to training without connecting it to the other essential steps of invitation, modelling and empowering. As we have articulated above, we cannot properly disciple people without engaging the whole of the person with the whole of ourselves. This can only be done when we vulnerably open up our lives to them to see Christ formed in us. Discipleship is not, strictly speaking, a student-teacher relationship. In a traditional mentality, the teacher does not and should not open the whole of their life to their student for them to examine and replicate it.

Our training in discipleship must include an active practice of invitation and a sharing of time, proximity and vulnerability with those we are discipling. However, it cannot end there. We must place critical importance on empowering the person to also walk as a disciple-making disciple themselves.

Third, we can run the risk of over-complicating the discipleship process. The Gospel is rich in diversity and deep enough to invest a lifetime of study and transformation. However, raising multiplying disciples does not require that they understand Hebrew and Greek or can articulate a perfect systematic theology. We may be tempted to move on from the basics of discipleship towards "advanced subjects." However, in many cases, the basics are where our energy needs to be focused. To see the 5 Discipleship Emphases of gospel fluency, secure identity, missional living, radical generosity and crucial conversations formed in those we are discipling will take many years of consistent faithful discipleship work. Often, there is a tendency to want to move on from basic ideas such as repentance, forgiveness, scripture study, prayer, generosity or the priesthood of all believers too quickly for the sake of 'more advanced' theology.

The illustration found in Hebrews 5:12 and 1 Corinthians 3:2 highlights the need of the church to continue to consume baby food: "milk" instead of mature food, "meat." In those cases, the believers were admonished to focus on the basics of avoiding worldliness and distinguishing good from evil. These are subjects that should dominate our discipleship process. In our pride, we can think that we should be focusing on advanced topics when, in fact, we haven't yet really grasped the basics. Of course, we do want to see our disciples mature, but it is in how they are transformed and empowered to see others impacted likewise — not in their technical theological prowess as a goal unto itself.

The sermon on the mount, for example, is profoundly simple in its concepts but will require a lifetime of discipleship to master. We can be tempted to engage in idle philosophical or theological dialogue as we disciple others and think that we are giving them "meat" to eat. We must be careful to remain focused on seeing our disciples grow in transformation through the beautiful simplicity of the Gospel and avoid fruitless theological debate.

The call to focus on the basics is tremendously empowering for the discipleship process. The concepts are straightforward to understand and, as a result, easy to transmit. Simplicity allows the multiplication process in discipleship to accelerate as quickly as it does and is critical to fostering a multiplying discipleship movement. The moorings in gospel fluency specifically, and the Discipleship Emphases generally, provide a helpful framework for focusing our discipleship training while avoiding getting stuck in the weeds.

Empowering

The final step in discipleship is the act of empowering the person we are discipling to begin to disciple people themselves. The importance of this step in discipleship cannot be overstated. It is in empowering those we are discipling to disciple others themselves, that we actualize a multiplying discipleship movement.

Paul's invitation to imitate him means that, in addition to inviting the Church to examine his life, he was also empowering them to continue the discipleship process in others. It was simultaneously an invitation and an empowerment. At the beginning of the letter to the Philippians, Paul highlights that he is in prison because of his proclamation of the Gospel. As he invites the church to imitate him, Paul is also empowering them to live missionally as he is! Paul is saying that they can do what he can do. This is remarkable, because Paul, the great church planter and evangelist, doesn't view himself as someone special but instead empowers the church to participate in the mission.

Jesus did not teach and train his disciples to merely comprehend or even be transformed by his teaching. Very early in the discipleship journey, he empowered the disciples to carry out the same work that he was doing.

Luke 9:1-2

Summoning the Twelve, he gave them power and authority over all the demons and to heal diseases. Then he sent them to proclaim the kingdom of God and to heal the sick.

He gave them real power and real authority to go on a real mission to genuinely proclaim the Kingdom to those who may not listen. Jesus' empowerment of the disciples was not a carefully sanitized micro version of ministry in which there was no risk. He sent them to those who could just as easily reject them. Early in the discipleship journey, Jesus empowers his disciples to do what he did. In fact, after just three years, he entrusted the entire mission to them! As Alan Hirsch says of Jesus' empowerment, *"talk about a baptism of fire."*[45]

In empowering the disciples, Jesus exposed them early on to three very important principles of discipleship. First, he demonstrated that they had a responsibility to the mission that went far deeper than merely following Jesus or doing what he said. They needed to become active contributors to the mission. There is no room in the Kingdom of God for experiences designed for mere consumption. Every one of us is called to ministry and as a result, must take on ownership of the mission of God to see people made fully alive in the hope of Jesus.

For many, an effective evangelistic season is often right after they have surrendered their life to Jesus, when they may know the least. As is clear from the 3 steps of inviting, modelling and training, the ability to make disciples is ultimately not dependent on our knowledge so much as it is dependent on our enacted desire to be formed in the image of Christ and inviting people to participate in that process with us. Knowledge is important of course, but even equipped with a little knowledge, a committed disciple can be tremendously effective for the kingdom.

By activating disciples to be making disciples themselves as early in the process as possible, we can establish a new norm by which they live and in turn raise disciples. If every disciple is sent to make more disciples as part of their first steps as a Jesus follower, then they will replicate that into others. When Jesus gives the great commission at the end of Matthew, "to go and make disciples," he was not asking the apostles to do something new; he was commanding them to keep doing what they had already done. If we incubate a disciple too long before empowering them to multiply themselves, it can be very difficult to properly mobilize the disciple.

As a second principle of discipleship, Jesus exposed them to the reality of failure. Discipleship is not a straightforward linear process in which the only direction we go is up. It is filled with ups and downs; there will always be both success and failures. When he sends the disciples, Jesus tells them to expect failure as a part of the process (Luke 10:10). By empowering disciples to go and make other disciples early in the process, we can create a more failure-tolerant culture in which people are more willing to put themselves out there at the risk of failure. If we withhold the empowering "go," aspect of discipleship too long it can become a theoretical commandment to which we do not attach any real action. This delay can result in the perceived negative consequences of stepping out in discipleship growing in the mind of the disciple to the point where they may be paralyzed by fear. The reality is that they *will* fail in their desire to disciple people. Jesus himself had a failed discipleship relationship with one of the 12 who were closest to him. The problem is not the failure itself, but rather how they respond to the failure. In empowering early in the process, the disciples are exposed to failure early and as a result become more resilient to it.

Third, Jesus exposed them to the joy of success on the mission. In the Gospel of Luke, Jesus sends out 72 disciples to proclaim the news about Jesus. When they return, they boldly proclaim that even the demons submitted to Jesus name! They quickly get a "win" under their belts which has the tremendous effect of emboldening them in their willingness to make disciples. Seeing someone respond to discipleship, whether it is a total life transformation in becoming a believer or grasping a small truth, is tremendously encouraging for the discipler. By empowering the disciples early in the discipleship journey, Jesus was inviting them to discover the joy of partnering with the mission of God. It is in this partnership that we invite our disciples to discover a whole new kind of joy! The greatest tragedy would be if we withheld from them the joy of seeing God move through them to transform someone else's heart.

Experiential learning is perhaps one of the greatest ways that we grow as disciples. The requirement to begin teaching, communicating and sharing our faith will actually result in refining our ability to do so. In discipleship, practice indeed does make perfect — or at least helps us grow closer to the perfect discipleship that Jesus modelled for us.

It is worth highlighting that the degree of empowerment should be closely related to the depth of transformation and formation. 1 Timothy 3:6 highlights that key leadership positions should not be given to new converts. This is crucial as increased leadership position correlates to increased influence. For those with great influence, we must exercise caution to ensure that the invitation to model will result in modelling Christ, rather than our sinful nature. We must be wary of applying these criteria too broadly, and inadvertently creating a culture where only the senior leaders are empowered to multiply. Multiplication must be an imperative that is given to everyone, we merely adjust the scope or platform for that empowerment so that it is appropriate.

Summary

When the four steps of discipleship work together, each disciple should become a disciple-making disciple. Jesus initiated the process of inviting, modelling, training and empowering with his disciples, and we walk in the rich history of millions of disciple-making disciples down through the ages. The inviting, training, modelling and empowering of disciples is not a one-time set of actions but a continual cycle of doing so with the people we are discipling. As we empower them, we also continue to invite them into relationship to continue to grow in their discipleship capacity. In this way those we are discipling are simultaneously activated for multiplication and continued personal formation. This is illustrated below.

188 | Discipleship Potential

4 Steps of Disciple-Making Disciples

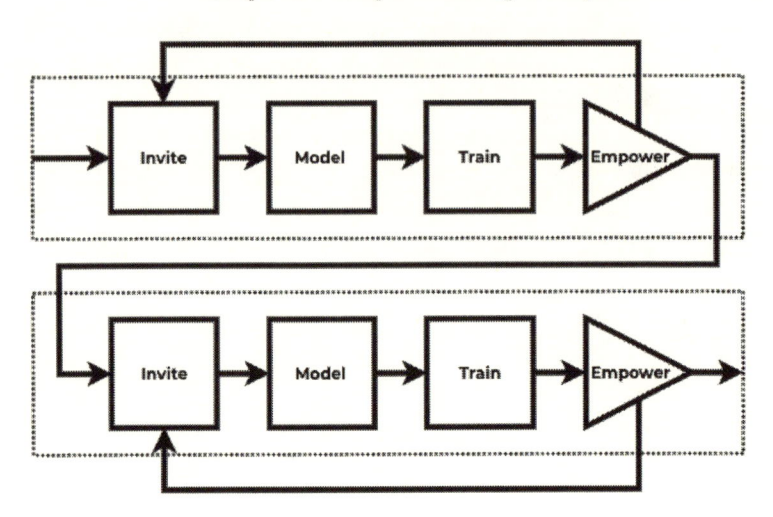

12

Discipleship Multiplication

Discipleship Potential articulates a process by which a person is consistently increasing their capacity and potential to be a multiplying disciple. As a person increases their Discipleship Potential across each of the 5 Discipleship Emphases, there is a sequence of distinct phases or levels on the Pipeline: Exposure, Understanding, Fluency and Multiplication. Each of these four phases highlights a different mandate to the disciple, and has a different degree of responsibility and influence.

Discipleship Potential

- Exposure
- Understanding
- Fluency
- Multiplication

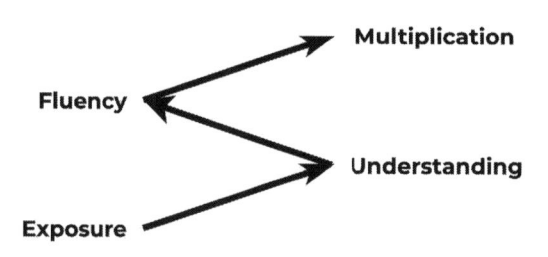

While growing through these four phases, both the inner and outer life of the disciple are transformed. As a disciple moves from exposure to multiplication, their identity, thoughts and actions are all transformed. Simultaneously, disciples should be growing in their ability to teach others to do likewise.

It is vitally important that every person on the pipeline has a responsibility and mandate for multiplication. Every person, from the moment they become a follower of Jesus, must begin the process of sharing and revealing Jesus to others. Everyone is involved in the Invite, Model, Train and Empower process. Everyone is invited to share time, proximity and vulnerability with those around them to see people grow in the 5 Discipleship Emphases.

In practice, those with understanding provide exposure to people who are new to Church. Those with fluency coach those who have attained understanding. Likewise, those who are at a multiplication level in their Discipleship Potential mobilize those who are fluent to in turn see people grow from exposure to understanding.

The call to be a disciple-making disciple needs to be deeply ingrained in the identity of the believer. This identity shift is not restricted as a part of advanced discipleship. In fact, if we try to mobilize people for mission only after many years of faith in Jesus, the transition will be tremendously difficult. As Alan Hirsch writes: *"Don't wait too long; as soon as people come to faith they should become part of the conspiracy of Little Jesuses."*[46] The call to be a disciple-making disciple is a tremendously costly invitation. Through inviting people to live into the reality of discipling others immediately upon coming to an understanding of Jesus' grace, the process of growing as a discipler becomes more natural and ingrained.

Discipleship Potential Phases

Where a disciple is on their discipleship journey can sometimes be difficult to determine. The goal in establishing these clear phases is to remove some of the ambiguity and subjectivity that can accompany discipleship. By breaking up growth in Discipleship Potential into distinct phases based on demonstrated fruitfulness, we can mobilize people for mission with a mandate appropriate to their capacity and depth as a disciple. These are designed to be somewhat objective in that we should be able to consistently test and elevate the most effective disciplers in the community.

Often a disciple grows in the different dimensions of transformation (sanctification and multiplication) at different rates. It is important that before we elevate someone to a higher leadership position with a greater mandate, that both their inner and outer life have grown to a corresponding level.

Discipleship Potential Phases

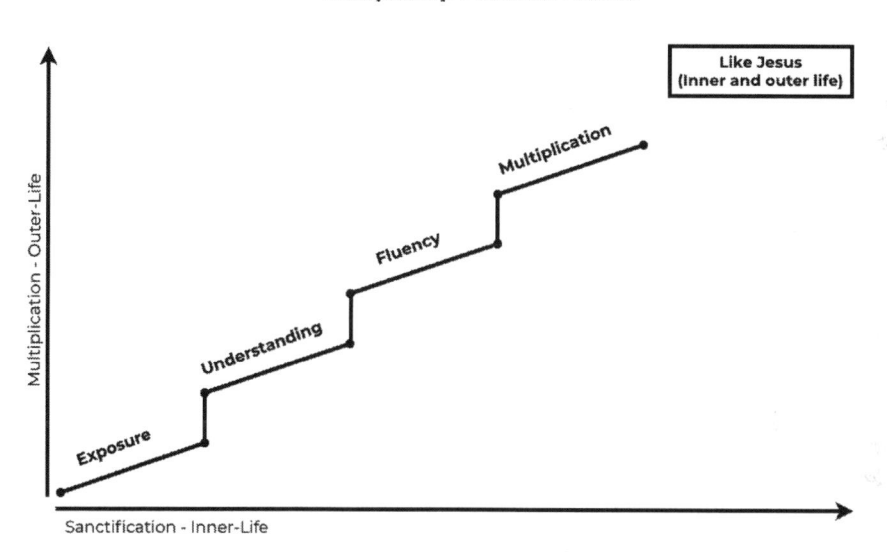

(Chart: A step graph with x-axis labeled "Sanctification - Inner-Life" and y-axis labeled "Multiplication - Outer-Life". Steps labeled from bottom-left to top-right: Exposure, Understanding, Fluency, Multiplication, leading to "Like Jesus (Inner and outer life)".)

As the diagram above illustrates, often a disciple takes a long time to internalize discipleship and to undergo the process of sanctification. To an outside observer it can seem as if very little growth is happening during this time, as much of their transformation has not yet become visible. During this time, it is tempting to give up or to assume that the effort of discipling an individual is wasted. We must avoid this temptation and understand that discipleship is a slow process that takes time.

With patience, the slow process of sanctification eventually results in something "clicking" and huge growth in their outer life follows rapidly. The temptation here is to assume that the rapid growth is not genuine or will not last. During this time we need to believe the best (See Chapter 14), and nurture their new growth as they enter the next phase of Discipleship Potential.

Exposure

The first phase on the Discipleship Potential Pipeline is Exposure. This is where every person starts in their discipleship journey. As the names suggest, people at this stage in their discipleship journey are being exposed to the Gospel for the very first time; they are not yet followers of Jesus. The primary objective when working with someone at an Exposure level is to see them move from merely hearing Gospel truths to understanding and accepting them as authoritative.

When someone is at the Exposure level, there is a significant gap between their thinking/living and the call of the Gospel. This can result in rapid growth for the person being discipled, as the disparity between them and what they read in Scripture is immediately apparent.

The temptation when working with people who are just beginning the journey is to lower the standard of Discipleship so that it is more palatable. We must follow the example of Jesus and resist the temptation to lower the bar (Matthew 8:22, John 6:60):

John 6:60, 66-67
On hearing it, many of his disciples said, "This is a hard teaching. Who can accept it?"... From this time many of his disciples turned back and no longer followed him. "You do not want to leave too, do you?" Jesus asked the Twelve.

To move people from Exposure to Understanding, rather than lowering the bar, we must instead consistently open our lives to the person we are discipling and show that although the way of Jesus is tremendously challenging, it is incredibly life-giving. To move people forward in discipleship, we expose them to the fullness of our experience in the Gospel through time, proximity and vulnerability; by inviting, modelling, training and empowering them in the way of Jesus.

As people at the Exposure level have not yet reached a point where they are actually in acceptance of the Gospel, the empowerment step of IMTE takes on a distinct shape. When we empower them, we are empowering them to ask questions and include others in the journey! It is very important that as a person is working towards understanding, they are free to ask open questions that receive genuine, thoughtful replies. A simple dismissive answer will not suffice; we must engage them in their questioning and demonstrate true concern and compassion as they wrestle to accept, or reject, an idea.

We can also empower them to invite others into the process. In Acts 13, Paul has arrived at Pisidian Antioch and is teaching in the synagogues. As he teaches, the crowds begin to grow and those who are being exposed to the Gospel for the first time are inviting others to come and hear about Jesus alongside them. As a result, many people came to faith. By mobilizing those who are just being exposed to the Gospel to invite those around them, the potential impact for the Kingdom is significantly increased.

Lastly, for someone who is already a follower of Jesus, the exposure level can also apply to one of the individual Discipleship Emphases that they have not been discipled in or taught. For example, a person may have an understanding and acceptance of gospel fluency but not yet have been exposed to or discipled in missional living or radical generosity. In such a case, we would continue to disciple them and help them grow in the Discipleship Emphases where they need to grow in order to help them become a healthy mature disciple-making disciple.

Understanding

The second discipleship phase is Understanding. This is the moment someone reaches a point where they comprehend and agree with the Gospel. At this point, their primary objections have been satisfied and they begin a journey of living into the 5 Discipleship Emphases.

It can be tempting for many raised with a transactional view of the Gospel to think of the Understanding phase as the goal of discipleship. If the Gospel is simply that Jesus paid a price for us, then when a disciple is 'saved' the journey of discipleship would be complete. As discussed in Chapter 6, this could not be further from the truth. It is of paramount importance that all followers of Jesus continue to engage in their own discipleship journey with someone farther along than them. They cannot, and must not, become an island unto themselves. They must continue to submit, in humility, to those who are discipling them to make sure they stay on the right track. They must be open to correction and steering in the 5 Discipleship Emphases.

If someone at an exposure level is having their thinking and worldview radically challenged, then someone at the understanding level is having the direction/orientation of their lives and decision-making processes completely rewired. Instead of living primarily for themselves, they are beginning to live with strategic Kingdom impact as the first priority of their lives.

There should now be a broad agreement between both the disciple and discipler as to what the objectives of discipleship are. This alignment creates space and permission for the discipler to have frank and poignant conversations that address the way the disciple is living and acting. A person with mere exposure likely will not have given permission to be directly challenged, but a person at the understanding level should be open to being pushed to live differently. This again reinforces the need for vulnerability in discipleship relationships, as frank conversations are much more effective in a relationship based on mutual trust and vulnerability.

At this point in the discipleship journey, a temptation is to postpone empowering a new disciple for mission, thinking that they are not mature enough yet. This is a grave mistake. The fastest and most sure way to move a disciple from understanding to fluency is to mobilize them in discipling others.

As a person who has attained understanding begins to live as a disciple and disciple others, the limitations of their knowledge and their need for continued sanctification will become immediately apparent to themselves and their discipler. This awareness of their need to grow and be refined is good news. Oftentimes, the person who has attained a level of understanding will begin to have an insatiable appetite for more knowledge and information. Similarly, they will be undergoing nothing short of a seismic shift in their lifestyle.

Not only is the mobilization beneficial for the growth of the disciple, but the ripple effect of this mobilization is catalytic for a movement. By actively mobilizing those who have reached a point of understanding in their discipleship journey to disciple those who are still at an exposure level, the discipleship process becomes a natural component of the disciple's life from the very earliest stages.

Fluency

The third phase of Discipleship Potential is Fluency. The term fluency typically describes a state of maturity where there is robust comprehension and communication skills of a concept or language. A disciple at the Fluency level of Discipleship Potential should have a robust understanding of the 5 Discipleship Emphases, exhibit accompanying personal transformation and demonstrate a marked ability to communicate these concepts and call others to similar transformation.

There are two key markers that differentiate between disciples at the Understanding and Fluency stages of Discipleship Potential. The first is that a disciple at the Fluency stage must have a demonstrated ability to see others move from Exposure to Understanding in their own discipleship journeys. The multiplying effectiveness of the fluent disciple is no longer evaluated solely on the basis of their own life, but on the lives of those they are discipling. It is not just their own formation that should be robust, but also the formation of those in the community around them.

At this stage of discipleship, making new disciples should become a natural, automatic part of the life of the disciple. Their impulse should be to live in a way that is consistently Inviting, Training, Modelling and Empowering those around them to grow in their faith. Discipleship must become their native language.

When someone is fluent in a language, their speed and efficacy in both comprehension and communication is significantly improved. The same applies to discipleship. When someone has reached a point of fluency in their discipleship, they can move more quickly in their discipleship relationships with others. They can quickly identify issues and work to see people mobilized. Due to their experience and depth of formation as they disciple others, their input is more valued and quickly adopted.

The second distinguishing characteristic of fluent discipleship is that the disciple should be developing a measure of self-responsibility. They should be able to discern, study and grow in their walk with Jesus somewhat independently; discerning truth from lies easily, having the ability to disciple others on their own, and being able to make wise decisions with minimal hands-on guidance.

This point of self-responsibility does not mean that they are not engaged in continued discipleship relationships; discipleship is always relational! Growing with a measure of self-responsibility does not mean that they are entirely independent or no longer reliant on others; rather, it means that they can grow on their own to a certain degree. Like an experienced athlete who trains on their own and makes their own training decisions but still depends on a coach, so do fluent disciples take a level of responsibility for their own growth in Jesus while still relying on other disciples for wisdom, guidance and accountability.

Multiplication

The Multiplication level of Discipleship Potential is what finally moves a moderately effective discipleship structure into a thriving discipleship movement. If disciples at the Fluency stage have begun to take an active and intentional responsibility for the maturity of those they are discipling, disciples at the Multiplication level must be actively creating an environment where those they are discipling, are discipling others, who are in turn discipling others.

Multiplying disciples will be discipling others in such a way that it is producing many generations of consistent, faithful, multiplying disciples. They are not measured on their life or even the lives of those they have discipled, but instead are measured on those they might not even have a direct connection to. Disciples at this level will naturally be developing an entire network of disciples whose fruit quickly multiplies beyond their direct influence; they likely will not even be able to measure the full scope of their influence for the Kingdom of God.

It is this network of disciples that amplifies the impact of the multiplying disciple. Multiplying disciples do not need to spread themselves too thin. Instead, they become specialists at highlighting and mobilizing the gifts of the people around them. The true multiplying disciple produces other multiplying disciples, not just fluent disciples.

Jesus was the ultimate multiplying discipler. He only lead a small group of people, but those people transformed the course of history. He invited them, modelled for them, trained them and then empowered his disciples to go and do likewise. Through this example of multiplying discipleship, the Church was born!

The multiplying disciple is someone who can very reasonably plant new churches. In fact, the only Biblical model of church planting is a multiplying discipleship movement. The example we are given in the New Testament is not one of exciting programs, fun events, great speaking or good music, but one of everyday ordinary followers of Jesus discipling others who disciple others who in turn disciple others! Instead of church planting being reserved for the elite or "strongest leaders," disciples who fully embody the Multiplication level of Discipleship Potential make church planting an accessible proposal for everyone.

An environment of multiplying disciples is, for all intents and purposes, a church. The powerful impact of activating multiplying disciples to plant churches is that these churches are formed with a multiplication mindset from the very beginning, and often go on to plant more churches. This is the power of a multiplying discipleship movement. This is the model that the early church and so many other church movements throughout history have used to change their world. This is the model that incredible church movements across the globe are using today!

True Kingdom impact does not take incredible amounts of money, leaders with tonnes of charisma, or attractional ministries. All it takes are multiplying disciples who in turn make disciples who in turn make disciples who in turn . . .

Discipleship Phases Rubric

The following rubric helps us identify the different characteristics of the discipleship phases:

	Exposure	Understanding	Fluency	Multiplying
Personal Growth	Rapid growth and challenging call to discipleship	High challenge, but now focuses on deep roots and application	Slower growth, but faster movement in their direct relationships	Slower personal growth, but much larger impact from the growth
Knowledge	Minimal knowledge, no acceptance	Minimal knowledge, but acceptance	Good knowledge, developing the ability to teach	Robust knowledge and training capacity
Behaviour	A large gap between behaviour and scripture	A mix of large and small gaps between behaviour and scripture	Small gaps between behaviour and scripture. "Above reproach"	Minimal obvious gaps between behaviour and scripture.
Approach	Peer-based through the unintentional yet contagious effect of excitement	Still primarily peer-based but invitational into their world through direct modelling	Begin to mobilize those they are discipling themselves in combination with their own direct modelling	A distributed network of multiplying disciples
Independence	No independence, apart from scripture study	Minimal independence — largely learning to master what they have been given	Some independent ability to self-study and move forward in discipleship	A large amount of independent thinking alongside a large network of accountability and support

Discipleship Emphases Growth

One way to think about the Discipleship Emphases relating to one another is by moving from a small pyramid to a large pyramid in our discipleship. We do not develop a disciple by adding layer upon layer. Instead, it is always a full pyramid. We are always working to see holistic, well-rounded disciples formed. The size of the pyramid is based on the breadth of each discipleship emphasis. Each discipleship emphasis provides the platform on which the next emphasis can build. Gospel fluency lays the foundation on which our secure identity is built, which in turn creates the platform for missional living, radical generosity and crucial conversations. Each emphasis naturally leads to the others being formed in us as well.

As we widen our understanding and integration of gospel fluency, the Holy Spirit will form our self-understanding in light of Jesus' work. The security of who we are in Christ, and the invitation to be children, servants and ambassadors, will naturally lead us to integrate every aspect of our lives so that others will know Jesus. The formation of a missional life naturally leads to a radically generous life. Giving our time, talents and treasures so that others will know Jesus is the natural next step for people who are formed by the gospel, secure in who they are in Christ and living on mission. Lastly, crucial conversations will flow naturally and healthily from the rhythm of a gospel-centric, secure, missionally generous disciple, thus further fuelling growth and maturity in discipleship.

Discipleship Emphases

- Crucial Conversations
- Radical Generosity
- Missional Living
- Secure Identity
- Gospel Fluency

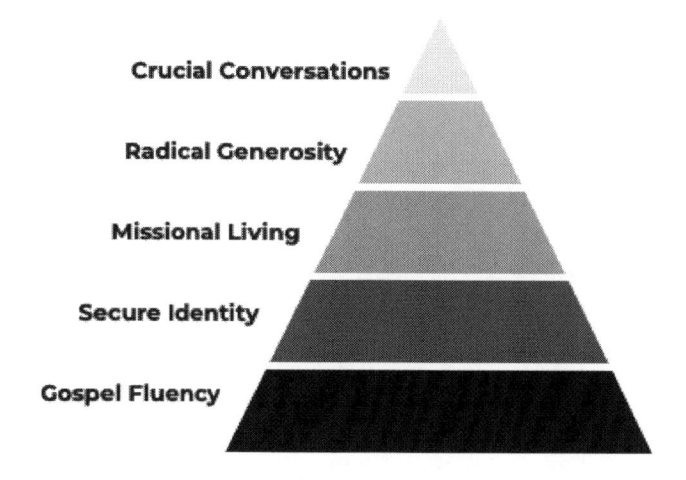

Instability in Discipleship

Oftentimes, when there is a breakdown in one of the higher Discipleship Emphases, it can be traced back to a breakdown in a lower emphasis. In fact, a particular issue may involve growth or maturation in multiple emphases simultaneously to really strengthen the disciple. For example, a disciple who struggles to receive crucial conversations may very well be struggling with an insufficiently developed identity in Christ.

Gospel fluency provides the overarching worldview into which our individual identities find meaning and purpose. This is crucial because without these foundational building blocks, the higher Discipleship Emphases do not make any sense; a missional life without knowing and receiving the unconditional grace of Jesus in gospel fluency or the Lordship of Jesus in our lives in security identity will be exhausting. The 'doing' Discipleship Emphases of missional living, radical generosity and crucial conversations must flow from a well-formed relationship with God and security in who we are.

When we try to build the Discipleship Emphases without the proper foundation, it leads to unstable discipleship. It may, in the short term, appear to produce fruit, as the language, actions and work of the person may appear healthy on the surface. However, if our discipleship is not built on a strong foundation, it will not stand the test of time.

For example, an identity without a gospel fluency will result in self-reliance and pride. Similarly, the call to a missional life without proper security in Christ will result in a form of works-based salvation where we are trying to gain self-confidence in our actions. Radical generosity without adequate formation for missional living will feel burdensome and weary, and we will resent it. Crucial conversations that flow from a robust gospel fluency, secure identity, missional living and radical generosity will be more productive, natural and powerful because they are flowing from a deep formation in every area of our lives by the Gospel. On the other hand, crucial conversations without the other emphases being formed will lack authority due to the visible hypocrisy in the disciple.

Part of helping a disciple grow is to identify where the breakdown is occurring in their discipleship and address the issue there. A lack of missional living may be the result of insufficient discipleship in that specific area, or it may result from an underdeveloped gospel fluency. Taking the time to understand the why behind the discipleship challenge is vital to help that person grow.

Typically, a person will have strengths in some Discipleship Emphases and weaknesses in others. This is why crucial conversations are so important as a discipleship emphasis. We must continually be engaging in discipleship dialogue to explore which area(s) of discipleship emphasis is limiting our missional impact and ask the Holy Spirit to continue to form us.

Immaturity to Maturity

All five emphases are necessary for every believer regardless of their stage on the journey. Radical generosity and crucial conversations are not "advanced discipleship." It is important, however, that radical generosity and crucial conversations are properly built on the capacity that has been formed in gospel fluency. We must call every discipleship to begin to wrestle in all areas of discipleship from the moment that they commit to Jesus as Lord. We must not wait to empower a disciple in the missional areas of discipleship until they are "fully trained." Rather, we must give them opportunities that are appropriate to their breadth of formation at that point in all discipleship areas simultaneously.

Discipleship Emphases Instability

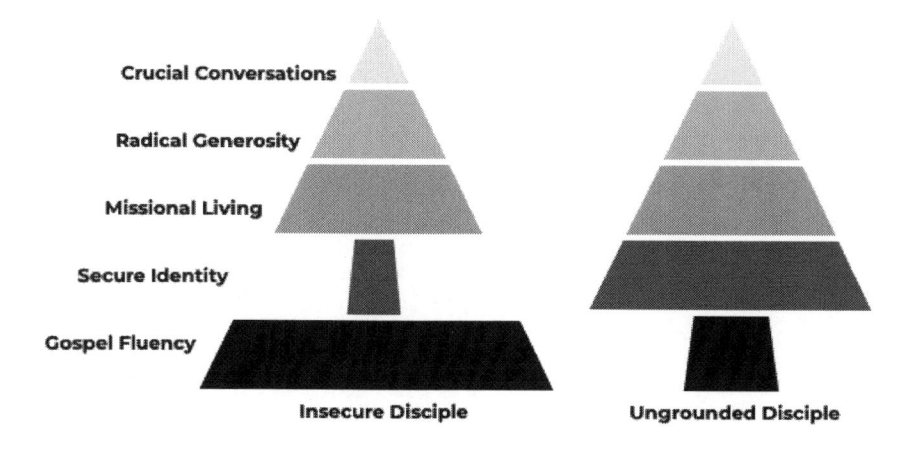

Crucial Conversations
Radical Generosity
Missional Living
Secure Identity
Gospel Fluency

Insecure Disciple   Ungrounded Disciple

Why is this important? Because we can mistake immaturity with instability in our discipleship. An immature disciple can still be a stable and healthy disciple — they just need to grow! A child, immature as they may be, is not unhealthy if they are growing and are exhibiting a robust development cycle. Consequently, a young or immature disciple can be given tremendous opportunities in discipleship in proportion to the size of their discipleship pyramid. We must not sideline them or limit them simply because they are young. In fact, if they are healthy and young, they may well be one of the best multiplying disciples in waiting!

Immaturity to Maturity

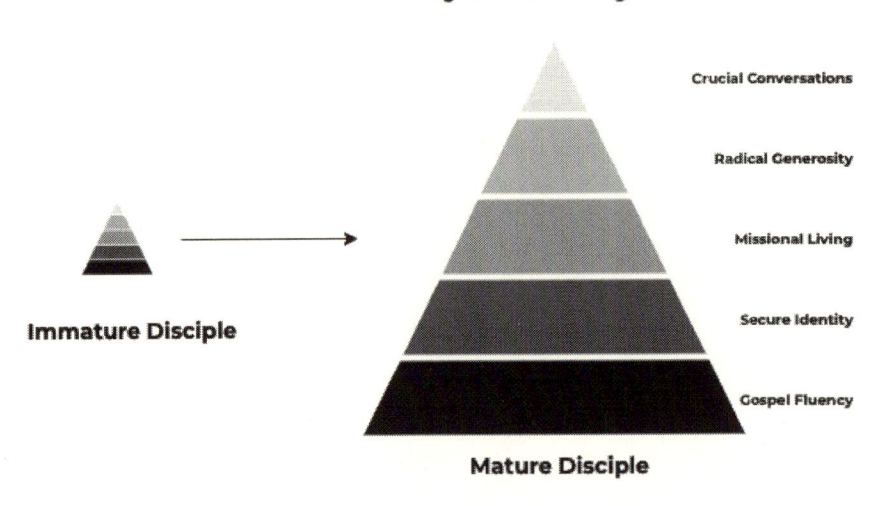

Immature Disciple → **Mature Disciple**

- Crucial Conversations
- Radical Generosity
- Missional Living
- Secure Identity
- Gospel Fluency

This concept of all 5 Discipleship Emphases being always present is what drives Everyone Sent to Multiply Everything. When a disciple has been given all 5 Discipleship Emphases, they will naturally begin to be missionally effective. Now, of course, if their foundation is not robust then their overall effectiveness will be limited, but they can still have some impact.

Part 3

Multiplication Power

13

How We Multiply: The N+2 Leader

Thus far, all of our focus on discipleship has been largely framed in one-on-one relationships. When discipleship works effectively, it will quickly lead to multiple people working together to further the name of Jesus — aka the formation of churches. How does discipleship work in the context of a broader community?

Discipleship is an incredibly influential way of mobilizing people for the mission of Jesus. However, discipleship as defined and articulated above, does not fully illustrate the extent of social influence that a discipler has. An effective discipler will have tremendous influence, but by itself, the process of inviting, modelling, training and empowering does not fully describe how a person can be effective in their discipleship. Discipleship Potential describes what we must do to be effective multipliers but not how we must do it, especially in a broader social context.

Unfortunately, many people have not been adequately discipled. Much of our thinking about discipleship and mobilizing the church is influenced by the goal of building large church services. Our thinking about discipleship can be reduced to a program or course. As a result, many people do not know how to operate as effective leaders and disciple-makers. This is reinforced by modes of church in the West that are largely consumerist and popularity driven. If discipleship is an activity restricted to the talented and gifted, then our ability to reproduce will always be limited to the reach of the few rather than the many. Likewise, if church is "for us" then we will never be able to produce effective disciples.

Multiplication Power is a way of articulating and encouraging the ability to influence disciples without artificially building it around personality or gifting. Of course, there are some who are natural gatherers, extroverts and social conveners. However, multiplying influence should not, and cannot, be limited to the obviously gifted; it is a call for each one of us. We are all ambassadors. We are all sent into the world to proclaim the name of Jesus. Only when our thinking about multiplication is deep enough so as to include everyone will we be able to truly see movements of disciples take shape. Without this, we will always be limited to some variant of producer-consumer thinking. Alan Hirsch describes the power of multiplying leadership:

> *Inspirational Leadership can be described as a unique type of social power that comes from the personal integration and embodiment of great ideas… It involves a relationship between leaders and followers in which each influences the other to pursue common objectives with the aim of transforming followers into leaders in their own right.* — Alan Hirsch[47]

In essence, multiplying leadership occurs when the deep personal formation of powerful ideas in a leader is combined with the invitation for others to be likewise formed by those ideas; deep inner-life transformation and multiplication in others through the power of discipleship (outer life). However, without training, this is very easy to say and much harder to do. We must ask, how does Multiplication Power work? How do we grow in it?

Multiplication Power Factors

In the same vein as Discipleship Potential, Multiplication Power has discrete phases and levels to help understand and communicate the degree of a disciple's ability to multiply. These Multiplication Power Factors correlate to the Discipleship Potential Phases discussed in Chapter 1 as well as the Leadership Positions in Part 4.

Multiplication Power

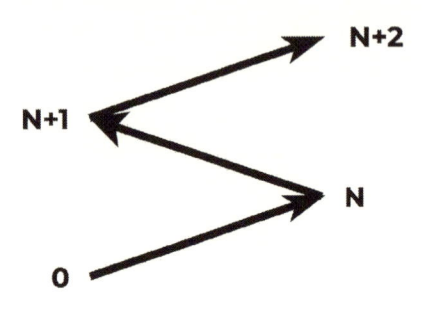

```
                    → N+2
        N+1 ←
                    → N
        0 →
```

The different levels of Multiplication Power, as illustrated in the diagram above, all follow a mathematical metaphor with "N" representing the disciple and the numbers following describing the degrees of separation of influence and leadership. We will briefly discuss the reach of influence of each level before dissecting the N+2 Leader in the next chapter.

Power of 0

The first phase of Multiplication Power is a Power of 0. This level corresponds to the Exposure and Attendee levels on the pipeline. As someone is just being introduced to the truths of the Gospel, they have do not have any Multiplication Power as the ability to multiply these truths is not yet developed.

Disciples with a Multiplication Power of 0 are still encouraged and empowered to invite others into their journey and questions. This phase is not to say that new disciples should be isolated or that they are alone in their journey; rather, that at this time, the brunt of their focus is on answering their own questions about faith, and their efforts should be directed at making commitments to the journey of discipleship. In mathematics, any number with a power of 0 results in an answer of 1. Likewise, someone with a

Multiplication Power of 0 is focused on answering the questions of 1 person: themselves.

Power of N

While a disciple with a Multiplication Power of 0 is focused on questions of what they believe and whether or not they will be committed to discipleship, someone with a Power of N will have answers to at least some of these questions. Corresponding to a disciple who has begun serving as a Team Member and has just gotten to a level of Understanding, a disciple with a Multiplication Power of N should be focused on self-leadership.

As mentioned many times, the journey of a disciple does not end with an acceptance of the Gospel; rather, that is when it truly begins. With this in mind, the focus of a disciple with a Power of N is growth. Again, they are encouraged to invite others into this journey with them; however, to truly multiply the Gospel into others, they must go beyond self-leadership to a place of leading others. In order to multiply, they cannot merely understand the Gospel, but must be fluent in it.

Power of N+1

A disciple with a Multiplication Power of N+1 will have gone beyond self-leadership and will have begun discipling others. The scope of their influence will now extend beyond themselves and into those they directly interact with. This power corresponds with the Team Leader position and Fluency phase of Discipleship Potential.

While certainly worthy of celebration, none of these steps (including N+1) has actually grown to the point where it is true multiplication. Thus far in Part 3, we have discussed fairly typical leadership development steps. However, it is in the N+2 Leader that multiplication truly begins, as their influence will extend beyond those they directly interact with. The N+2 Leader is what makes a discipleship movement possible.

The N+2 Leader

At the bedrock of the concept of Multiplication Power is the concept of the N+2 Leader. The N+2 Leader is a leader who can consistently lead people who lead others in turn; or in our context, make disciples who then make other disciples. The influence of an N+2 Leader is substantial because his/her influence is accelerated beyond the direct teaching, personal relationships and capacity of the person themselves.

N+2 Leadership

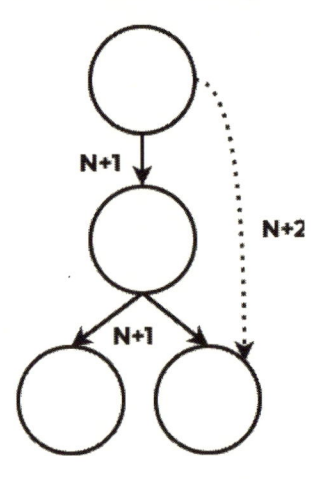

The "+2" in N+2 refers to the fact that the leader is able to influence someone at 2 degrees of relational separation. The separation means that the N+2 Leader may not have any direct influence, relationship with or even knowledge of the people who are being reached by those they are directly leading. Therein lies the power of N+2 Leadership: the N+2 Leader is able to activate those who they are leading to reach and impact their own networks without engaging those networks directly themselves.

The N+1 leader is the leader that can rally people to them. They are often charismatic, gifted and talented. People enjoy following N+1 leaders because they provide a context of safety and security. The N+2 Leader does not gather followers so much as they mobilize leaders. They specialize in mobilizing the collective influence of those they are leading. N+1 Leaders rely on their gifting, knowledge and wisdom to move forward — like a genius with a thousand helpers. The N+2 Leader activates the capacity of those around them.

N+2 Leadership is an invitation to rethink our understanding of influence and leadership through the lens of multiplication instead of addition. We are so conditioned to attract followers and build crowds that listen to us that we fail to see the power of true mobilizing leadership. The N+2 Leader is able to mobilize those around them to lead and disciple beyond their own abilities and gifts. The ability to mobilize people means that while their direct influence may be somewhat limited, their network influence can be substantial. An N+2 Leader may not have any form of public platform but still have a substantial cultural impact.

The N+2 concept was developed to help multiplying leaders think about their indirect impact, not just their direct impact. By continually reminding and focusing N+2 Leaders to think beyond one degree of separation, their impact becomes one of fostering reproducing disciples rather than consumers of a product. All of their discipleship focuses on training those they are discipling to think about others rather than themselves. N+2 Leaders focus on raising selfless leaders rather than self-absorbed ones.

Jesus was the ultimate N+2 Leader. Yes, he attracted large crowds at times, but his influence in those crowds was actually not as substantial as we might immediately think. It turns out that attracting a large crowd does not mean that any transformation has occurred (John 6:67). In fact, attracting large crowds can be antithetical to the discipleship process, as leaders inevitably end up pandering to the mob rather than mobilizing them for mission. Jesus instead invested very intentionally in a small group (the 12 disciples and to a lesser degree the 72) and mobilized them for mission. Jesus was ultimately a specialist at activating people; his entire ministry was shaped and defined by it. It is after Jesus' ascension that the disciples began to be truly effective in mission. Jesus, having intentionally invested into his few followers, released them for their own ministry. The Apostles repeat this process in Acts 8. When persecution comes, instead of centralizing their leadership, the people scattered and mobilized for the mission.

This is shocking. The church did not grow by great preaching or emotionally sung musical worship (although Peter and John did preach and songs of worship were sung). The Holy Spirit ultimately saw fit to mobilize the entire body for mission. The fact that persecution was the tool that the Holy Spirit used illustrates how counter to our natural tendencies it is to think as N+2 Leaders instead of N+1. N+2 Leadership is challenging to the leader because the praise and adulation that comes from successful leadership will largely be received by the N+1, not the N+2. N+2 Leaders derive their satisfaction from seeing others thrive and succeed. As noble as this sounds, it presents a real challenge, as the N+2 Leader must learn to serve and lead sacrificially, often without recognition or gratitude from those that are impacted.

Let us discuss three primary properties of the N+2 Leader: Everyone Sent, Faith and Grit.

Everyone Sent

The foundation for the N+2 Leader is what they believe about other people. In order to be an effective N+2 Leader, we must have a deep conviction that all people are included and equal participants in the mission of God.

One of the most important principles in the New Testament is the priesthood of all Believers. In the Old Testament, priesthood was restricted to a specific tribe (Levites) in a specific nation (Israel). This limitation meant that only a very few people could minister on behalf of the Lord, and an even smaller number of people, the High Priests, could even enter the presence of God; even then, only once a year after a complex set of elaborate sacrificial practices (Leviticus 16).

Jesus' work on the cross fundamentally changed this relationship. We no longer need a priest to be a mediator; instead, Jesus is our mediator! Everyone now has direct access to the creator of the universe, and each one of us has been invited to participate in the work of including people in the mission of God (1 Timothy 2:5).

We, as the body of Christ, form a nation of priests where we are all ministers and missionaries (1 Peter 2:9).

This theology matters so much because we so seldom live it out. When someone arrives in a church community, do we truly view them as someone who is invited into the mission of God and view our job as activating them for that mission? The importance of seeing everyone sent can be challenging because it essentially requires that we recognize that we are not that special or unique in our ministry callings. We are all called to be ministers which means that, to be frank, the key leaders are not that special.

When we meet people, our job is to see by faith what others may not see. We must learn to see the Holy Spirit-empowered potential which resides in every follower of Jesus — every follower. The N+2 Leader is someone who can see that potential and encourage, inspire, lead and challenge the person to see it themselves. The N+2 Leader is someone who sees in people what they likely do not yet see in themselves. This means that we must learn to look beyond first impressions, sinful habits or social inadequacies. That is not to say that impressionability and sin are irrelevant, but that we must not allow people's deficiencies to define our perspective on their capacity. We must learn to see people as Jesus sees them: as collaborators for the Kingdom of God.

Jesus' selection of his disciples is very telling. He selected religious zealots, fishermen, a tax collector (aka traitor/thief) and prostitutes. Notice that he did not select the religious elite, gifted communicators or well-liked individuals? Clearly Jesus was evaluating on a different paradigm than their performance or their talents.

This is part of a broader scriptural narrative: in ourselves we have absolutely nothing to bring to the table. God routinely selects those who are not that gifted or qualified for the job that he invites them into. See Abraham, Joseph, Moses, Rahab, Naomi, David, Jeremiah, Isaiah or Paul as a few examples of who were not qualified but that God used for his purposes. All of them had major black-marks against them that should have disqualified them for being used for God's eternal purposes. By contrast, from a worldly perspective, people like Esau, Samson, Solomon, King Saul and the Pharisees were all ideal candidates for selection but failed miserably in their leadership. What if we learned to view people from the lens of the Gospel as described in 1 Corinthians 1:

1 Corinthians 1:27-31

Instead, God has chosen what is foolish in the world to shame the wise, and God has chosen what is weak in the world to shame the strong. God has chosen what is insignificant and despised in the world—what is viewed as nothing—to bring to nothing what is viewed as something, so that no one may boast in his presence. It is from him that you are in Christ Jesus, who became wisdom from God for us—our righteousness, sanctification, and redemption, in order that, as it is written: Let the one who boasts, boast in the Lord.

God's paradigm is redemptive in nature. By his grace, he invites people to participate in his mission, not on the basis of their performance, but by his redemptive work in their lives. The fact that God can use literally anyone, even a donkey (Numbers 22:21-39), for his purposes is a key part of the narrative of scripture. N+2 Leadership is about learning to live in such a way that we understand that it is not about us or our gifts, but about the body of Jesus working together in harmony — every piece doing its part for the glory of God (Ephesians 4:16).

One point of clarification: the N+2 Leader does not immediately activate everyone into a position of leadership but disciples those around them towards being multiplying disciples. Leadership is a substantial responsibility that requires wisdom and experience (James 3:1). The job of the N+2 Leader is to invite people to progress towards being an effective disciple-making disciple. The N+2 Leader is wired to value and mobilize people, and as a result, is uneasy when those around them do not take intentional steps towards being activated in their own callings.

Faith

The second key mark of the N+2 Leader is that they are fundamentally people of faith. They learn to see and work towards that which does not yet exist. Their vision remains fixated on Jesus and his promises. After describing the hall of faith, the author of Hebrews invites us to fix our eyes on Jesus, the author and perfecter of our faith. Everything that is accomplished in the Kingdom of God is done so through faith. In fact, without faith, it is impossible to please God or to multiply at all.

The N+2 Leader is always thinking, deciding and acting on the basis of faith. Faith provides the lens through which they see the world around them, including other people and situations. Being saturated in and convinced of, the power of God, they literally live by faith not by sight (2 Corinthians 5:7). The N+2 Leader is constantly seeking to maximize their Kingdom impact. This is accomplished through living by faith. The N+2 Leader is someone who integrates gospel fluency, secure identity, missional living, radical generosity and crucial conversations into a life that is driven by faith.

N+2 Leadership is not just good strategic leadership, though it may be that as well. It is a way of living that is lead by the Holy Spirit. Faith and optimism are not synonymous. Optimism is a decision to see the best possible outcome in a situation. Not all N+2 Leaders will be optimistic by disposition. Faith, by contrast, is a choice to believe that regardless of the outcome, God's purposes will still be achieved. Faith is the decision to remain hopeful regardless of circumstances. This is not blind and senseless optimism; rather, our hope is based on the resurrection of the Son of God and his promises to build his church (Matthew 16:18).

The N+2 Leader is rarely in active control of their situations. They have chosen to live missionally and radically, so their lives are often dependent on the sustaining power of the Holy Spirit and his provision. Further, everything they do is actualized through empowering and encouraging others. The N+2 Leader cannot control people; they can only invite them to participate. This means that N+2 Leaders must continually trust their lives into the Lord's hands and his ability to use them for his glory.

Grit

The third property of the N+2 Leader is Grit. By grit, we mean a combination of endurance, tenacity, faithfulness and conviction. The call to multiplication is certainly not an easy one. There are likely to be regular setbacks and frustrations. People and situations will disappoint, criticisms will come and reasons to give up on the mission of Jesus will be plentiful. Failure, in a momentary sense, is inevitable for those living to mobilize and multiply others for the kingdom. Rather than sugarcoat the reality of serving Jesus, the N+2 Leader looks at the cost and still says, "Jesus, you are worth it!" Jesus himself promised substantial challenges in our efforts to follow him. He said that the world would hate those who follow him (John 15:18), and even that there would likely be family tension as a result (Luke 12:53). In fact, the call to follow Jesus will cost us our lives.

N+2 Leadership is about embracing of all of the mess and confusion with courage and faithfulness. The N+2 Leader puts faith in the promise of Jesus in John 16:33: that although challenges will come, Jesus has ultimately overcome them. Romans 5 puts this in a particularly powerful way, highlighting that, as our satisfaction is found in Jesus, he will work to refine and transform us, often through tremendously difficult situations.

> **Romans 5:1-5**
>
> *Therefore, since we have been declared righteous by faith, we have peace with God through our Lord Jesus Christ. We have also obtained access through him by faith into this grace in which we stand, and we rejoice in the hope of the glory of God. And not only that, but we also rejoice in our afflictions, because we know that affliction produces endurance, endurance produces proven character, and proven character produces hope. This hope will not disappoint us, because God's love has been poured out in our hearts through the Holy Spirit who was given to us.*

We live in a world where comfort is a priority, and the easy path is preferred. There is nothing comfortable or easy about the path of an N+2 Leader, as it depends on mobilizing people, not programs.

People are fallible, including, perhaps most importantly, ourselves. Our fallibility as humans means that mistakes will be made in the process of making disciples, and hurt will occur. The N+2 Leader is not defined by that hurt.

The N+2 Leader has the grit and perseverance to continue, even in the face of great challenges. Those challenges may be financial, circumstantial, mental, emotional, social or spiritual. Regardless, the N+2 Leader does not give up or give in to the pressure that comes from leadership and multiplication. There are always reasons to have self-doubt, but a gritty leader will prevail through their own doubts.

Faithfulness, like endurance, is a difficult character trait to develop because it is only developed through challenges (James 1:3). It's easy to be faithful when things are going well. Leadership is easy when people are following us willingly, reproducing consistently and speaking well of us. However, all leaders will face a point where the challenges come. It is in those challenges that grit is developed. It is very tempting when difficulties come to seek self-pity or to find someone to complain to, yet the N+2 Leader instead views the challenge as an opportunity to be refined and made stronger.

Furthermore, the N+2 Leader is able to help develop grit in those he/she is leading by leveraging the challenges that inevitably come in everyone's life. If not careful, this multiplying of grit can be done callously or even selfishly. Seeking to multiply grit into others does not mean the N+2 Leader does not care, is "hands-off" or is not active in the lives of those they are leading — quite the opposite! Multiplying grit is not about taking it easy but about equipping those they are leading to grow in their relationship with Jesus and develop the ability to persevere. Done effectively, the N+2 Leader will help the person they are leading move beyond the situation, by faith, to see the hand of Jesus in it and invite him to redeem that circumstance or challenge for his glory (2 Corinthians 4:15-17).

Such grit and determination does not arise from within but is actually found in Jesus himself! For the *joy* that was before him, Jesus endured the cross. N+2 Leaders are motivated by a joy in

Jesus and the reward that is knowing him. Jesus fills their frame at all times.

> **Hebrews 12:1-2**
>
> *Therefore, since we also have such a large cloud of witnesses surrounding us, let us lay aside every hindrance and the sin that so easily ensnares us. Let us run with endurance the race that lies before us, keeping our eyes on Jesus, the source and perfecter of our faith. For the joy that lay before him, he endured the cross, despising the shame, and sat down at the right hand of the throne of God.*

Grit does not come from sheer force of will, but from a deep and profound satisfaction in the things of Jesus. By continually keeping their vision on Jesus, the N+2 Leader is satisfied in him, not their successes. As a result, they are also not defined by their failures. Endurance, perseverance and grit come from a deep, well rooted and well formed relationship with Jesus.

Effective Multiplication

Effective multiplication is a product of the way we relate to other people, the way we lead those people and the language we use to do so. Multiplication starts with valuing people and inviting them to join the mission. However, one can believe that everyone is an equal participant in the mission of God, as discussed above, but still have difficulty actually living that belief out. Seeing the value in people, especially as potential multipliers themselves, is a skill that the N+2 Leader must learn. Similarly, the process of inviting other people to join the mission is also something of an art and must be honed. We will discuss both below with practical advice, as well as a valuable comment about the language we use.

Seeing Everyone

The first component in growing in our multiplication power is to address our implicit biases and barriers when it comes to who we can multiply. Perhaps one of the greatest limitations to our multiplication power is when we automatically, consciously or not, exclude people from the process. We will not be able to multiply effectively if we exclude ourselves or others from the mission. Our multiplication power can be detrimentally impacted by our predispositions towards certain types of people or groups. There could be a host of reasons for this, but there are a number that we can highlight here.

People Not Like Us

We, entirely naturally, tend to want to be around people who are similar to us. We look for lines of commonality and then build relationships around those lines. Most of the world, both inside and outside the church, tend to associate along tribal lines. They may be something as obvious as ethnicity, education or social status. We might also associate along more subtle lines such as our personality preferences. This exclusion stems partly from automatic assumptions.

While we cannot possibly do a full treatment of the psychosocial dynamics around subcultures and ethnicity, it is a critical point to highlight since our exclusion of those not like us is profoundly anti-Gospel. The Gospel, as discussed in the dialogue regarding the reversal of Babel, is about bringing humanity together under a common King, Jesus. Paul writes in Galatians that the racial, ethnic and gender lines that formerly excluded people from participation in the mission of God have been gloriously undone under the grace of Jesus.

> **Galatians 3:28**
>
> *There is no Jew or Greek, slave or free, male and female; since you are all one in Christ Jesus.*

N+2 Leaders intentionally seek out and build relationships with those who are not like them. They recognize that our collective diversity is a strength to be leveraged. By activating people not like them, the N+2 Leader can reach people who may be outside of their personal social-network or be closed off to them.

The key with this point is that it is intentional. The N+2 Leader must continuously remain vigilant to their bias for comfort and uniformity in their relationships. They must seek to activate and mobilize people who are not like them. Whatever their individual comfort zone is, they must be willing to go outside of it to reach those not like them.

Effective multiplying leaders must be wired to watch-out for those who are under-engaged or under-challenged. This wiring for the excluded people means that when they view crowds of people, instead of looking for those who already belong, they look for those who do not belong. Especially in social situations, those with high multiplication power have trained themselves to be on the lookout for the creation of cliques or closed off groups and work to integrate people rather than isolate them.

This intentional erasing of the lines that divide us also speaks volumes to the world around us. Almost every major movement of the Gospel over the last 2000 years has been accompanied by a radical inclusivity. In the midst of cultural racism and sexism, the Gospel always brings people together. Seeking out people not like us is an essential part of any discipleship movement, and thus it is vital that our N+2 Leaders live this out.

Over Emphasis on Charisma and Attractiveness [48]

Much of the Western church is built around what happens on a public platform. Leaders who are celebrated tend to be leaders who are comfortable and natural in front of large groups of people. As a result, we tend to think that charisma is a key ingredient in N+2 Leadership.

It is not.

Similarly, it can be tempting to believe that leaders can be selected based on having a magical "it factor" or some form of "cool" that causes them to gain followers naturally. The N+2 Leader is not a leader who attracts followers by force of their personality but one who mobilizes those who are around them for greater impact. The N+2 Leader is one who can activate others for mission, not build a following around themselves. The job of the leader, as described in Ephesians 4, is to equip others for ministry, not to do it themselves. Too often we celebrate the N+1 leaders in our discipleship environments when we should be celebrating the N+2 Leaders, whose influence may be entirely unnoticed by the crowds.

It is the cultural emphasis on these charismatic, talented leaders that results in many people assuming that they simply could never be a leader or plant a church. We must ask: on what biblical basis are we basing the assumption that church planting or multiplying leadership are somehow connected to personality? As we have already discussed, there is a great deal of Biblical material communicating precisely the opposite!

In many ways, charisma can serve as a liability for multiplication because the charismatic leader is wired to attract attention to themselves. They are essentially saying, "follow me" over and over again. Attracting attention can cause the charismatic leader to build discipleship around themselves, rather than mobilizing and multiplying new leaders in their gifts.

Communication and leadership skills will be a vital component of a fully activated N+2 Leader. However, these can be developed in even the most introverted, shy, non-charismatic person. In short, communication and leadership can be learned skills, not innate ones.

In highlighting the over-emphasis on charisma, we must be careful not to swing the pendulum the other way and begin to penalize the charismatic, attractive leader prematurely. The emphasis in this section is to try to shift our propensity away from our wiring for exclusively attractive leaders, and to help us realize the people who God has entrusted to our care are far more capable than we realize.

Boldly Making 'The Ask'

The multiplication process always begins with an invitation. Just as Jesus said to his disciples "come follow me," so too must we invite people to join us on the mission. The invite step discussed under Discipleship Potential is a largely personal one-on-one invitation to begin a discipleship journey together. Partnership in leading may be a component of this invitation as well. From the perspective of the multiplying leader, 'the ask' is an invitation to give time, talent or treasure towards the specific work they are doing. The ask is the moment where the multiplier has identified an opportunity to mobilize someone for mission. The ask can be one of the most influential and essential tools in our toolbox.

These asks could be something as simple as joining a team, serving our city or taking a leadership role in a Simple Church. However, they can also include a request for a substantial financial sacrifice, the request to move cities or the ask to give up a job to invest in the mission. Big invitations or small ones are all built on the same theological foundations.

When we invite someone to participate in the mission, we are almost always inviting someone to do something they have not done before. It will likely be challenging, uncomfortable and require a measure of sacrifice. If asking did not require taking a step of faith, the person we are asking likely would have done it already! When we make an ask, we do so based on faith. For the multiplying leader to be effective in making the ask, it is crucial that we do so from a place of firm conviction and faith.

Start With Why

The basic building block of the ask is a clear and well thought out vision for what we are inviting someone into. For better or worse, our culture is wired to ask "why" to almost every question. It is crucial that in every invitation we start with why, not what. The specific action that we are inviting people to take will require a well thought out reason for why they should join in this mission. Nearly all asks will require the person we are asking to give something up, be it time, money, prestige or opportunities. If we are unsure of why we are inviting someone and unclear with what we are asking them to do, we will struggle to be effective with the ask.

Identifying Gold

Oftentimes, when we make an ask, we are inviting someone to take a step into the unknown, and our ask may be met with the response of "I could never do that" or "I don't know how" or "there must be someone better." Notice how all of those objections have to do with some sort of inadequacy in the person we are asking, whether it is perceived or real. The job of the multiplier is to call the person to that which they would otherwise not do. Multiplying leaders help people see in themselves what they had never seen before. They identify and draw out the very best in people! Oftentimes, there will be just a small glimmer of the potential a person has and an effective multiplier will help that glimmer genuinely shine.

Part of effective multiplication is helping people believe that what the Lord can do in them is greater than they realize. It is this Jesus-centric self-confidence that enables someone to begin to take bold steps in their faith. By affirming and speaking into the way that God is moving in someone's life and calling them to continue to develop their skills and abilities in that area, we can multiply strong and capable leaders. Encouragement may be one of the most powerful tools that we can use to help make our asks effective.

Sacrifice is Worth It

As mentioned, when we invite someone to participate in the mission, it will almost certainly require some kind of sacrifice. Many people will feel guilty for making the ask and either water the ask down to something more palatable or take the extra load onto themselves. Few things can derail an effective ask as much as a sense of personal guilt accompanying it. When we are inviting people to participate in the things of Jesus, we are ultimately inviting people to do what is best for them, even if it is sacrificial. Jesus himself has called us to pick up our cross and follow him. Any ask that we make is simply a piece of the bigger ask to give our lives for the cause of Jesus. We must be absolutely convinced that serving Jesus with our whole lives is the best possible way to spend them. This conviction forms the basis of understanding that the invitation to sacrifice our lives for the name of Jesus is worth it.

The invitation to serve others is not a burden we are laying on people. It is merely an invitation to live the Gospel and to exercise the 5 Discipleship Emphases in practice. Without an invitation to actually put those emphases into practice, most people will just continue on the same worldly trajectory. The invitation to give their lives for the Kingdom of Jesus may be one of the greatest gifts we can give people. Jesus himself has said that his "yoke" is not a burden but in fact life-giving and restful (Matthew 11:28-30). Jesus made this statement knowing that those he was inviting would pay a steep price for doing so.

In making the ask, we are fundamentally beginning the process of shifting people's attention from themselves to the Kingdom of Jesus. At first, this appears to be unnatural and difficult, but given time, people will begin to value things of eternity instead of this world. Is there a better gift that we could possibly give people (Colossians 3:2)?

A culture of sending is built in a culture of sacrifice. Effective multiplication will always result in some form of sending others to go and bring the Gospel to a place where it has not yet been brought. By making small asks, we are actually preparing people to live sent into their world. As people practice sacrificing in small ways, this prepares them to sacrifice much larger areas of their life later. We cannot see people sent unless we first invite them to let go of what they are holding onto. For this reason, 'the ask' is not just a tool for multiplication; it is a crucial part of discipleship.

We are Better Together

The ask is always an invitation to community and relationship. We ask people to join the mission as a double-sided affirmation of our care for them and our passion for the mission. We do not ask people simply because we have a task that needs to be completed and they are a convenient solution. Multiplying leaders must value people, not tasks, projects or opportunities. However, it is through the task, project or opportunity that the gifts, talents and passions in the person are activated. The multiplying leader will affirm the intrinsic and inherent value in the individual by inviting them into a secure and loving relationship. Simultaneously, the multiplying leader will activate that person to do more than they can on their own. In this way, the multiplying leader is inviting people to be fully alive by providing the relational environment for people to live with purpose.

To live a purposeful life requires that we exist in meaningful community and complete meaningful work (Genesis 1:22, 2:18). The multiplying leader creates space for both of these necessary requirements to exist simultaneously.

Success, No Matter What

Because the process of making an ask is grounded in recognizing the value in a person and inviting them to relationship and participation in the purposes of God, the ask is one of the most life-giving things that we can do for a person! Appropriately done, when a multiplying leader invites someone to the mission, it should be received as an affirmation and an encouragement to the person. When our identity is secure in Jesus as sons and daughters of the King, it will provide us with a platform by which we can invite others. In doing so, we are extending the Love of God to them, helping them see that they, too, are invited to be sons and daughters of the King. We do not ask from a place of lack, need or poverty. We ask people because it is good to do so, both for them and for us! In this case, even if we are rejected and the answer is an emphatic "no," we still have affirmed, encouraged and invited someone to the mission.

The ultimate goal in making the ask is not to see a task accomplished, but rather to see people made fully alive in Jesus and in so doing, see Jesus glorified. Yes, tasks, projects and goals are a part of that, but they are the means, not the end. We must resist the urge to be frustrated or discouraged when we are rejected, but instead, as Jesus says, dust ourselves off and keep going (Matthew 10:13-14).

No Is Rarely NO!

With all of the above affirmed, having someone say "no" to the ask is not always the end. In fact, "no" can be the beginning of a conversation. When someone says "no," they are really saying that the invitation as they understand it and their priorities do not align. The "no" could come from all sorts of reasons. It is important that we take the time to understand the reason behind the "no" and not just take it at face value. A "no" could be rooted in deep insecurity that they are not capable; in which case, we must encourage them, reminding them that the Holy Spirit empowers us when we are weak and explaining that we will journey with them as well. A "no" could flow from a misplaced set of priorities, in which case the "no" may be a gateway to a healthy and fruitful crucial conversation. A "no" could come from a simple logistical challenge, in which case it may be an excuse so we should work to get past the logistics to understand the real issue at play, or it could be as simple as finding a solution to that challenge that they had not thought of yet. A "no" may also be due to another desire or work that they were hoping to do, in which case we should encourage them to take decisive steps towards that work.

We could enumerate many possible reasons that a person says "no." The key idea is to view "no" as an opportunity to better understand, disciple and challenge someone to continue to surrender their life to Jesus. If we learn to consider "no" as an opportunity instead of a barrier, our multiplication power will increase.

Language

The New Testament has a fascinating use of language. When the church leaders, particularly Paul, John and Peter, wrote to the churches, their language was very intentional. In almost every case where they write to the church, they address them as "fellow brothers and sisters" or "saints."[49]

Much of our language in the church is very hierarchical, with there being a clear distinction between pastors and volunteers. While the leaders in the church did occasionally leverage a title (e.g. Apostle), they regularly placed themselves on the same footing as the rest of the church with language such as "fellow servant".

Our language, in many cases, serves a contrary narrative to the priesthood of all believers. We do not volunteer for the church, nor do we "work" for the church — both of those are words that connote pay and salary. Regardless of the question of being paid or not, we are commanded to give our lives for the service of the

Kingdom of God. The invitation to be a multiplying leader is not some form of Christian volunteerism or do-good-ism. We are commanded to serve the poor, proclaim the Gospel and love one another as a way of life. Our lives must be structured to maximize our impact towards that end. Words such as "staff" and "volunteer," and honourifics such as "Pastor" serve to reinforce the divide between the clergy and laity. They may arise from good intentions, but given the substantial barriers that exist in getting people to normalize a high-call, high-sacrifice Christian life, any and all barriers that cause people to think they are not "called" to the same degree is problematic.

First and foremost, the church must live and act as a family of disciples who live on mission together. It is crucial that our language reflects the call to be a family on mission, not an organization that offers goods and services.

14

Multiplication Imperatives

To help encourage multiplying leaders in their day to day decision making, we have come up with nine statements to serve as reminders to the multiplying leader. We call them the 'Multiplication Imperatives' and they help leaders operate in the context of community in ways that help maximize their Multiplication Power. When every leader operates in harmony while living into these values, these decision making habits help create a culture of multiplication.

1) Multiply Everything

Multiply everything is the starting point for the multiplying leader, so naturally it is the first Multiplication Imperative. The multiplying leader is constantly looking for opportunities to see others activated, stretched and mobilized to participate in the mission of God. The imperative, multiply everything, is another way of saying Go Make Disciples. The multiplying leader is the master discipler.

Multiplication means that we look at who Jesus has put into our life, both believers and non-believers, and ask ourselves the question, *"How can I help the people around me know Jesus and participate in his mission?"* Multiply everything is something that is designed to occur in our natural rhythms of life. The invitation to multiply everything is an invitation to structure our lives so that we can be effective multipliers. A caveat here is that we need to prayerfully and humbly recognize that sometimes our rhythms are anti-multiplication. Anti-multiplication moments are when we reject our God-designed nature to be creators, learners and disciplers. A typical expression of this is the shift from multiplier to consumer in our mentality. Consuming is the ultimate anti-multiplication strategy.

This imperative applies to all multiplying leaders in all spheres of life. The true multiplying leader views every role, task or situation as an opportunity to strengthen the body of Christ and see the Church thrive. The imperative to multiply everything is to see our lives through the lens of multiplying discipleship.

The imperative to multiply everything means that our lives must be lived in a way that is inclusive. We invite people into our world, to come and join us as we chase after Jesus. This starts in incredibly mundane moments: work, the grocery store and even the gym are examples of mundane moments that we can invite others into. Multiplication can happen in the routine as well as unexpected moments as we open up conversations with complete strangers. Multiplication can happen in our workplaces as we naturally and transparently open up our lives. Multiplication can happen on creative teams, one-on-one discipleship, technical teams or in music. We can multiply everything because in everything we do we are given the opportunity to invite and mobilize the gifts, talents and passions of others.

It should be apparent that multiply everything is also a fantastic strategy to build healthy teams even in a non-Christian environment. This is because multiplication is about inclusion of others into what we are doing. Regardless of the situation, multiplication naturally results in healthy teams.

Multiply everything means that we look to include others into our teams or serving opportunities. We understand that our job is not just to complete the task, because the task is never the goal. Loving, valuing and mobilizing people is always the goal. To multiply everything means that regardless of what we do, we seek to value and include others in the process. The task provides a natural and simple opportunity to include someone in what we are doing. The task, however, is not the goal; neither is a big team or a successful program. The ultimate goal is passionate followers of Jesus raised and sent from us, and who in turn do the same . Only in keeping that goal front and centre is our work truly multiplying.

2) Pull Together

Multiplying leaders always work as a part of a larger team, considering that pulling together is a way of encouraging robust teamwork in everything that we do. Pulling together alludes to a vision of a team pulling on a rope all together at the same time and in the same direction; connected to that rope is the mission at hand. The value of Everyone Sent means that our objective is to see every person engaged in the life of mission that Jesus has called us to. Naturally, as people are mobilized, chaos can ensue if we are not going the same direction together. We must all pull together in the same direction, towards the same goals. Of course, one aspect of this is leadership, but the attitudes and ways in which we work together are just as important as the leaders who set the vision and direction.

Diversity

One of the guiding principles of pulling together is the necessity for diversity in both our teams and our work. No one person, team or group is capable of fulfilling the full mission that Jesus has called us to. We need each other's gifts, talents and abilities.

> **1 Corinthians 12:12**
> *For just as the body is one and has many parts, and all the parts of that body, though many, are one body—so also is Christ.*

Our multiplication power substantially increases when we value diversity in the body of Christ. It is what allows us all to collaborate and understand what each person brings to help us thrive. Even if we engage someone who is not a good fit strategically, relationally or competently for what we are personally working on, our valuing of the body compels us to find a place where that person can thrive. It is in these moments that we can help accelerate the health of the whole body of Christ and not just ourselves and those like us.

There is no room for "greater" or "lesser" roles. The multiplying leader understands that every person, no matter how diverse or different, is a valuable and important contributor to the Kingdom. There is no room for "more important people" or "more honourable roles"; every person is called to fulfill a critical and valuable role in the whole. When one person is not working properly with the others, it significantly affects the ability of everyone to make disciples.

Unity

Pulling Together means that we all work together in the same direction for the benefit of the whole. There is no room for personal ambition in a multiplying movement. It is always about "we," not "I." One of the most important principles that Jesus outlines in his instructions to his disciples is the necessity for unity in their lives and work (John 17:23). Something powerful happens when we are all working together without selfish-ambition corrupting our work (Philippians 2:13).

Bitterness can very quickly seep into things when we are working on a team and feel like we are not getting a fair deal or like we are doing more work with less reward than others. It is in these moments that we are formed by the Gospel. The Gospel is unfair; unfair because Jesus did for us what we did not deserve or earn. Fairness is not always the goal in the context of a team; the mission is the goal! The first course of action to take when we feel the unity being threatened is to immediately uproot the bitterness and replace it with an intentional and willful joy (Hebrews 12:15).

Ownership

Part of pulling together is that each person has been empowered and entrusted with a specific set of responsibilities and people to disciple. Each person has their specific part of the 'rope.' It is absolutely critical that our teams are empowered to own their part and that their energy is focused on the people and responsibilities that are in their hands. Such ownership means having the ability to make and execute decisions while being willing to be held accountable for those decisions. Ownership and accountability go hand-in-hand.

Awareness

The need for each of us to take ownership of the specific people and opportunities in front of us can lead to an isolationist or siloed way of working together. A popular phrase to encourage this ownership is "stay in your lane." This can have a negative effect of leading people to only work on their projects or their people without an awareness of how others around them are doing or how their decisions affect other people.

In reality, isolation and independence is impossible; everyone has to work cross-functionally to some regard. We need to have our eyes up to see how the people around us are doing and seek to thank them and support them in their work. Practically, this can mean asking if we can help or serve them when we have downtime or asking if there is anything we can do better to support or encourage them.

3) Believe the Best

In our work as multiplying leaders, we are required to trust those around us to make disciples, fulfill their responsibilities and communicate clearly with the rest of the community. Inevitably, there will be moments where that trust is tested, stretched or broken. There will be all kinds of moments when those around us will frustrate or even hurt us: both unintentionally and sometimes intentionally. It is in these moments that our resolve to be like Jesus is genuinely tested. Our attitude in those moments is a choice. When we do not know someone's motives or intentions or are tempted to be bitter, we can make a choice about how we will respond. We can either respond by choosing cynicism and anger, resulting in passive-aggressive or even aggressive responses, or we can choose to believe the best about that person.

What we choose to believe is always a decision that is in our hands. When we do not know all the facts conclusively, we can choose to view things through a lens of optimism, grace and trust. By always choosing to believe the best, it helps to structure our relationships on a foundation of trust versus suspicion. This trusting foundation in turn provides the firm footing to navigate conflict when it inevitably arises. Many of us, by default, operate from a paradigm of hurt due to our past experiences. Through prayer, we must intentionally seek a paradigm shift in our communities to a paradigm of trust.

This does not mean that we whitewash the facts or take a naive approach to every relationship. Rather, the invitation to believe the best means that in the absence of clarity we make the choice to trust and be gracious.

There is a special case of Believing the Best as it applies to the people who are leading us. Oftentimes, our leaders may not be able to communicate clearly why something is happening or happened. Further, they are likely navigating complexities that we do not fully understand in their decision making processes. Their decisions and actions may be wise and prudent, but we may struggle to see how that is the case without knowing all the facts and challenges that they do. It is in these moments that we must choose to maintain unity and believe the best about that that are leading us. Multiplying leaders will carry a tremendous burden and one of the best ways to support them is to choose to believe the best and encourage others to do the same.

With this in mind, there are four steps we can take to help us believe the best in the context of our relationships.

Seek Understanding

When we are unsure what is happening or why something happened, our first job is to graciously and patiently seek to understand what is happening. We do so with the base assumption being one of optimism and trust. As we seek to understand, we do so through a lens of relationship.

Communicate Transparently

When we are seeking understanding or navigating a challenging conversation, we must communicate openly and transparently. We need to carefully communicate what we are feeling and why we are feeling it. Sweeping the issue under the rug will never resolve it so we must clearly communicate our perspective. If both parties resolve to believe the best and are committed to the relationship, open communication will only serve to strengthen the relationship.

Forgive Quickly

Regardless of the situations and the facts, we are commanded to forgive (Colossians 3:13, Matthew 6:14). We cannot hold on to the wound or the issue hoping that in doing so we will be vindicated. The cross compels us to forgive, so we must forgive. We must extend the hand of forgiveness and release the issue from our control.

Never Ever Gossip

Lastly, we must never ever gossip. Few things are as toxic and destructive to a culture of multiplication and trust as gossip. However, very few people will acknowledge they are gossiping; normally it is disguised under the veil of "venting" or "getting something off my chest." If there is an issue with someone, talk to them about it directly or raise it with a leader. However, in most cases, it will either boil down to an invitation to humbly get over it or to raise a legitimate issue directly with the person. See Matthew 18 for Jesus' counsel on how to navigate these issues.

One comment for the multiplying leader: if someone is routinely causing a breakdown in trust, then discipline may likely be necessary, be it removal from the team, a firm rebuke or another form of discipline. The invitation to believe the best is not an invitation to be complacent or to lower the bar of expectation.

4) Celebrate the Best

Celebrating the best is an invitation to be people who celebrate others' successes: big or small. In a world of self-promotion, celebrating the best is an invitation to promote others! The multiplying leader never leads so as to serve themselves; they are always working to see those around them succeed and thrive. There are a million reasons to be critical or negative about a situation or a person. By encouraging and championing a culture of celebration, we can place the focus on the positive rather than the negative.

> **1 Thessalonians 5:12-13**
>
> *Now we ask you, brothers and sisters, to give recognition to those who labor among you and lead you in the Lord and admonish you, and to regard them very highly in love because of their work.*

People will be much more likely to emulate what they see celebrated in others. By specifically and clearly identifying where someone has "hit the target," we can encourage people to keep going. The goals in multiplication can be fuzzy and confusing for people initially as they are so counter-cultural in many ways. By celebrating people, we can help provide clarity around what a multiplying discipleship movement actually looks like in reality, not just theory.

An important consideration when celebrating the best is to be as specific as possible. The goal in celebration is of course to encourage the person, but it is also to help reinforce for the whole community the kinds of actions and decisions we want to see multiplied. Celebrating the best requires thought and intentionality to identify the specific area in which someone can be celebrated and then to articulate why they are worth celebrating.

Our goal in celebrating is to paint a picture of the goal and invite people to continue to take a step towards it. The objective is not so much to celebrate people's perfection as it is to celebrate that fact that they are "directionally correct." Perfection is very rare, especially in young, fast-moving, multiplying communities. The objective is not perfection, per-say, but to ensure that people are headed in the correct direction. Celebration is a powerful tool that we can use to encourage people to persevere in that direction. With this in mind, it is also important to celebrate both "big" and "small" victories. While it is encouraging to celebrate notable and significant achievements, these larger moments only come as a result of numerous small steps and everyday decisions. When we only celebrate "big" moments, it can have the result of discouraging those who feel like they are not able to accomplish "big" victories.

One of the most powerful tools in celebrating the best is the power of story or testimony. By encouraging people to share their success, we give them permission to bring what they have been working on into the light so that others can be inspired and encouraged. Without the invitation to celebrate, this kind of storytelling is likely to be misunderstood as self-promotion. Testimonies are also powerful because they help to diversify the voice of the multiplying leader. Rather than one or two leaders always speaking and people getting fatigued by listening to them, by inviting others to share their own stories, the multiplying leader is able to demonstrate what the goals look like, and in so doing, normalize those actions in the community while also reinforcing a culture of Everyone Sent to multiply everything.

5) Make it Better

There is always room for improvement, both as disciples and as multiplying leaders. We need to constantly be growing and developing both as individuals and corporately. Until every tribe and tongue has responded to the grace of Jesus, our mission is not complete. In order to fulfill that mission, we will need to bring innovation and creativity to the table. In our mission to see Christ glorified in his church, we must constantly seek to ask the question, *"How can we improve?"* Continuous improvement is a well-worn tactic in the manufacturing and business world that allows for a constant feedback loop between coming up with an idea and improving it. It is only sensible that we ask the question, *"How can we be more effective?"* in our leadership.

Innovation & Creativity

In order to reach people who we are not yet reaching, multiplying leaders must do things that we are not yet doing. Innovation in the context of multiplying discipleship is absolutely paramount. We must be willing to do things we have not done before by improving upon the work that we have already done.

There is always room for improvement and creativity in the work that we are doing, especially discipleship. It is often in the creativity that comes from a desire to 'make it better,' that we find ourselves the most energized in our work. God invited us to partner with him in discipleship as free and creative moral agents. God gave us creativity for a reason: to use it so that he can be glorified.

Part of creatively improving that which we are responsible for is a willingness to sometimes break the unwritten social and organizational "rules" that confine our thinking. Of course, multiplying leadership cannot be rebellious, but at times we will need to challenge the status quo and suggest improvements.

It is very tempting, largely because of the amount of effort involved, to allow the status-quo to rule in the things that we are leading. Innovation is hard work. However, as the idiom goes, "If it was easy someone would have done it already." A multiplying leader will not despair in the face of the challenges presented by improvement. Instead, the challenges will cause them to galvanize their resolve and press forward until a solution is found.

Reflect

In order to catalyze the innovation process, the multiplying leader will need to reflect upon areas of weakness that need improvement. A multiplying leader must be willing to take an honest and critical look at the things they are leading and ask questions of themselves and their team. Multiplying leaders constantly are asking, *"How can we make it better?"* The reflective process should be both intentional and regularly occurring. A multiplying leader must step back and examine their work and the attitudes and work of others and ask how the entire team and community can improve.

The desire for improvement is not a mere matter of applying human effort with greater precision and effort. Rather, we invite the Holy Spirit to grant us the wisdom to understand our own weaknesses and seek his wisdom in our decision making. Continuous improvement in the context of discipleship is not just a human endeavour but one of partnership with the Holy Spirit. It is this partnership that liberates us from an overtly performance centred mindset; instead, focusing our attention on the joy that comes from glorifying Jesus. The objective in our improvement is not human glory but Jesus' glory.

The crucial component in making it better is that it is a solution-oriented imperative, not a problem-oriented or critical one. Of course, part of improving things is identifying areas of weakness, but the multiplying leader approaches those weaknesses with the confidence and resolve to create a culture where the entire team or community believes a solution can be found.

6) Best Idea Wins

Naturally, as we begin to ask the question, "*How can we make it better?*" both fantastic and less than great suggestions will be tabled. A multiplying leader has the responsibility to ensure that there is an environment where the best ideas are the ones that are accepted and celebrated. The best idea wins is about having the humility to submit to others' ideas for the sake of innovation.

Multiplying leadership, by nature, is not a selfish leadership where things like recognition or praise are particularly relevant. A true multiplying leader derives joy from seeing others ideas thrive, not just their own. Multiplying leaders create an environment where the team works together to arrive at the best possible outcome. When every person at the table brings their best ideas and insights, confident that they are loved independent of their performance, the best ideas can rise to the top.

As we seek the best possible ideas, the multiplying leader must keep the emphasis on the goal — on the people, not just the task at hand. We must continually remember the "why" behind the particular challenge that is in front of us. By focusing our attention on the big-picture motivations behind what we are doing, the tendency to become defensive or territorial can be mitigated.

To create an environment where the best ideas win, we will need to cultivate a secure identity in those we lead: security in Christ as well as security in the broader family of God. The acceptance, or rejection, of someone's ideas, does not speak to their intrinsic worth or value. Many immature leaders will struggle to follow when their ideas are not accepted because they cannot distinguish between themselves and their ideas. If their idea is rejected they take it personally and feel offended. Part of discipling multiplying leaders is helping them navigate rejection of their ideas.

There are three crucial ingredients to getting to the best idea: listening, advocating and deciding.

Listening

For a team to get to the best possible ideas, we must stop and listen to the ideas. To listen to an idea means that we hear it and understand the idea. In many cases, as good ideas are brought forward, they arrive in a nascent form, underdeveloped and poorly articulated. But it might be a great idea!

For this reason we need to explore and dissect ideas as they arrive, patiently asking questions, adding value and testing to see if the idea holds any merit. For a vocal leader, the listening phase of an idea can prove challenging. They may want to automatically move on to their ideas without waiting for a more timid member of the team to present or share their thoughts. The multiplying leader must help mediate the team to ensure that as people share ideas, the best ones are fully articulated.

Advocating

The best idea can only win if the idea is shared! Many of the greatest ideas remain locked up in the minds of those who did not share them! Part of learning to be a multiplying leader is developing the skill of sharing and advocating for your ideas. Advocating for an idea can be difficult because as we advocate for an idea, we become personally invested and attached to that idea. Our passion for ideas can be fuel for tremendous creativity, but we must be careful that as passionate as we are about our ideas, we carry them with a humble heart, willing to submit to the rest of the team and the greater good with a positive attitude.

Advocating and listening must go hand-in-hand. We must both present ideas as well as listen to others. A multiplying leader will know when to listen and when to speak.

Deciding

Finally, for the best idea to win, we must actually make concrete decisions. It is in this phase that the challenge of leadership arises. The multiplying leader must be able to make concrete, specific and actionable decisions.

Decisions are often unpopular, and rarely will everyone feel entirely satisfied with the course of action. Leadership is not about arriving at a perfect consensus on everything. Rather, multiplying leaders create a space where the entire team feels secure to share and articulate their ideas. Once the brainstorming or ideation phase is complete, the multiplying leader must make a decision and act on that decision. We must actually select the best idea in order for the best idea to win. Multiplying leadership requires the courage to make difficult decisions.

7) Take the Leap

If the best idea wins, then we must take the leap to execute that idea. Multiplying leaders are leaders who, through the ideas, passions and creativity of others move problems to solutions and solutions to reality. We reach a point where the time for planning, dreaming and talking are over and we must take a step of faith: believing that even though we do not have certainty of the outcome, we trust that Jesus will be glorified in our work.

Taking the leap is all about faith. We choose to believe that what may seem impossible without God will be possible because of his grace and goodness. We choose to be a people of faith — people of hope. As Hebrews 11:1 invites us, we choose to be confident and full of hope, believing that what cannot yet see will come to pass. Hebrews pushes this idea so far to say that without faith, it is impossible to please God (Hebrews 11:6). At a basic level, the faith that Hebrews is talking about is faith in the saving grace of Jesus' work on the cross. Without faith in his grace, we cannot glorify God. But the faith described in Hebrews is not just faith in that past action of Jesus; it is faith in his future goodness as evidenced in our actions! Hebrews makes it abundantly clear that God is pleased when we choose to build our lives upon his promises. God is pleased when we choose to trust him with our lives, livelihoods, futures, insecurities, hopes and dreams!

One of the most precious promises we can depend on as a multiplying leader is that of Jesus in Matthew 16:18 where Jesus says, *"...I will build my church and the gates of hell will not prevail against it!"* We take bold steps of faith because Jesus has promised to build his church and nothing will stand in the way. While we may fail momentarily, we can be bold because we know the end of the story; Jesus wins!

Taking the leap may involve considerable risk to our individual reputations, finances and livelihood, as the Apostle Paul highlights in Romans 16:4 in celebrating the risks of Priscilla and Aquila for the cause of the Gentile churches. Taking the leap does not come with a guarantee of the outcome. We cannot predict how people will respond or what unforeseen challenges will present themselves.

Taking the leap is not just about the success; it is actually about obedience to the leading of the Holy Spirit. As sent people, we must go to the world with the unchanging message of Jesus in creative, innovative and new ways. We must enter every sphere, domain and people group, calling them to Jesus. We must extend the invitation to our brothers and sisters in the faith to take up the call and serve our King wholeheartedly. Why? Because Jesus has said we must and he is our King.

We do not jump without careful consideration or exercising wisdom. We wrestle to make sure the best ideas have been explored and the poor ones discarded. We bring to bear the best research, insights and input that we can put our hands on. As we prepare to take the leap, we take the command to steward our lives and our resources seriously. However, we cannot allow fear to rule or slow us down. We must be bold, decisive and unafraid in our moves to see Jesus glorified. We must invite others to put their hope in Jesus and step boldly into the future that he has called us to.

8) Fail Forward

Short-term success in the mission of multiplying disciples is by no means assured; rather, the opposite is true. In desiring to see people know Jesus, we will certainly make mistakes, drop the ball and let people down. In many cases we will take the leap and be met with failure. The failure in many cases will be very real. It may be costly relationally or financially. Our failure will certainly come with hurt and grief. There are some Christians who are uncomfortable with calling our missteps "failures" because they can be redeemed — and they can! However, in calling our mistakes failures, we are acknowledging that there is a serious pain that can come when our dreams turn into nightmares.

The Gospel reminds us that sin is real and that failure is real. The goodness of the Gospel is not found by watering down sin or failure so much so that it no longer is noticeable. We do not dismiss it as a figment of our imagination. Instead, the Gospel faces the full horror of sin and failure and declares that Jesus is greater! It is in our weaknesses, sin, brokenness and failures that the glory of the Gospel shines the brightest. The Apostle Paul points to his own weaknesses in 2 Corinthians 12.

> ### 2 Corinthians 12:9-10
> *Therefore, I will most gladly boast all the more about my weaknesses, so that Christ's power may reside in me. So I take pleasure in weaknesses, insults, hardships, persecutions, and in difficulties, for the sake of Christ. For when I am weak, then I am strong.*

We will also run into situations where our weaknesses are exposed through our mistakes and failures. However, as multiplying leaders whose hope is in Jesus, we do not despair or lose heart.

Our hope and security is and always will be in Jesus, not in the outcome of our efforts. While that truth does not necessarily alleviate the pain of failure, it does give us a footing to stand on when we feel weak and insecure.

We are wired and taught to believe that something is inherently wrong when challenges are encountered. We naturally seek out the easiest and most comfortable path and think that pain is something to be avoided. This leads to a desperate search for purpose without suffering, challenges or trials, which, in turn, results in the accompanying anxiety created by the fear that our lives will amount to nothing. The Gospel releases the pressure of performance and striving for value by providing us with the mandate that all of our efforts are for the glory of Jesus and not ourselves. When our identity is firmly rooted in Jesus, we do not have to fear failure. Jesus owns both our successes and failures and is able to make even our failures work out for his glory.

When we fail, big or small, we are presented with the opportunity to decide how we will respond to the failure. It is certainly tempting to become angry, embittered or cynical when our efforts do not produce fruit. However, we are actually called to look at our mistakes with an attitude of joy (James 1:3).

Why is that the case? Through our failures, we are given the chance to develop perseverance and be refined in our character. It is our failures that present the opportunity for us to be made more into the image of Christ, both as individuals and also collectively as a family of disciples. We respond to failure as Jesus has instructed us in Matthew 10:14, by "shaking the dust from our feet." We dust ourselves off and continue to press into the purposes and plans of God in our life. This attitude allows us to be shaped, even by our failures, into disciples more resembling Christ. Simply, we fail forward because as we fail, we can be made more like Jesus.

We also fail forward because as we fail, we learn from our mistakes. We can quickly dismiss this statement as trite or reductionist. However, failure is a necessary teacher. We can and should reflect on what has happened to cause failure, be it relational or circumstantial, and personally take responsibility for the mistakes. A crucial part of multiplying leadership is taking responsibility for our failures. We celebrate the success of others rather than ourselves. On the other hand, we directly take responsibility when there are shortcomings in our own planning or character.

In his book, *Good to Great*, Jim Collins talks about how effective leaders will look "in the mirror" at their mistakes and "out the window" for the success of others. They will look outwards when there are successes and inward when there are failures. When this practice is executed from the security we have in Christ, it becomes a truly formative and life giving model of leadership.

9) Lead Fearlessly Urgent

The ministry of the Apostle Paul was characterized by a sense of urgency. He knew that his life was short, and he sought to make the most of the time that he had been given. For example, when he has a vision of the people in Macedonia calling him to bring the Gospel, he is described as "immediately" springing into action (Acts 16:6-10). In Colossians 4:5, Paul urges the church to "act wisely toward outsiders, making the most of the time." Time is precious, and the need to multiply leaders to proclaim the Gospel into unreached places requires urgency. We call this leading fearlessly urgent. Urgent, because time is short. Fearless, because we know that Jesus is in control.

Fearless urgency is what happens when we lead with a healthy measure of Godly wisdom combined with Holy Spirit led urgency. Fearless urgency is simultaneously urgent and wise. It is not reckless, foolish or panicked. Instead, fearlessly urgent leadership is decisive, resistant to laziness and apathy, time-sensitive and willing to put in the long hard work to make sure the mission succeeds.

Fearless Urgency Grid

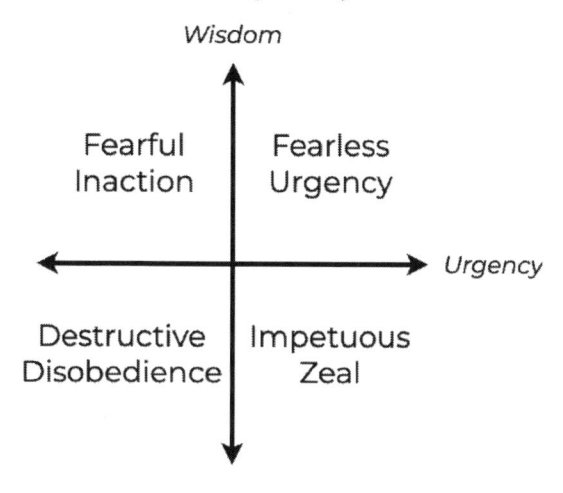

```
                Wisdom
                  ↑
    Fearful       |    Fearless
    Inaction      |    Urgency
                  |
  ←───────────────┼───────────────→ Urgency
                  |
   Destructive    |    Impetuous
   Disobedience   |    Zeal
                  ↓
```

These two properties of leadership can be modelled as the diagram above shows: When we lack urgency, we will tend to fall into Fearful Inaction. On the other hand, when we are decisive but unwise, we will be impetuous and unreliable. Of course, if we lack both wisdom and urgency, then we are causing harm to ourselves and others in our disobedience.

Fearful Inaction

Fearful Inaction is what occurs when we do not allow ourselves to be grounded in the previous imperatives that aid in teamwork and decision making. Specifically, believing the test, taking the leap and failing forward. We will always be a people of faith. We must also be people of action; we cannot allow fear to paralyze us. Fear can halt us in our tracks for reasons ranging from fear of failure, fear of man, fear of success or fear of the unknown. We are called to be people of action, not people of fear. Paul knew that Timothy, his protege, may have been tempted to fall into fearful inaction, so he reminds him in his final letter to lead decisively and confidently. He declares, *"Therefore, I remind you to rekindle the gift of God that is in you through the laying on of my hands. For God has not given us a spirit of fear, but one of power, love, and sound judgment."* (2 Timothy 1:6-7).

Impetuous Zeal

On the other end of the spectrum of urgency from Fearful Inaction is Impetuous Zeal. These are the leaders who are eager to jump into new initiatives or proclaim their faithfulness as quickly and loudly as possible. However, the leader who operates with Impetuous Zeal lacks tenacity, faithfulness and grit. Impetuous Zeal is marked by the habit of emotional instability or a lack of long-term commitments.

Leadership is hard work, and leading fearlessly urgent requires a high degree of grit and tolerance for our own failures and others' mistakes. When we do not count the cost carefully before we commit, we hurt ourselves and others by failing to be trustworthy with the people who we are entrusted with. When we operate with impetuous zeal, we are like the person who proclaimed that they would follow Jesus wherever he went, but when push came to shove, or it was inconvenient for them, they were no longer committed. Jesus has some serious words for this kind of disciple, "But Jesus said to him, "*No one who puts his hand to the plow and looks back is fit for the kingdom of God*" (Luke 9:57-62).

We must count the cost as we follow Jesus. We must be willing to commit for the long-term to the mission he has put in front of us. Equally important, in the context of multiplying discipleship, we must be faithful and committed to our church family. We cannot effectively disciple people if we are not faithful, patient and committed to the church we are a part of. Discipleship is not a work of convenience, it is a call to give our lives for the benefit of others in the context of a broader church family.

Destructive Disobedience

The greatest threat to effective multiplication in discipleship is not likely our lack of wisdom or our lack of zeal. The greatest threat is apathy or good old-fashioned laziness. We demonstrate what we truly care about in our actions. We must continually allow our desires to be brought into alignment with the heart of God. Apathy and laziness are often not conscious decisions. Instead, they set in through the subtle infiltration of broader cultural values or compromises along the way. Our culture is constantly pressuring us towards the pursuit of comfort and experiences, promising that fulfillment is found in more. Instead of cultivating a heart for evangelism, discipleship, missions or service of the poor, we cultivate hearts that yearn for better jobs, nicer homes and fancier vacations. The love of these things above Jesus is the root of all kinds of evil, and it causes great harm to ourselves and others (1 Timothy 6:10).

Destructive disobedience is routinely evidenced in our actions. They demonstrate that we care more for ourselves and our own comfort than we do for seeing people come to know Jesus. We must take up the call of Christ to give our lives in the service of others. We must develop the habit of daily giving up ourselves for the benefit of others. We must be vigilant against our apathy for the cause of Christ. We must discipline ourselves, and our minds, to be after the things of Christ (1 Corinthians 9:27).

Fearless Urgency

Fearlessly urgent leadership is decisive, compassionate, sacrificial, wise, tenacious and faithful. The New Testament is full of leaders who operated with fearless urgency, be it the disciples who dropped everything to follow Jesus, Peter who seizes the moment to proclaim the Gospel in Acts 2, Paul who gave his life for the cause of the church, or of course Jesus who lead with precision and patience. Jesus did not lead with a sense of panic, but he was also not slow in his work. In some cases, Jesus acted immediately to deal with an issue, such as driving the money changers from the temple with a whip (John 2).

In Jesus, we see a crucial point; the call is to lead fearlessly urgent, not follow fearlessly urgent. Jesus was careful to set the agenda to lead those around him. He would respond graciously to those around him, but he would not allow them to set his schedule or drive his intentions. He would listen to the needs of others but would also discern how to best respond, without fear or panic. He is informed that his friend, whom he loved, was dying. Rather than panicking and running off to heal him he responds by saying ,*"This sickness will not end in death but is for the glory of God, so that the Son of God may be glorified through it"* (John 11:4).

Jesus was neither lulled into inaction nor was he impetuous. He was intentional in seeking to glorify God in all of his actions. He was intentional to ensure that those around him would be discipled into multiplying disciples themselves. He led with fearless urgency. Fearless, because he was secure in his relationship with the Father. Urgent, because he knew what his life was about and that it was his time to inaugurate a new Kingdom on earth.

Multiplication and Discipleship

Leading fearlessly urgent is a good example of how the Multiplication Imperatives and Discipleship Emphases intertwine and interact. When a leader is living in either Fearful Inaction or Impetuous Zeal, it is likely that the root of this issue can be found in their identity not being secure in Christ. While it is useful for teaching to expound on multiplication and discipleship separately, we must always remember that they must always be deeply intertwined, and we must always be keeping both in mind when trying to form these imperatives in others.

15

Thriving as a Multiplying Leader

Developing grit occurs in the context of community; it is rarely something that we can develop on our own. As grit is being developed in someone, it is invariably discouraging, frustrating and even painful. In the process of learning to live as servants of Jesus, there are many moments where we will want to pull the plug or throw in the towel. It is in these moments of discouragement that there are four simple steps that we can do in our church family to help us stay the course over the long term.

With the high-cost, fast paced, rapidly changing environment that is characteristic of multiplying movements, it is crucial that we have a way to identify and shut-down negative thought patterns as quickly as possible.

Take The Thought Captive

The first step in the process is to identify our patterns of thinking and learn to choose to intentionally guide our own thoughts.[50] When we are discouraged, it is easy to become enslaved to our own patterns of negative thinking. As we dwell on what is frustrating us or discouraging us, it can build up until we are utterly and totally convinced the issue is unsurpassable. The process of allowing our thoughts to build up pressure and overwhelm us can happen regardless of the issue at hand. Relational, logistical, team-related, leadership, cultural or financial challenges are all susceptible to this process.

Jesus teaches that it is out of the abundance of the heart the mouth speaks (Luke 6:45). When we dwell on a problem and focus on it, that problem will inevitably begin to drive our actions, behaviours and decisions. This creates a feedback-loop as we dwell on the difficulty of a problem, and continually thinking about that problem only serves to reinforce our negative beliefs on that issue.

This feedback cycle is the birthplace of bitterness. As we repeat the cycle on our frustrations, bitterness begins to form deep roots in our hearts, infect our thinking and drive our actions. Our thoughts do not only affect our own lives, but the lives of the entire community. What we set our hearts on will inevitably affect the people around us. What we dwell on, we will multiply, both the good and the bad.

We must uproot or tear out that root of bitterness as early as possible and replace it with truth and joy. We must, as 2 Corinthians 10:5 instructs, take the thought captive and submit it to Jesus. When we take a thought captive, we refuse to allow it to roam free in our minds, destroying everything in its path.

We must allow the truths of scripture to begin to define our thinking. It is clear that our Discipleship Potential and our Multiplication Power are clearly intertwined. In order to thrive in multiplication, we must know scripture and be formed and defined by it. God's word must become the ultimate authority in our lives; we must submit to it and let it mould us.

James 3 describes a juxtaposing picture of negative thoughts producing toxicity, versus Christ-like thinking producing all kinds of beautiful fruit.

James 3:14-18

But if you have bitter envy and selfish ambition in your heart, don't boast and deny the truth. Such wisdom does not come down from above but is earthly, unspiritual, demonic. For where there is envy and selfish ambition, there is disorder and every evil practice. But the wisdom from above is first pure, then peace-loving, gentle, compliant, full of mercy and good fruits, unwa-

vering, without pretence. And the fruit of righteousness is sown in peace by those who cultivate peace.

We know that our thinking is healthy when it produces peace, unity, mercy and faithfulness. Verse 17 in particular suggests that our endurance and faithfulness actually flows from our thoughts. If our thought processes are producing disorder or disunity in those around us, then we know that the real problem is not the issue at hand but is our thinking! On the other hand, even the most complex and challenging issues can be navigated with grace, mercy and gentleness if we can learn to surrender our thoughts and pride.

There are two primary modes that these negative thoughts can take. First, we can focus on ourselves: for example, our inadequacy or ineffectiveness. As we do so, we can begin to feel guilty or like a failure. For these types of thoughts, we must return to our secure identity in Christ and meditate, dwell on and pray into those truths.

Second, we can focus on the failures and inadequacies of those around us: either those we are leading or those leading us. We can begin to resent others or assume the worst about them. In Matthew 5, Jesus gives us a powerful tool to maintain a pure and joyful spirit in addressing our relationships, even with our enemies. He instructs us to pray for those who are against us, even those who persecute us. A key component of taking a thought captive is that we do not blame those on the outside. Many bitter thoughts will arise in the form of blaming the church, the employer, the boss, the leader or the friend. When we find ourselves resenting or blaming others, we must immediately stop and begin to pray for those people, especially our leaders.

Reach Out

Our ability to see the truth or stop that cycle of bitterness or discouragement can be very difficult on our own, especially if we have allowed it to continue for some time unabated. It is in these moments that we must reach out and seek wisdom from those who are leading us. One of the most challenging things to do when we are struggling is to admit it. However, in order to thrive, we must learn to admit to our leaders when we are not doing well, ideally before it is a major issue. We normally want to be strong, secure and capable. Admitting we are struggling is often viewed as weakness and as a result, we often delay reaching out for help and instead seek to resolve the issue on our own.

We may reach out to peers in these moments, and in many cases that can prove to be tremendously valuable. However, in reaching out for help, we must make sure that we are open and honest with those who are leading us, as they are the ones who are both responsible for and empowered to care for us. Peers tend to be primarily supportive whereas our leaders have the responsibility and capacity to help us make decisions that are the best for both the individual and the community.

Our culture tends to be highly individualistic and autonomous, so the idea of submitting to our leaders, especially in our weaknesses, is very challenging. It is important that we create a culture where there is no shame in acknowledging that we are disheartened, weak or struggling. 1 Thessalonians 5 encourages us:

1 Thessalonians 5:14-15

And we urge you, brothers and sisters, warn those who are idle and disruptive, encourage the disheartened, help the weak, be patient with everyone. Make sure that nobody pays back wrong for wrong, but always strive to do what is good for each other and for everyone else.

The responsibility of the leader is to care for the person they are leading by helping them see and receive the truth while making an action plan to help them thrive. In a normal case, the action plan will involve continuing to persevere with a few minor tweaks to help the person they are leading remain healthy. By providing a listening ear and helping them see the truth, a great deal of care and encouragement can be provided.

However, it is absolutely critical that the leader has the boldness to identify and correct an issue that is untrue, harmful or hurtful. These types of issues can be challenging because the person who is struggling must be open to being corrected and pointed towards truth in a clear and direct manner. Said another way, the leader must help the person uproot the bitterness before it infects the person more deeply and hurts others as well. The process of reaching out must be accompanied by a willingness to believe, even an assumption, that we are wrong and seek to be pointed in a better direction.

This process of reaching out for support does not just apply when things are going wrong but should include our broader decision making practices. Multiplying leaders do not function as lone islands but as part of a broader community. As such, they make decisions with humility and vulnerability to that community.

Take a Break

The normal Christian life is a life of service and sacrifice, and as a result, it will be challenging and difficult. Part of sustaining a lifelong journey of ministry is discerning when we need to take a break from the tasks and people who we are responsible for. Part of creating a healthy multiplying environment is affirming and creating a space for people to rest and recover. These breaks could be as short as a morning or an afternoon, a week or even months. Sometimes a simple reset is all that is required; other times, a longer time-off may be required.

A mature multiplying leader will be able to self-diagnose when a break is needed and calmly take the break to restore their soul. Each person has unique warnings signs that indicate they are getting tired and need a break. Part of developing as a multiplying leader is learning to identify those signs early and develop habits for taking that break.

Guilt

For some, there can be a sense of pressure and performance that says, "Unless I perform I am not valued." That is a lie. The reason we work hard to multiply disciples for Jesus is not so that we can prove our worth to ourselves or others. We multiply because we want people to know the goodness of Jesus — that is it! In these moments, we must remember that we are not valued for what we do, but for who we are as sons and daughters of the King. Multiplication does not mean we are more loved or treasured by Jesus or by our community.

Again, the verse in 1 Thessalonians paints the picture beautifully: we must create space and be patient with those who require a break or are discouraged. We were not made to be idle, but that does not mean that our value is found in producing, either. Rather, we were made to be fully alive in Jesus; part of that is being secure in him, and part of that is partnering with him.

Pride

For high-performance, high-capacity leaders, the idea of taking a break can be very challenging as it can be thought of as a form of failure or weakness. Yes, we work hard, but we will tire in moments and we will need time and space to draw close to the Father. Perseverance and endurance are important of course, but there are seasons where we must allow others to carry the load so that we can be restored. We must choose to release control of what is in our hands and trust those around us.

> **2 Corinthians 10:9**
>
> *But he said to me, "My grace is sufficient for you, for my power is perfected in weakness."*

Taking a break does not mean that we are weak or that we have failed; in fact, it can prove to be a tremendous opportunity to mobilize others for the Kingdom. Jesus can actually use our weakness to see others thrive in their ministry callings.

Stay Close

This final point may be one of the most important, but often forgotten, components of thriving while multiplying: we must stay close. Many people, when they are hurt, struggling or confused, will isolate themselves as a form of self-protection. This isolation often happens unintentionally or subconsciously as we allow space to develop between ourselves and those in our community who could challenge us or are frustrating us.

Discipleship, church, multiplication and community are all intimately intertwined concepts that centre on the same basic foundation: relationships! When we are struggling as a multiplying leader, it is our relationships that will be the most threatened by the distance that is created in our struggling. We call this process drifting. A boat without an anchor will drift from the shore and ultimately end up lost and alone at sea. Our Church family is designed to provide an anchor for us so that we can navigate the storms that come our way. We were not designed to, nor intended to, ever struggle alone.

Hebrews 10:24-25

And let us watch out for one another to provoke love and good works, not neglecting to gather together, as some are in the habit of doing, but encouraging each other, and all the more as you see the day approaching.

If we are tired and need a break, we must press into our community and stay close during that time. We must allow them to care for us, support us and encourage us. In short, healing happens best in the context of relationships. Instead of allowing distance when we are struggling, it is in these moments that we should press into relationship the most deeply.

As Hebrews implores us, we must "watch out" for one another in the process. When we see this drifting process occurring, we must address it. At first it can appear slow and innocuous and almost imperceptible. It is these moments that we must open up a dialogue with that person and encourage them to continue gathering in community. It will likely be painful and difficult, but it is through hearing encouragement, care, love and truth in our church family that we can thrive the most.

Staying close when we are weak is an active and intentional choice that we must make. However, it is a hard decision to make, so we must identify and engage those who are struggling and invite them to that relationship. We must see them at their moment of weakness and intentionally choose to engage, encourage and support them

Part 4

Leadership Position

16

Empowering to Multiply

Discipleship Potential shaped the question of what we seek to multiply, and Multiplication Power described how multiplication actually happens. We have sought to describe and articulate the shape of a discipleship movement where multiplying leaders are equipped and empowered to raise and send disciples. We must now return to the questions that started the discussion: How do we create a scalable environment where everyone is sent to multiply everything? How do we strategically ensure that everyone is sent? How do we know what they are multiplying? How do we ensure that those with the greatest ability to multiply the most desirable discipleship qualities are given the greatest influence?

The toolbox has been filled in with the 5 Discipleship Emphases, four discipleship steps, three discipleship ingredients and nine Multiplication Imperatives. Creating scalable discipleship and multiplication environments requires infrastructure: systems and structures that help organize our relationships. Organizing hundreds, if not thousands, of people in a discipleship movement requires that every person understand how their unique gifts, story and experiences contribute to the whole. Such a robust understanding of how people fit together and relate to one another on a larger scale is crucial for them to continue to reproduce.

Moses famously found himself leading the Israelites but was struggling to keep up with the demands as the judge and decider of the people (Exodus 18:21). His father-in-law, Jethro, gives him the relatively simple advice of organizing the people of Israel into groups of thousands, hundreds, fifties and tens. On the surface, it appears to be a pretty basic leadership pipeline. However, Jethro's advice was more profound than the basic organization of people; he was inviting Moses to empower the people of Israel to discern and enact the leading of the Lord. Jethro's advice was a picture of Everyone Sent to Multiply Everything. Jethro was inviting the nation of Israel to be multipliers and contributors instead of demanding consumers.

Systems and structures in a multiplying environment exist to draw out the unique role of every person. Everyone Sent to Multiply Everything requires that every person is equipped, trained and sent to make disciples in some capacity.

Anecdotally, in the 21st-century Western world, many are predisposed to be somewhat deconstructionist or anti-establishment. We often bristle at the idea of organizing people, as it means that we cannot do whatever we wish. Systems and structures are often seen as the enemy in the church as they can stifle creativity, limit passion and control people when improperly implemented. However, as we discussed at length in Discipleship Potential, discipleship relationships require that we submit ourselves to a broader community for the benefit of the Kingdom. We give up some of our autonomy to be a part of something far greater. When we make this sacrifice we find, contrary to our sinful impulses, that submitting to one another through relationships implemented in systems and structures actually provides an environment to thrive, as opposed to squashing our creativity. Such thriving occurs because we learn to draw on the strength, creativity and passions of the whole.

Ephesians 4:16

From him the whole body, fitted and knit together by every supporting ligament, promotes the growth of the body for building up itself in love by the proper working of each individual part.

In Moses' case, the initiation of systems and structures was precipitated by conflict. Especially in cases of conflict, clarity of relationships is essential to provide clear pathways for reconciliation. Likewise, one of the most common causes of conflict is the lack of clarity around who is responsible for decision making. Again, clear leadership structures are essential in limiting conflict and providing clear pathways for reconciliation.

Leadership Pipelines

With this background in mind, we can begin to think about empowering disciple-makers through recognized leadership. The Leadership Position dimension of the Discipleship Pipeline ensures that each person clearly understands their responsibilities, expectations, and opportunities for growth within the church.

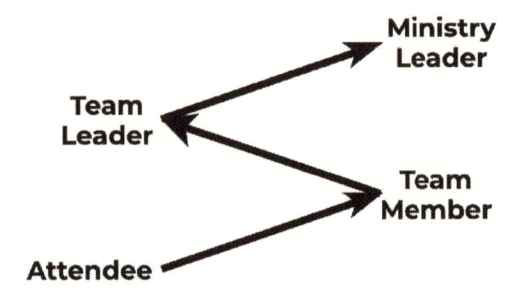

In nurturing a discipleship movement, we require a clear process for leadership development that is effective and efficient.[51] Ultimately, our best leaders will not be found externally from other churches; they will come from within our own church! A healthy and thriving leadership development process is the ultimate solution to this challenge as it provides a means by which we are continually developing leaders. A leadership pipeline is just that, a process for consistently developing and empowering leaders for both the present and the future. This pipeline is shown in the diagram below.

Leadership Position

Attendee → Team Leader → Ministry Leader → Team Member → Team Leader

A leadership pipeline, through leadership positions, ensures that each person clearly understands their responsibilities, expectations, and opportunities for growth within the church. It also helps establish what each person should be primarily focused on and concerned about. Leadership Position is a vital component to making sure the Disciple Potential functions to its fullest effectiveness. If leadership positions work as intended, they ensure that the breadth of priorities and concerns are covered in a healthy and sustainable manner. The pipeline also defines the processes by which we can clearly identify who each person is accountable to: both in fulfilling their role and also in ensuring their spiritual, emotional and physical health.

As a leader begins on the pipeline, they are initially responsible for only themselves. Initially, they are formally responsible solely for ensuring that they are fulfilling their specific responsibilities and contributing to the team appropriately.

As leaders move up the pipeline, the number of people who they are responsible for increases significantly. As a result, the attributes that they multiply are very quickly distributed throughout the church. The potential impact of positive actions and attitudes is tremendous. However, so is the potential negative impact. One of the objectives of the pipeline is to define a process whereby leaders have the training and equipping necessary to effectively handle the responsibilities and opportunities that they have been given.

A good question for a leader to ask themselves is: "*What if those who I am responsible for were to emulate my actions and attitudes?*" This powerful question helps to illustrate the power of leadership. It is important that at each layer of the pipeline, a leader has an awareness of their potential impact.

For this reason, we regularly celebrate the best aspects of our leaders that we wish to see multiplied. However, it is equally important that we do not tolerate actions and attitudes that undermine the leadership process, regardless of where a leader is on the pipeline.

Skill Development

The leadership pipeline exists to empower people to lead others in a role that is appropriate to their discipleship and leadership development. Each distinct role on the leadership pipeline has a set of leadership specifications. Each position requires new skills, knowledge and know-how. As people move upwards through the leadership pipeline they are empowered to lead on a new level and will need to acquire an entirely new set of skills and adapt to new responsibilities and expectations. Similarly, as disciples move upwards through the leadership pipeline, the rigour of accountability must increase to match the degree of influence that they have.

Empowering Leadership

Leadership positions are a tool to empower people for the work of discipleship. Beyond creating clarity around systems and structures, at its very core, leadership positions are an invitation to a life of discipleship! When we observe Jesus' ministry, it is abundantly clear that discipleship can only happen in the context of a relationship. The power of leadership position is only activated when it is mediated through deep, vulnerable and authentic discipleship relationships.

Every role on the pipeline is crucial to building a healthy and thriving church that can continue to plant new churches. The roles are designed to fit together to ensure that we have proper coverage across the many concerns, tasks, discipleship relationships and responsibilities involved. In organizing people into leadership positions, there are five leadership questions that each person needs to ask. Each of these questions are accompanied by leadership specifications that establish a clear standard that everyone in the discipleship movement agrees to. The work of developing a robust leadership pipeline is equal parts establishing clarity around roles and creating a discipleship environment to develop those roles. The following questions are a mix of inner and outer life discipleship; they focus on both "being" and "doing." Expectations and Qualifications are attributes of our inner-life, or sanctification journey, as leaders. Values, and Responsibilities are primarily questions that involve our outer-life or the role we play in multiplication. Accountability involves both our inner and outer-life. The pentagon diagram below illustrates how the five leadership questions work together to produce a holistic leadership framework.

Leadership Specifications

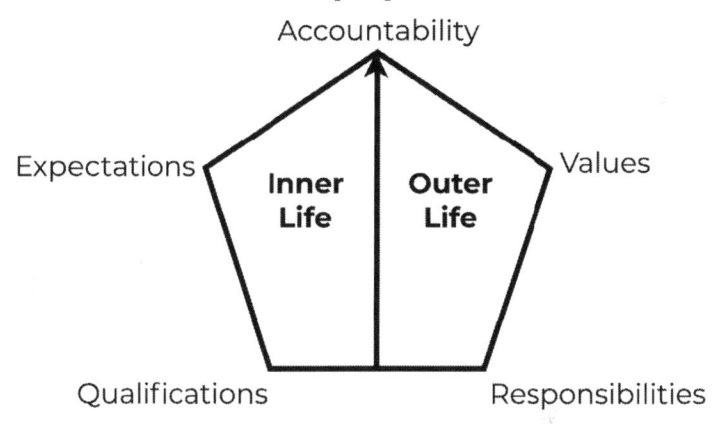

```
                  Accountability
                        ↑
Expectations ┌─────────────────┐ Values
             │ Inner  │ Outer  │
             │ Life   │ Life   │
             └─────────────────┘
       Qualifications      Responsibilities
```

Values: What do I care about?

Answering this question helps properly align one's current set of values with his/her role. Value alignment is one of the primary, if not the central, issues at stake when evaluating where to position someone for influence in a discipleship movement.

Further questions to explore are: what does the church value and how does that fit with my personal values? Is there alignment and agreement regarding what matters the most? Are the questions I'm asking appropriate for my leadership position? Am I thinking more about tactics or strategy (details or big picture)?

Qualifications: Where am I at?

Answering this question helps each person in the Church develop a self-awareness of the extent to which they are engaging and committing to community and the process of discipleship.

Further questions to explore are: is my identity rooted in Christ? Do I have a home at church? What am I passionate about? What am I good at? What do I want? Do I know what it means to be a part of a church?

Team Responsibilities: What do I do?

Answering this question helps us ensure that the wide array of talents, gifts and passions of our teams are properly integrated into the church, while simultaneously ensuring that the breadth of responsibilities necessary to fulfill our mission are fully carried out.

Further questions to explore are: what am I responsible for? What tasks do I need to prioritize? Is there anyone I can multiply into my position?

Individual Expectations: What's expected of me?

Answering this question helps us establish clarity for what is expected. Setting clear expectations helps to prevent feelings of guilt for failing to meet unclear expectations, while helping to shape discipleship conversations around shared goals.

Further questions to explore are: what does the community expect from me in terms of growth in my faith, commitment to the community, and other marks of discipleship? Do I understand what the standard is?

Accountability: Who cares for me? / Who do I care for?

Answering these questions helps us make sure that every person in the church is integrated into healthy discipleship relationships.

Further questions to explore are: what do I do if I have a need? Who should I be discipling? Who is discipling me? Who should I hold accountable and who is holding me accountable?

Values

Ultimately, a multiplying discipleship movement is a gathering of disciples who are committed to a unifying objective together. However, what ultimately holds us together is deeper than mere agreement on primary objectives or outcomes. The underlying motivations and values (the "hows" and "whys") are just as important as the physical outcomes, if not more important! As we reproduce disciples, we are producing people who have a shared set of values. There are many ways to plant churches and make disciples. In cultivating a discipleship movement, we seek to empower disciples who share the underlying value system with the rest of the movement.

In the specific case that we have been discussing, the core value of Everyone Sent to Multiply Everything is a central tenet that unifies all the disciples. We must empower every believer, ministry and mission without exception. In a discipleship movement, every believer must share the value that every person be trained and sent to reproduce disciples. Without agreement on this core value, the mandate of discipleship will naturally begin to centralize around those who are gifted or hold key leadership positions.

In empowering people for leadership, we must stop and carefully evaluate if they share the same core value of reproduction, multiplication and empowerment in people. As people increase in influence, misalignment on such a significant core value will create massive issues within the broader network. Beyond a shared belief in the Apostolic Imperative, there must be a shared belief in Multiplication Imperatives that shape how we think about reproducing disciples. Whether it is taking the leap, believing the best or leading fearlessly urgent, each disciple that is empowered to lead must do so with agreement on *how* they will lead, not just *what* they will lead.

When there is alignment on what we value and how we multiply, then we can increase a leader's formal influence in the discipleship movement with the confidence that they will be leading people in the same direction as the rest of the movement.

Valuing at the Correct Layer

There are many considerations in each layer of leadership. Each layer in the pipeline must be properly thinking about each of the considerations appropriate to their role. Confusion of values is one of the primary causes of breakdown in the Discipleship Pipeline. By making sure that everyone is asking the appropriate questions for their role within the pipeline, we can be assured that we have proper coverage and empowerment in people.

A common mistake is when a leader values questions more appropriate to a role higher on the pipeline. In short, a leader who should be primarily task-oriented or team-oriented becomes vision or strategy-oriented. While they may certainly have valuable insight, it is important that they spend the bulk of their energy investing in the questions appropriate to their layer.

Likewise, another common mistake is when a leader who should be functioning at a strategic layer operates at a task layer. As a result, important strategic questions are left unanswered or unasked. A leader will simply not have the time or energy to set the culture and vision of the church if they are constantly focusing on small details.

These breakdowns in the pipeline cause frustration as leaders regularly invest large amounts of energy in areas that do not yield a good return on their investment. Thus, it is important that everyone at every layer in the pipeline understands their role as a part of the whole.

Qualifications

How do we know when a leader is at the point where they can make a "turn" or "move up" the Discipleship Pipeline?

There are three primary components that each leader must demonstrate to an appropriate level for their position: commitment, character and competence. The goal is to develop '3C' leaders at each layer of the pipeline. At each layer in the pipeline, we seek to have leaders who have an appropriate and sufficient commitment, character and competence. The discipleship process is intentionally oriented to see leaders grow in each of the three categories.

Commitment

For a team member to be qualified for the role, there must be demonstrable commitment and reliability that is appropriate for their role. Commitment is the first component that we evaluate when examining qualifications. Commitment is a way of ensuring that people are invested in the long term when we work with them and that they will persevere when there are challenging moments or even seasons. A person may have a high character or even competence, but without commitment, there is no way to integrate them into the church. There are three specific types of commitment that we evaluate, in order of importance:

1) Commitment to faith and discipleship

They must approach their role with a humble attitude where they are committed to learning and growing. They must demonstrate that they are faithfully pursuing a relationship with Jesus and exhibit growth all 5 Discipleship Emphases, from exposure towards multiplication. It is important that they recognize and are sincere about intentional discipleship in their own life. They may have the need for improvement or growth in areas of character or competence. Still, regardless, they are actively demonstrating that they have a teachable spirit that is being moulded by the Holy Spirit.

2) Commitment to the church family

They must demonstrate that they are committed to the church. This commitment must not be solely out of emotion or a sense of being a part of something popular or socially beneficial, but rather must be rooted in a clarity of understanding that the Holy Spirit has planted them into a faith community that they are called to serve. Are they more committed to the church than they are to their particular role? Do they demonstrate a heart for the church beyond their direct responsibilities or involvement? Do they value discipleship and multiplication, and is that evidenced in their life?

3) Commitment to the role

They must demonstrate reliability and commitment to the role. This includes fulfilling the basic components of commitment, including reliability, timeliness, preparedness and eagerness. A person who routinely arrives prepared and always fulfills their responsibilities is a team member who is demonstrating a capacity for increased leadership. Further, they must demonstrate that they are committed to navigating the challenges and difficult seasons associated with the role.

Character

After Commitment, the next qualification we evaluate is one's Character. Character is a growth area for every person following the way of Jesus. However, scripture makes it clear that those with increased leadership responsibilities are held to a similarly significant expectation regarding their character development. A person may be reliable, committed and capable. However, if their character is not aligned with Christ, or at least moving in that direction, then we cannot elevate their leadership mantle.

Character can be challenging to identify. In moments of low-stress and relative calm, many people will appear Christ-like. When pressure increases, our real character comes out. This should cause us to ask questions when evaluating the character of a leader: How do they respond when things are not going well? How do they handle criticism? How do they speak of others that they are in conflict with?

In Christian leadership, there is no divide between our formal leadership role and the private dimensions of our lives. Everything is connected. When examining character, we do not just look at their character in leading others, but also the overall Christ-like quality of their life.

An important note about character: when an issue is identified, we must have the courage to speak to it. It is the responsibility of the leader to continually encourage and challenge those they are leading to become more like Christ. This must be done with grace, recognizing that we are all being refined by the Holy Spirit on a daily basis.

Competence

The final dimension of evaluating a leader's qualifications is that of competence. Do they have the necessary skills and abilities to fulfill their role? It is important that team members are serving in areas in which they are skilled.

Competence is often perceived to be the most important qualification, but it is actually the least important. Competence is the easiest of the qualifications to train. We can develop skills in people much more easily and far faster than we can develop their commitment or their character.

That said, competence is still of great importance. Allowing someone to serve in an area where they do not have sufficient skills will result in team frustration, low morale and poorly invested resources. Psalm 78 ends with a statement of how David led his people with both an upright heart as well as skillful hands! It is important for commitment and character to come first in our evaluations, but competence is just as critical and biblical. Before placing someone in a role, we must sufficiently train them to fulfill that role. Training a person includes equipping them in both the skills particular to that role, as well as the logistical infrastructure associated with that role.

Creating clear processes to train our team members is important. They need to be given the skills to complete their job, as well as the awareness of how their role fits into the larger picture of creating and caring for a discipleship movement.

As a leader moves through the Discipleship Pipeline, it must not be assumed that because they were successful in one role, they will automatically be successful in a role higher up on the pipeline. We need to be intentionally training leaders to develop the competencies specific to their role.

For example, a talented musician (Team Member) may be highly competent at their instrument. However, the role of Team Leader requires a number of competencies of team leadership, including administration, leading meetings and identifying abilities in others. This is a vastly different skill set, and intentional development must take place to train and equip them for such a role.

A second example: a long-time Christian may be very comfortable in prayer and have a thorough understanding of scripture. However, when they join the prayer team as a Team Member they need new skills including sensitivity training, counselling fundamentals and handling confidential information. These skills cannot be assumed to be acquired on a de-facto basis and must be intentionally communicated and trained.

A third example: a new team member on a serving team may love our church and be committed to serving faithfully. However, they must be trained on the process of online engagement tools, scheduling and communicating availability in order to be effective contributors to the team. We cannot assume that they will figure out this information by themselves.

Responsibilities

The team responsibilities define the specific items and tasks that a person is responsible for. Each layer of the pipeline must have clearly established responsibilities that they own. Each person must be able to clearly understand what it is that they are being asked to accomplish. At a basic level, each person in the pipeline must be aware of what exactly they are responsible for and have an idea of what others are in turn.

In many ways, responsibilities are the most practical of the leadership specifications and the easiest to understand. It is not especially difficult to articulate what specific responsibilities a disciple must carry as part of their role in the church. Task completion, however, is not the only goal. We must think more intentionally and carefully when we empower people to accomplish responsibilities with a multiplication mindset.

Every task or responsibility must connect back to the primary objective of the discipleship movement, demonstrate the core value of the Apostolic Imperative and substantially mediate the Multiplication Imperatives. A responsibility exists so that discipleship occurs; it does not exist for its own sake. As we communicate responsibilities, we must ensure that each disciple understands how exactly the responsibility fulfills the mission, no matter how small or insignificant the task may appear. A disciple that is carrying out a responsibility without understanding why they are doing that task will not be able to train or empower others to carry that task properly. Ultimately, the goal is always about empowering new leaders and disciple-makers, so any breakdown in that process must be taken very seriously.

By training and empowering leaders to lead with multiplication and discipleship at the forefront of their leadership roles, rather than the task by itself, we ensure that the entire system of discipleship has the capacity and potential for continued and sustained reproduction.

When evaluating if a person is fulfilling their responsibilities, we must consider *how* they accomplish it, not just *if* they accomplish it. By evaluating success on the basis of "how," we are opening up all sorts of character and discipleship opportunities. We must resist the temptation to accept high-quality execution of responsibilities in a manner that does not reflect who we really are. How a task is fulfilled is just as important as if it is fulfilled.

Part of leading effectively is raising leaders who accomplish their responsibilities in a way that is reflective of the core values of the entire body of believers. As leaders progress through the pipeline, their leadership responsibilities will change. However, their values will not substantially change. It is critical that discipleship and multiplication are central values that determine how they execute their responsibilities from the outset. Failure to do so will inevitably result in either ineffectual leadership due to the inability to empower others, or divisive leadership due to value misalignment. As Peter Scazerro says, "*immaturity rooted in unresolved issues in their family of origin, trauma, issues with authority and faulty thinking, for example, will reveal themselves sooner or later.*[52]"

The Multiplication Imperatives and Apostolic Imperative help to create a clear framework to answer the "why" and "how" behind the "what" that is articulated in a disciple's responsibilities. When we are empowering people, we need to continually remind them of their mandate to develop new leaders and disciples in their own right. Further, the Multiplication Imperatives are a crucial anchor when considering how a leader fulfilled their obligations. It is remarkably easy when we are focused on completing a task, to forgo celebrating the best, pulling together, taking the leap, failing forward or leading fearlessly urgent. However, these imperatives help ensure that the responsibilities that a disciple is charged with are part of the larger goal of mobilizing others to know Jesus.

Each responsibility provides an opportunity to see the Discipleship Emphases formed in those we are discipling. As people work as part of a team to accomplish a goal, we, as disciple-makers, must be on the lookout for opportunities to affirm or correct how the Discipleship Emphases are being expressed. The call to be an ambassador and a slave for Christ as a part of their secure identity will naturally be challenged or affirmed as people execute their responsibilities. It is far too easy for those we are discipling to be secure in what they do and the praise that accompanies it, rather than in Christ. These are tremendous discipleship opportunities. Similarly, it is far too easy to allow those we are discipling to be enticed with the allure of comfort in our culture and consequently compromise their responsibilities and their call to a missional life.

Jesus has a profound encounter with Peter in Matthew 16:13-28. Peter has recognized who Jesus is, and has been commissioned for a leadership role, but declares that he will not let Jesus give his life for others. While appearing noble, Peter had misunderstood the commitment of Jesus to be a suffering servant in his leadership. Jesus takes the opportunity to rebuke Peter firmly, saying, *"get behind me Satan"* and then re-affirms to him that a disciple must pick up their cross and follow him. Jesus does a brilliant job confronting Peter's value misalignment and correcting that his responsibilities must be fulfilled in light of a broader value-set (servanthood).

It is through using leadership responsibilities to teach the Discipleship Emphases and Multiplication Imperatives that effective and efficient multiplication can occur. Emphasis on recruitment, empowerment, discipleship and multiplication in Leadership Position are the essential ingredients that distinguish a multiplying discipleship movement from a mere organization. In a multiplying discipleship movement, the organizational structure itself exists to produce reproducing disciples and leaders.

Expectations

As discussed above, the responsibilities and potential influence of our leaders increase significantly as they move through the pipeline. Biblical instruction is that those in leadership positions live lives that are worth emulating (Titus 1:6, 1 Peter 5:1-3), though we recognize that this is a discipleship process governed by grace. A new team member may be new in the walk with the Lord, struggling with questions and working to develop healthy spiritual practices. However, as a leader works their way through the pipeline, the expectation is that they are growing in their faith and living a life worth emulating.

While responsibilities are about the tasks that a disciple fulfills, expectations define the unifying expectations for belief and lifestyle in a broader sense. Establishing, communicating and holding disciples accountable for expectations can be an intimidating prospect. Establishing expectations can be challenging as it may feel as though we are drawing a circle that excludes people from participating. This kind of exclusion may appear to be elitist or legalistic at first glance. However, established expectations are ultimately liberating for the community of disciples. The life of discipleship is a life that is committed to the worship of God by participating in the mission of Christ. By definition, discipleship is about adopting a set of values that influence our behaviour. If we do not articulate how our scripturally founded values change our behaviour, then our values will inevitably be found to be worthless.

It is through clearly set expectations that our values and commitment to discipleship find a means of expression through the actual lives of disciples. Without setting and holding disciples accountable to expectations, values are merely wishful thinking. It is through clearly defined expectations that our individual and collective commitment to scripture is tested and validated. It is easy to talk to a good talk about where we are at in our faith, but it is by holding people accountable to real expectations that we get a glimpse into their actual heart position.

Jesus demonstrates why expectations are important in Luke 9:62. A man desires to follow Jesus, but Jesus clearly establishes a standard of expectation that reveals the man's true intentions. Following Jesus is costly! Clearly set expectations allow us to ensure that the true cost of discipleship is not hidden from view.

As discussed in Discipleship Potential, when a person begins their journey with Jesus as a disciple-maker, they will need to undergo a substantial degree of sanctification. As such, expectations are not uniformly applied to all layers of leadership position. As a leader's influence increases, we must hold them to more stringent expectations and a higher degree of accountability.

Oftentimes, this process can be tricky to measure as each person is on their own walk with the Lord and navigating unique questions and concerns. We all have areas of sin where we need grace. In order to assist this process, we can use the Discipleship Emphases to help ensure leaders are moving forward in their pursuit of the way of Jesus and inviting others to do likewise.

Generally speaking, a leader must demonstrate a movement from exposure to understanding to fluency to multiplication in each of the Discipleship Emphases: gospel fluency, secure identity, missional living, radical generosity and crucial conversations. When setting expectations, we are specifying how each of the Discipleship Emphases influence the specific ways that we behave as a community. Expectations are not just about a moral standard. On issues of sin, for example sexual promiscuity, lust or drunkenness, the standard is uniformly set in scripture. A new believer does not get a free pass to lust just because they are new in their faith. When discussing leadership, however, the standard is not always clearly set or uniform.

When considering gospel fluency, we are setting theological belief and teaching expectations. In secure identity, we are considering commitment and consistency in presence with church commitment, behaviour and conflict management. In missional living, we are setting expectations around the nature of a leader's lifestyle, especially in what might be considered "private" affairs. Expectations in radical generosity establish a standard around giving of time, talents and treasure. Lastly, expectations in crucial conversations help us to establish expectations around teachability and evangelism.

The primary motivation for setting clear expectations surrounding church engagement is to ensure the spiritual, emotional, and physical health of each person who is serving the church. The desire is to see every person who is serving be integrated into the church such that it functions as a healthy family. The roles that every person fills are a part of a bigger picture where the objective is to see a thriving church. If people are serving in a role but are not integrated into the church properly, they will ultimately end up simply doing a job but not receiving proper encouragement, accountability or care.

To build a healthy church requires that we are committed to one another; that we are more committed to each other than we are to the particular role that we fill. While roles, opportunities, and circumstances change, our love and support for one another must not.

We cannot provide pastoral care or encouragement to those who are only partially connected. We cannot ensure that we are caring for people if they are not a regular part of the church, and therefore we are unaware of the details of their lives. We cannot hold people accountable if there is not a high degree of trust fostered through a mutual commitment to each other.

Accountability

The final area of leadership specification is that of accountability. Accountability means that those who are empowered to lead and disciple are actively fulfilling and multiplying in their domain of influence. A healthy accountability process requires three crucial components. The first component in a robust accountability environment is a clearly defined set of values, qualifications, responsibilities and expectations as outlined above.

Accountability Relationships

The second component is that of clear lines of relational accountability. Accountability, especially in a discipleship environment, is all about relationships. Accountability without relationships will merely degrade into a legalistic application of quasi-utopian ideals. In the real world, there are many shades of grey in holding people accountable. It is only through relationships that meaningful accountability can be established. Relational accountability means that a person knows who to talk to if they have a question, an issue or an item to celebrate — both up and down the pipeline.

When we are fostering a discipleship movement, we need to ensure that we are first and foremost nurturing deep relationships with each other where we are known for more than just what we do. Accountability must extend to values, qualifications, responsibilities and expectations. Merely considering the responsibility angle does not provide sufficient depth for a true discipleship movement. We may be able to host good events or accomplish a great deal of work for the Kingdom; however, unless we have deep relationships where our lives are open to one another and are truly known, then our discipleship will only be partial.

For accountability relationships to function, it must be clear to everyone who each person is accountable to and for what. Every person must have someone who they are accountable to and a group of people they in turn hold accountable. Every person must be empowered to hold others accountable and be held accountable, and it must be clear who those people are. This is the nature of discipleship, as the Apostle Paul writes in 1 Corinthians 11:1: *"Be imitators of me, as I am of Christ."* Ambiguity in this area will result in relational drift, and ultimately people feeling valued only for what they do, not for who they are.

Accountability Processes

The final component of robust accountability is an effective accountability process. Effective accountability requires clarity surrounding what a person is held accountable for (values, qualifications, responsibility and expectations), who they are accountable to and for and finally, how they are held accountable.

It is tempting to think that because a discipleship movement is all about relationships that accountability can be purely relational without the need for any systems or processes to help manage that accountability. However, as movements scale, so also does the impact, complexity and challenge of maintaining unity and evaluating progress. A robust process of accountability is necessary to ensure that what we say we are going to do and what we actually do are in alignment.

A process of accountability must include clear scheduling, metrics and follow-up. We must ensure that there is a well understood rhythm of accountability so that it happens on a predictable and repeatable basis. Over time, the value of taking regular measurements on a repeatable schedule helps create a sense of expectation and the ability to evaluate progress by taking measurements at consistent intervals. Accountability without attaching dates and schedules is merely aspirational in nature. By creating a clear schedule to which we will hold people accountable, we can move the "some-day" to "on this specific day".

An accountability process also requires clear and consistent metrics. What we measure we celebrate, and what we celebrate we replicate. We must create a process for measuring discipleship in a manner that reinforces multiplication over addition in our thinking. The business world makes judicious use of Key Performance Indicators to evaluate performance over periods of time. Why should discipleship movements be any different? Performance in discipleship does not add to our personal security in Christ or our value as a human being, of course. However, not all discipleship is equally effective and not all initiatives produce the same quality or quantity of results. Only when we actually measure our quality and quantity can we make great improvements.

Lastly, when developing an accountability process, we need to repeatedly follow-up on our conversations. One conversation is rarely sufficient to produce the necessary progress. Accountability processes are iterative; each conversation produces a future conversation. Persistence and patience in accountability relationships is so important. Discipleship takes a significant investment of time. That is why accountability, like discipleship, can only be done with a limited amount of people at a given point in time.

Leadership Turns

When a leader is demonstrating effectiveness in all five of the above specifications (Qualification, Responsibilities, Expectations, Values and Accountability), it is an indicator that they may be ready for a leadership 'turn.' A turn is the point where a leader moves from one layer in the pipeline to another, as demonstrated in the diagram below.

Leadership Position Turns

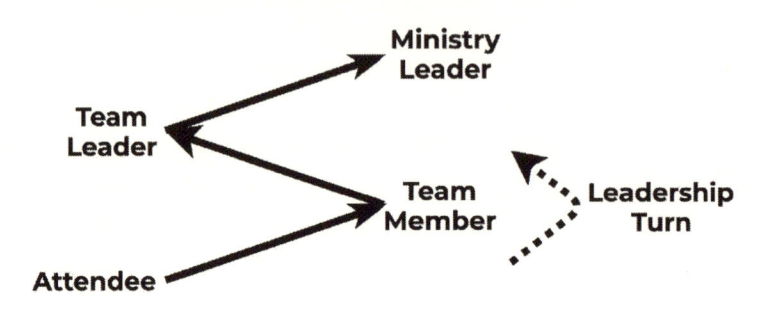

Attendee → Team Member → Team Leader → Ministry Leader → Team Member (Leadership Turn)

While the pipeline does facilitate a process by which people "move up," a person cannot graduate to increased responsibility until they have demonstrated effectiveness in their current position. When the Discipleship Pipeline is properly understood, leaders should not "skip layers." By not-skipping levels, we ensure that every leader properly understands the specific culture of the discipleship movement and how every area of leadership fits together.

One of the grave mistakes that we can make when developing and advancing leaders is to think that merely because someone was effective in their previous position, they will be successful in their new one. That is not the case, and an effective leadership development process must raise leaders who can adapt and be coached to lead in new roles despite success in former ones.

Raise and Replace

Multiplying movements require that every person is simultaneously student and teacher: both a disciple and disciple-maker. In a healthy multiplying environment, leadership transitions are an essential component of raising new leaders. When a leader takes a leadership turn or steps into a new role, they must also have developed a leader to take their place. When we step into new leadership roles or step out of a position for a break, we will leave a hole. There will be relationships and responsibilities that we were caring for that no longer have a clear point of contact. A true multiplying leader will always have developed someone to take their place when they make a leadership change. The leader must think about the health of the whole team instead of just their part. A true multiplying leader understands that their responsibility is to develop and disciple people, not just to accomplish tasks. For this reason, when they make a leadership change, they do not make the fulfillment of those responsibilities or care for those relationships someone else's problem. Instead, they work to ensure that there is a smooth hand-off of duties to someone who they have personally invested in, discipled and trained for leadership.

The simple principle that leaders take responsibility to replace themselves is what transforms a basic organizational structure into an efficient and thriving leadership development environment. When a replacement leader is inadequately trained, leadership changes are disorienting and confusing, as responsibilities and relationships are mishandled. However, when leaders take responsibility to disciple people to take over from them, the transition becomes a powerful tool for leadership development. We should expect leaders to regularly be changing roles and responsibilities as they train those to take over from them. It would be alarming, from a leadership development standpoint, if a leader remained in the same position for a long time as that would signal that that leader is either unable to raise leaders or is finding security and identity in their current role in a way that is detrimental to discipleship and leadership development.

Fruitfulness

Ultimately, leaders and disciples must be measured based on their output or effectiveness, not their words or intentions alone (Luke 6:43). Jesus promises in John 15:5-8 that true disciples will be fruitful in producing disciples. The measure that Jesus has set up for measuring effectiveness in discipleship and leadership is fruitfulness; we would be wise to follow his lead.

Many people can talk a good line or may be attractive and come with "star power." However, have they actually lead anything substantial? Have they led people to know Jesus directly themselves? Have they mediated or managed conflict? Have they been hurt and been required to extend grace and forgiveness in a costly and sacrificial way? These are all part of leadership, and allowing a disciple to assume too much leadership when they have not demonstrated a Christ-like witness in the above questions will inevitably lead to a great deal of pain.

Teachability

Perhaps one of the most important character traits when evaluating whether or not to allow a leader to take a turn is teachability. As mentioned above, a new role will require a whole new set of skills. A leader who is not willing to humble themselves and to adopt the posture of the servant and the student will inevitably fail under the weight of their arrogance.

Many leaders will struggle in their new roles initially. Rather than be shocked and surprised by this, we should anticipate the challenges and graciously come alongside them as an encourager and coach. We must generously help them see their areas of strength in addition to their areas of weakness. Perhaps most importantly, we must listen attentively and carefully as they process and ask questions or seek guidance.

Teamwork

Before a leader is selected or approached with the option of making a leadership turn, there should be an open discussion between the leaders of the individual. The persistent attitude of all leaders must be to consider what is the best outcome for the church as a whole and what will allow the leader to thrive the most effectively. As a result, when a leader moves upwards on the pipeline in one area, they may need to take a step back on another.

These conversations can, at times, be difficult and require a high degree of transparency, humility and trust. It may feel like there are winners and losers in these conversations, but we must resist this false dichotomy and adopt a broad Kingdom perspective.

Failure After a Turn

One unique aspect of discipleship movements versus traditional corporate pipelines is that we cannot simply fire people for poor performance. The starting point of a discipleship movement is the body of Christ, and we cannot just chop off our arm because it is not working the way we want. A leader who is not leading well should be coached, corrected and encouraged as much as possible. However, at a certain point, it may be more unhealthy to allow them to continue in their role.

The value of Everyone Sent to Multiply Everything does not cease to be a guiding value merely because someone is struggling. When that person is struggling in an unhealthy way to themselves and others, we must give them the gift of liberty from their role and reposition them or give them a break. There is no shame or guilt in taking a break or recognizing that the role was a poor fit. In fact, those failures can be fantastic teaching points for all involved.

These are difficult conversations, and we must hold our roles with open hands. We must never allow our identity or sense of value and purpose to be tied up in our role. A leadership role is a gift that we are given to glorify God. If the opportunity is taken away or changed, we must be grateful and gracious for the joy of being able to lead in a new way.

The one exception to this process of repositioning is a continued failure in the area of individual expectations and unrepentant sin, as discussed above.

Summary

An effective reproducing leadership system where every person in the discipleship movement understands the values, qualifications, responsibilities, expectations and accountability systems is vital to continued health. Leadership positions exist to properly empower those with a proven track record of multiplication to yield greater influence. Likewise, leadership positions are a powerful tool for developing disciple-makers in a real-world setting. Leadership Position must never be about the hierarchical path towards the top, nor does it exist merely to foster organizational efficacy. Leadership Position in a multiplying movement is a means to see everyone sent to multiply everything. It is through leadership structures that the rest of the Discipleship Pipeline finds a framework for continued multiplication.

Part 5

Apostolic Life-Cycle

17

Apostolic Life-Cycle

Put together, Discipleship Potential, Multiplication Power and Leadership Position, as guided by the Apostolic Imperative, is a way of leading and contributing to a multiplying discipleship movement. Through Discipleship Potential, we have a clear and emphatic means by which we are thinking about and reproducing discipleship. In Multiplication Power, we have established a definitive culture and values around how we multiply that discipleship. Through Leadership Position, we empower and organize leaders according to their multiplication fruitfulness.

The entire system is designed to be a simple, scalable and sustainable model of discipleship that has the potential to be simultaneously viral and sustainable. For example, the Moravians in the 18th century essentially used the Apostolic Imperative as their operating system and had a tremendous Kingdom impact as a result. The Moravians pioneered more new ground in the 20 years from 1732 to 1752 than all the other movements combined in the previous 200. How? By mobilizing and sending ordinary believers who had been transformed by the grace of Jesus into new places so that others could also encounter Jesus.[53]

The Price of Sending

Where do we start? We start with the end in mind, and we start right where we are. Whenever we are thinking about discipleship systems, we can so easily be distracted from the necessity and mandate for multiplication and sending. Sending people to new places is a noble idea and easy to champion, but in practice, it is costly, risky and painful.

It is painful due to the distance that is introduced between those who were once in close discipleship relationships. Regardless of geographic implications, sending is relationally painful because those who we are very close with are sent to a new place to reach new people, so the time, proximity and vulnerability we once shared becomes strained or even broken. We must resist the urge to be so comfortable in our relationships that we fail to mobilize and send those we are discipling properly. We must prepare them, as we would our own children, to one day leave our care and reproduce on their own in new and uncharted territory.

Sending is risky because we cannot be assured of the success of those we have discipled. Challenges from outside and weaknesses and sin from inside threaten to derail the sent disciple. As disciple-makers, we must be willing to release those we are discipling to the potential of failure and even hurt. Of course, we train them with every hope they will succeed, but there are risks that we cannot account for in advance. There are some challenges that they will have to walk through for the first time on their own.

Sending is costly in both a human sense and a financial sense. Sending is costly because we send talented, gifted and able contributors to our work to go and pioneer new ground. When they go, they will leave a genuine operational and relational hole that we will need to work to fill. Of course, sending is also a financially risky decision, and we support new disciple-making initiatives with the financial resources necessary for them to succeed without the assurance that there will be a return on the investment.

If we are not careful, the practical reality of these pain points in our situations will allow us to delay multiplication indefinitely, or rationalize it away using such pseudo-spiritual nonsense as "it is not the Lord's timing." Jesus has given us an unequivocal mandate to produce multiplying disciples; we have no other job! If we are not serious about discipleship multiplication, what on earth are we doing?

We must continually and prayerfully return to the Discipleship Emphases, particularly missional living, to stay focused. We must routinely invite the Lord to mould our individual and collective desires to think about others and the work to which our Lord has commissioned us.

A Sending Process

A simple, repeatable process for multiplication is tremendously powerful in helping to focus our multiplication efforts on a large-scale. Sending disciples will inevitably result in planting more churches. The process for multiplying new churches can be described using the following 7 step process called the Apostolic Life-Cycle:[54]

1. Send Disciples
2. Establish Authentic Relationships
3. Share Gospel
4. Plant Church
5. Develop Foundations
6. Multiply Leaders
7. Send Planters

The Apostolic Life-Cycle is a process that can be implemented at both a macro and a micro level. At the macro level, large churches can leverage the process to guide the planting of other large churches. Similarly, a small church, say ten people, can use the same process. The only major difference is the scale of systems, not the substance of the process.

Depending on the unique application and context, each step may take varying amounts of time, ranging from days to years! The point is not so much the speed of the process, but that we are intentionally discipling leaders from no knowledge of Jesus to be sent and multiplying disciples in their own right.

1) Send Disciples

The first step in the process is to send and commission disciples to go to a new location to make new disciples. That new location may be in the same neighbourhood or city. Equally, it may also be on the other side of the world. The nature of the new location is inconsequential from a sending standpoint. An essential aspect for sending is the clear mandate for disciple-making. Without stating it openly, many church growth strategies are built upon transfer growth from other struggling churches or collecting disaffected Christians. While every Christian needs to find their home in a vibrant, missional and multiplying church family, discipleship movements must be primarily built upon seeing brand new believers invited to know Jesus.

The sending of disciples must be saturated in prayer as we seek the Lord's blessing, covering and protection as they begin the difficult work of breaking ground for the Gospel.

2) Build Relationships

The second step in seeing a discipleship movement thrive is building relationships. As we have discussed, seeing people know Jesus requires a revelation by the power of the Holy Spirit and the willingness to surrender all of our lives to him. For our message to be received, we must earn the trust of those we wish to reach. The content of our lives must verify the message before it will be accepted into someone else's life. The missional living everyday practices are, of course, the starting place, but the role of compassion cannot be overstated.

One of the best ways that we can win the trust of those we desire to reach for Christ, is to meet the tangible emotional and physical needs that they are immediately facing. It is through our genuine, honest and sacrificial compassion that our true intentions of seeing people made whole and redeemed can be demonstrated in our actions (James 1:27). An important facet of meeting their needs is actively listening and learning. It can be tempting to assume we already know the needs of a group of people, but we must always come with a posture of learning, and a willingness to serve on their terms.

Discipleship movements rely on healthy relationships more than attracting crowds, as it is through those relationships that we raise future disciple-making disciples. We must have the relational capacity and intentionality to ensure that every person we seek to reach can be mobilized and sent with the Gospel themselves. Without the relationship base from which we can disciple those we aim to reach, we will not be able to mobilize for mission. It is through the power of these relationships, which become discipleship relationships, that we can move from addition to multiplication for the Gospel.

3) Share Gospel

Sharing the Gospel, calling people to repentance and inviting them to accept Jesus as Lord, is a crucial transition phase from seeing people sent and fostering relationships, to seeing new disciples of Jesus formed. We must actually tell people about Jesus and call them to surrender before his throne. As we share the Gospel, we leverage the evangelistic capacity we have developed through our own crucial conversation discipleship in union with the Holy Spirit.

There is no formula for how long the building relationship phase will take before we can effectively share the Gospel. Each context is different, with unique barriers to overcome. The Multiplication Imperatives that help shape and inform our thinking about risks, urgency and failure are particularly helpful at this phase. We remember to lead fearlessly urgent in our desire to share the Gospel. Fearless urgency coupled with taking the leap allows us to live as people of faith, trusting that salvation is a work of the Holy Spirit and not our intellect (1 Corinthians 2:4).

By God's grace and his promises, we can be assured that eventually people will respond to the Gospel wherever we have the courage to proclaim it!

4) Plant Church

The planting of a church, especially in a simple or house church format, is perhaps the most effortless and most natural step in the process. By "planting the church" we mean the organizing and covenanting together of these new believers for discipleship, as defined as glorifying God by following and being transformed by Jesus while inviting, modelling, training and empowering others to do likewise.

The reason this is a natural step is that if we have built relationships and effectively shared the Gospel, then we will likely already have integrated these new disciples into covenant community. In this thinking, "planting the church" is the formal recognition of what already exists: a covenant family of believers on mission together!

Crucially, the church plant begins with an immediate eye to repeating the process and raising and sending a disciple. In seeing a new church planted, no matter how big or small, we must think about mobilizing and reproducing a new plant. Planting a church is the middle of the process, not the end. Only when a church plant has successfully reproduced itself by sending new believers to reach new people can we consider the plant successful. We must not compromise on this criteria or we will very quickly begin to think that the church exists for its own sake rather than the mission of Jesus. The need to reproduce is not connected to size; a church of 10 people and a church of 1000 people have the same mandate to multiply and make new disciples.

5) *Disciple Believers*

As the new church learns to walk together in that covenant community, the work of discipleship continues in earnest. It is at this phase that the quality and depth of those we have reached with the Gospel is tested in the context of church family (Luke 8:4-15). As we begin to train disciples in gospel fluency, secure identity, missional living, radical generosity and crucial conversations, there will be challenges to overcome and intentional work to do.

As the believers learn to work together on mission, the Discipleship Emphases must be continually honed so that they are learning to be formed by them and develop them in others at the same time. As we disciple new believers, those same believers are also being sent to reach those around them with the Gospel. In this way, the Apostolic Life-Cycle is an iterative and parallel process.

As we begin to disciple the new believers, all manner of sin, pride and selfishness will rise to the surface. The temptation to compromise in discipleship or lower the bar of missional living will be very tempting as we seek to maintain peace in the community in the short term. As we disciple believers, we must ensure that all five emphases are being substantially formed in and through every new disciple. As we do this discipleship work, not all disciples will continue to walk in relationship with us, and that is ok. We must remain faithful to the task and mission to which we have been sent. We must think about preparing each of our disciples for a life of discipleship multiplication themselves.

6) Multiply Leaders

As the community grows and thrives, the need for structure, leadership and systems will become increasingly important. We do not start by building systems and structures as that will stifle both relationship and creativity. However, as the community grows, we must bring in the Leadership Position aspects of the Discipleship Pipeline through systems and structures. We must ensure that each person can identify the values, responsibilities, qualifications, expectations and accountability relationships within the church plant.

As we multiply leaders, the need to be crystal clear on values and the Multiplication Imperatives is vitally important, particularly the Apostolic Imperative: Everyone Sent to Multiply Everything. As the community grows, the job of the leadership is to maintain unity by providing clarity surrounding the long term vision.

It is through the combination of clear values and effective structures that we can intentionally multiply committed and competent leaders for the future of the discipleship movement. It is those leaders who will carry the future responsibility of multiplication.

7) Send Disciples

Finally, we return to the beginning; we send new disciples to a new place to reach new people and start the process afresh. It is with joy that the disciples who were originally sent can send their own disciples. This is not the end for the original disciples or those they have now commissioned. Of course, the new disciples are sent to initiate the multiplication process themselves. However, the original disciples must continue to raise and send new disciples. The responsibility to send is not a one-time event but a continual work to which they commit their lives and empower those they are leading to do likewise.

Conclusion

Discipleship is a beautiful and life-giving process of seeing people discover the glorious hope of Jesus and invite others to know that hope as well. We have attempted to demystify the process of making disciples so that any disciple, anywhere, is empowered to go and multiply more disciples. We must resolve to keep the emphasis that discipleship is an act of worship that is equal parts sanctification and multiplication. We must remember that every disciple has the call, and the mandate, to see themselves grow closer to Christ as their inner and outer life are moulded into a life of worship.

The Discipleship Pipeline helps to organize, steer and empower disciples to be disciple-makers themselves. It is merely a tool so that we can clearly articulate where a discipleship movement is headed and how we will get there. Each of the Discipleship Emphases, Multiplication Imperatives and leadership positions must be contextualized and adapted for the unique people who are involved in discipleship.

The goal must not be to deliver a program or deploy a system; systems do help to organize discipleship and discipleship movements, but they are not discipleship in and of themselves. Discipleship is always about worship, sanctification and multiplication through a relationship with God and others. The goal must always be to see people know Jesus personally, intimately and authentically so that they can invite others to do likewise. The world around us needs to know Jesus. He is life, he is hope, he is joy and he is goodness. The Discipleship Pipeline is a tool to help that happen.

Let us pray the Lord will continue to raise and send disciple-makers into this world so that a harvest of righteousness can be reaped for his glory. The harvest is indeed plentiful, so we pray to our Lord that he would raise more workers. We pray that we see everyone sent to multiply everything.

Appendix: The Story of Scripture

The Gospel, is of course a story, that can be summarized as follows.

In the beginning was God: We believe in God, who is love and is the creator and sustainer of all things. He exists in perfect harmony as three persons-in-one (we call it the Trinity). The Father, Son, and Holy Spirit: a perfect, loving and glorious relationship. Distinct among his creation, God made…

You and I: We believe that we were created for relationship with God: to love and know him, each other, and ourselves. In our pursuit of this, we were meant to be creative and adventurous. However, we decided that we were better off, and we…

Rejected God – and became alone: We believe that we have rejected relationship with God, and as a result are separated from him. We have a broken relationship with each other and the world around us. This rejection of relationship with God is the root of what the Scriptures call sin, and within ourselves, there is no solution. Thankfully…

We were given a promise: We believe that God immediately began a process of redemption to restore relationship with mankind. This was documented in what Christians call the Old Testament which still speaks to us today. God's promise to restore relationship culminated in…

A solution – JESUS: We believe Jesus is the complete, perfect and the only answer. As God himself, Jesus lived roughly 2000 years ago revealing the character of God, dying so that we could be forgiven and being resurrected to life forever, conquering sin, death and the spiritual enemies of this world. Because of this…

We can respond: We believe that to live in relationship with God, we need to first acknowledge our living apart from God, and then put faith in Jesus. When we do so, we are forgiven of our sin, brought back into relationship with God and are filled with the Holy Spirit. This is called the Gospel – the Good News. As a sign of our faith in Jesus we are baptized in water, publicly declaring that we now live for Jesus, helping others experience him and collectively becoming…

The Church: We believe that the Church exists so that others could know the hope of Jesus. To help make this happen, Jesus gave supernatural ability to the Church as we carry out his mission. We will continue this mission until…

He Returns: We believe that Jesus will return to bring final justice to creation. There will be a new heaven and earth where those who have put their faith in Jesus will enjoy him forever, and those who have not will be forever separated from him.

We believe the Bible teaches these things: It is accurate and authoritative in our lives. We read it often to better know God and walk in relationship with him.

Scripture Index

Old Testament

Genesis
1:1	61
1:22	223
1:26-28	62
1:27-28	29
1	31, 32, 72
2:18	223
2	61, 72
3:12-16	65
11:4	30
11	32
12	90, 143

Exodus
3:14	62
7:3	165
18:21	257
23:19	145

Leviticus
16	19, 210
20:26	64
21-22	20

Numbers
16:3	20-21
16	19
18:20	20
18:1-3	19
18	138
22:21-39	212

Deuteronomy

6:6-9   80-82

Judges
21:25   65

2 Samuel
12   158

Psalms
27:1	50
51	81
78	267
90:12	140
119	76-79
133:1	120

Proverbs
3:9	145
9:10	62
29:5-6	114

Ecclesiastes
12:12-13   107

Isaiah
43:7	61
47:8	143
49:3	45
49	45
64:6	64
66:1-2	22

Ezekiel

36:26	49
36:27	165

Micah

3:10	143
6:8	106

New Testament

Matthew

4:19	177
4:17-19	14, 669
5:1-11	67
5:1-16	71
5	249
6:6	116
6:10	116
6:14	232
6:21	134, 143
6:24	134
6:33	113
6:34	114
6:1-4	134
7:1-3	152
8:22	192
9	22
10:4	241
10:8	136
10:16	159
10:39	86
10:13-14	223
11:28-29	173
11:28-30	221
12:41-44	134
13:22	134
13:44	134
16:18	149, 213, 239
16:23	182
16:24	181
16:13-28	270
16:20-21	149
17:24-27	135
18:15-17	155
18	232
19:21	134
20:27	139
20:26-28	98
20:27-28	138
21:12-13	134
23	148, 153
26:57-68	18
27:51-53	22
28:16	68
28:19	3, 32, 62, 186
28:16-20	44

Mark

1:16-20	168
1:29-31	125
10:17-27	135
10:28-31	120
11:15-18	135

Luke

3:14	134
6:35	136
6:43	278

6:45	248	14:25-26	69
8:4-15	287	15:8	51, 52
9:26	113	15:18	214
9:62	272	15:5-8	278
9:1-2	185	15	50, 51
9:57-62	244	16:33	214
10:10	186	17:1	45
10:1-17	186	17:18-20	96
10:29-37	135	17:23	229
11:42	145		
12:33	134	**Acts**	
12:53	214	2:4-5	32
14:27	46	2:36-38	67
14:28	134	2:42	70, 115
14:26-28	46	2:45	128
15	131	2:46	124, 137
16:13-15	134	2:47	130
21:1-3	144	2:42-47	114, 124
22:19	68	2:42,46	118
24:44-45	73	2:44-46	121
		2	114, 130, 245
John		4:24	116
1:14	121, 148	6:1-7	37
1	65	7:60	46
2:17	22	8:1,4	32
2	245	8	209
3:16	85	13:28-32	66
4	182	13	193
6:44	115	16:6-10	242
6:60	192	17:16-34	161
6:67	209	17:25	136
6:66-67	192		
7:38	112	**Romans**	
7	112	1:19-20	63
10:10	45, 176	1:21-23	86
11:4	245	1	86
13:35	94, 119	3:25	18

5:8	135	10:31-11:1	178, 179
5:10	64		
5:17	67	**2 Corinthians**	
5:1-5	214	4:15-17	215
5:3-5	103	5:7	213
6:11	88	5:17	71
6:13	88	5:20	96, 97, 181
6:22	49, 98, 99	9:7	137, 144
6:23	64	9:8	144
8:17	47, 91	9:6-8	144
8:39	91	9:11-12	138
8:22-24	72	9	138, 143
8	81	10:5	248
10:9	67, 86	10:9	252
12:1	26	11:28	107
12:4	26	12:9-10	175, 240
12:6-8	69, 142, 143	13:13-14	61
16:4	239		
		Galatians	
1 Corinthians		3:13	23
1:18-20	165	3:14	91
1:27-31	212	3:28	92, 217
2:4	286	4:19	95
3:2	183	4:4-6	90
5:12	152, 162	5:22-23	69
5:13	155	6:10	140
6:19	18		
6:19-20	24	**Ephesians**	
9:19,22-23	137, 161	1:5	90
9:27	245	1:7-9	136
11:1	274	1:13-14	68
12:1-11	69	2:19	92
12:7	142	2:4-5	58
12:12	228	3:10	47, 70
12:7-11	142	4:11-13	69, 71
12:24-26	36	4:14	60
14:12,25	117	4:15	148

4:16	212, 257	2:7-8	123
4	218	5:12-13	233
5:21	95	5:14-15	250, 252
5:25	133		
5:15-33	93	**2 Thessalonians**	
6:12	164	1:11-12	48
6:18-20	165	1	51

Philippians

1 Timothy

1	184	2:5	210
2:5-11	666	3:6	187
2:7	133	6:10	245
2:8	135	6:17-18	144
2:13	77, 229	6	143
2:17	27, 137		
3:17	176	**2 Timothy**	
3	109	1:6-7	243
4:12	50, 129	3:16-17	75, 155
4:13	105		
4:11-13	27, 105	**Titus**	
		1:6	159, 271

Colossians

Hebrews

1:21	135	4:16	23
1:9-10	57	5:12	183
1:27-28	53	9:22	21
1:28-29	53	9:28	72
2	129	10:10	26
3:2	129, 222	10:25	94
3:13	93, 232	10:24-25	253
3:17	88	11:1	238
3:1-3	144	11:6	239
3:1-4	106	12:2	137
3:1,5	87	12:11	154
3	87	12:15	229
4:5	159, 242	12:17	155
		12:1-2	215

1 Thessalonians

12:7-8,11	101
12	100
13:17	95, 152

James

1:3	215, 241
1:4	50
1:27	285
1:2-4	102
3:1	212
3:26	51
3:14-18	248
4:13-17	111
5	143

1 Peter

1:6	46
2:9	18, 118, 210
2:11	25, 97
3:14-16	161
3:18-20	22
4:10	141
4:11	47
5:5	151
5:1-3	271

2 Peter

3:13	72

1 John

2:15-17	145
3:1	90
4:9	135

Revelation

1:6	18
1:5-6	118
7:9	70
12:11	158
19:15	88
20:11-15	72
21:34	73
22	112

Endnotes

[1] Barth, Karl. Church Dogmatics: A Selection with Introduction by Helmut Gollwitzer. WJK Press, 1992, p72

[2] Greear, J.D. Gaining by Losing. Zondervan, 2015, p 70

[3] Sailhamer, John H.. The Pentateuch as Narrative. Zondervan Academic, 1992, p392

[4] Abernethy, A.T. The Book of Isaiah and God's Kingdom: A thematic-Theological Approach. IVP Academic, 2016, Kindle Edition, Loc 2145

[5] Bruce, F.F. The New Testament Development of Old Testament Themes: Seven Old Testament Themes Perfectly Fulfilled in Christ. Kingsley Books, 2017, Kindle Edition, Loc 1419

[6] Adapted from the translation of C. M. Jacobs (Works of Luther, Philadelphia: A. J. Holman Company, 1915), found online at: http://www.iclnet.org/pub/resources/text/wittenberg/luther/web/nblty-03.htm

[7] Silva, Moises. Philippians (Baker Exegetical Commentary on the New Testament), Baker Academic, 1988, Kindle Edition, Loc 3372

[8] Luther, Martin. The Epistles of St. Peter and St. Jude Preached and Explained. Kindle Edition. p70,71-72

[9] Comer, John Mark. Garden City. Zondervan, 2015, p38

[10] Teja, G, Wagenveld, J. Planting Healthy Churches. Multiplication Network, 2017 p55

[11] Abernethy. Loc 2721

[12] Peter Scazerro develops a similar idea of inner and outer life in his book The Emotionally Healthy Leader.

[13] Bridge Johns, Cheryl. Pentecostal Formation: A Pedagogy Among the Oppressed. Wipf & Stock, 2010, p35

[14] Lewis, C.S. Mere Christianity. HarperOne, 1952, 2001, p176

[15] Pearcy, Nancy. Love Thy Body. Baker Books, 2018

[16] Wright, N.T. Paul, Fortress Press, 2009, p 35

[17] Blomberg, C. L. The Historical Reliability of the New Testament, B&H ACADEMIC, 2016, Kindle Edition, Chapter 14

[18] N.T. Wright, The Resurrection of the Son of God, 707. Cf. Russ Dudrey, "What the writers should have done better: A case for the resurrection of Jesus based on Ancient Criticism of the Resurrection Reports" Stone Campbell Journal 3 (2000) p55-78

[19] Teja, Wagenveld, p50

[20] Lewis p199

[21] Wright. Paul. p114

[22] Newbigin, Lesslie. The Gospel in a Pluralist Society. Eerdmans, 1989, p92

[23] Gaffin, Richard. Biblical Hermeneutics 5 Views ed. Porter and Stovell. IVP Academic, 2012. p99

[24] Newbigin, Lesslie. Foolishness to the Greeks. Eerdmans, 1986. p58

[25] Quoted in Fernando, Ajith. The Call to Joy and Pain (Kindle Locations 393-394). Crossway. Kindle Edition.

[26] Newbigin, Lesslie. Foolishness to the Greeks. Eerdmans, 1986. p86

[27] Lewis. p98

[28] Fernando, Ajith. The Call to Joy and Pain. Crossway, 2007, Kindle Edition. loc 387-388

[29] Soren Kierkegaard, Kill The Commentators, ericsenglish.com/kill-commentators-text/

[30] Barth, Karl. The Epistle to the Romans. Oxford University Press, 1968, p53

[31] Keller, Tim. The Meaning of Marriage. Riverhead Books, 2011, p185

[32] Butterfield, Rosaria Champagne. The Gospel Comes with a House Key. Crossway, 2018 Kindle Edition.

[33] Grieg, Pete. The Vision and the Vow. Relevant Books, 2004, p129

[34] Guder, D. Missional Church. Eerdmans, 1998, p189

[35] Finney, Charles. Lectures on Revival. Bethany House, 1988, p22

[36] Grieg. p19

[37] Butterfield.Ch. 5

[38] Ibid.

[39] Ibid.

[40] Note: this is not to say that we do not consider if there is Godly stewardship of the resources we give. We have a responsibility to give radically to those who will steward those resources well.

[41] Scott, Kim. Radical Candor. St. Martin's Press, 2017

[42] Newbigin, Lesslie. The Gospel in a Pluralist Society, p189

[43] Bonhoeffer, Dietrich. The Cost of Discipleship (SCM Classics) . Hymns Ancient and Modern Ltd. Kindle Edition.

[44] Ignatius' *Letter to the Romans*, quoted in John R. Tyson, Invitation to Christian Spirituality, Oxford University Press 1999, p55

[45] Hirsch, Alan. The Forgotten Ways: Handbook. Brazos Press, 2009, p78

[46] Ibid 79

[47] Ibid 66

[48] Some of this content was developed with Jim Collins' *Good to Great* in mind. The N+2 Leader and what he calls the "Level 5 Leader" are somewhat similar. Collins highlights the over-emphasis on charisma, and his discussion of the "Stockdale Paradox" is similar to our discussion on Faith and Grit.

[49] Romans, 1 Corinthians, 2 Corinthians, Galatians, Ephesians, Philippians, Colossians, 1 Thessalonians, 2 Thessalonians, 1 Timothy, 2 Timothy, 1 Peter, 2 Peter, James, 1 John, 2 John, 3 John and Revelation all leverage this familial language!

[50] This is not to say that major mental health conditions are not a factor. Exceptional situations such as an anxiety disorder, will require more nuanced course of action. However, in healthy and mature multiplying leaders the ability to manage one's emotions and thoughts is a necessary requirement.

[51] Some of the ideas for Leadership Pipelines were built upon the work of Ram Charan in his book The Leadership Pipeline.

[52] Scazzero, Peter. The Emotionally Healthy Leader. Zondervan, 2015, p224

[53] Hesselgrave, David. Planting Churches Cross-Culturally. Baker Academic, 2000, p75

[54] The Apostolic Life-Cycle is an adaption from David Hesselgrave's Planting Churches Cross-Culturally. The intent is to rework his fairly denominational/ecclesiological framework for more multiplication oriented thinking. See: David Hesselgrave, Planting Churches Cross-Culturally, Baker Academic, 2000, p47

Made in the USA
Monee, IL
11 February 2020